TWENTIETH CENTURY VIEWS

The aim of this series is to present the best in contemporary critical opinion on major authors, providing a twentieth century perspective on their changing status in an era of profound revaluation.

Maynard Mack, *Series Editor*
Yale University

OTHER VOLUMES IN THIS SERIES

CAMUS, edited by Germaine Brée
T. S. ELIOT, edited by Hugh Kenner
ROBERT FROST, edited by James M. Cox
PROUST, edited by René Girard
WHITMAN, edited by Roy Harvey Pearce
STENDHAL, edited by Victor Brombert
HEMINGWAY, edited by Robert P. Weeks
FIELDING, edited by Ronald Paulson
THOREAU, edited by Sherman Paul

SINCLAIR LEWIS

SINCLAIR LEWIS

A COLLECTION OF CRITICAL ESSAYS

Edited by

Mark Schorer

Prentice-Hall, Inc., *Englewood Cliffs, N. J.*

LIBRARY OF CONGRESS CATALOG CARD NO.: 62-9311

Printed in the United States of America

81037-C

Acknowledgments

This book was prepared with the assistance of Miss Nancy Ann Goolsby, to whom I am deeply indebted.

I am also grateful to the following writers, agents, and publishers for permission to print the works in question.

Richard P. Blackmur and *The Nation;* "Utopia, or Uncle Tom's Cabin," by Richard P. Blackmur, *The Nation,* October 30, 1935, copyright 1935 by *The Nation.*

Mrs. Janice Biala Brustlein; *"Dodsworth,"* by Ford Madox Ford, *The Bookman,* April 1929.

Robert Cantwell and Malcolm Cowley; "Sinclair Lewis," by Robert Cantwell, *After the Genteel Tradition,* edited by Malcolm Cowley, W. W. Norton and Company, Inc., copyright 1937 by Malcolm Cowley.

Columbia University Press; "Sinclair Lewis and the Method of Half-Truths," by Mark Schorer, *English Institute: Society and Self in the Novel,* edited by Mark Schorer, copyright 1956 by Columbia University Press.

Malcolm Cowley and *The New York Times;* "The Last Flight from Main Street," by Malcolm Cowley, *The New York Times Book Review,* March 25, 1951, © 1951 by The New York Times Company, reprinted in *Highlights of Modern Literature,* edited by Francis Brown, New American Library, 1954.

William G. Frederick, Mercantile-Safe Deposit and Trust Company, Baltimore, Trustee of the Estate of H. L. Mencken; "Consolation," *Smart Set,* January 1921, and "Portrait of an American Citizen," *Smart Set,* October 1922.

Maxwell Geismar, Houghton Mifflin Company, and Russell & Volkening; "Origins of a Dynasty" and "The Land of Faery" from Chapter 2, *The Last of the Provincials: The American Novel, 1915-1925* by Maxwell Geismar, Houghton Mifflin Company, 1947, copyright 1949 and 1950 by Maxwell Geismar.

Harcourt, Brace & World, Inc.; part of Chapter 9 from *American Humor* by Constance Rourke, copyright, 1931, by Harcourt, Brace & World, Inc.; renewed, 1959, by Alice D. Fore.

Harcourt, Brace & World, Inc.; "Sinclair Lewis: Our Own Diogenes," from *Main Currents in American Thought* by Vernon L. Parrington, copyright 1927, 1930, by Harcourt, Brace & World, Inc.; renewed 1955, 1958, by Vernon L. Parrington, Jr., Louise P. Tucker, and Elizabeth P. Thomas. First appeared as Number 5 of *University of Washington Chapbooks,* 1927.

Harcourt, Brace & World, Inc., and Edward Arnold, Ltd.; "Our Photography: Sinclair Lewis," from *Abinger Harvest* by E. M. Forster, copyright, 1936 by E. M. Forster. First appeared in New York *Herald Tribune Books,* April 28, 1929.

Harold Ober Associates, Inc., for the Estate of Sherwood Anderson; "Sinclair Lewis" from "Four American Impressions," *Sherwood Anderson's Notebook,* copyright 1926 by Boni & Liveright, Inc., first published in *New Republic,* October 11, 1922, and most recently reprinted in *The Portable Sherwood Anderson,* edited by Horace Gregory, Viking Press, 1949.

William Heinemann Ltd. and Frederick A. Praeger, Inc.; "Sinclair Lewis: A Lost Romantic," by Geoffrey Moore, *The Young Rebel in American Literature,* edited by Carl Bode, published by William Heinemann Ltd., 1959, and Frederick A. Praeger, Inc., copyright 1960 by Carl Bode.

Alfred Kazin and Harcourt, Brace & World, Inc.; part of Chapter 8, "The New Realism: Sherwood Anderson and Sinclair Lewis," from *On Native Grounds* by Alfred Kazin, copyright 1942 by Alfred Kazin.

Joseph Wood Krutch and *The Nation;* "Mr. Babbitt's Spiritual Guide: A Review of Sinclair Lewis's *Elmer Gantry,*" *The Nation,* March 16, 1927, copyright 1927 by *The Nation,* and "Sinclair Lewis," *The Nation,* February 24, 1951, copyright 1951 by *The Nation.*

Mrs. Robert Morss Lovett; "An Interpreter of American Life," by Robert Morss Lovett, *The Dial,* June 1925.

The Macmillan Company; "Sinclair Lewis," from *Men of Destiny* by Walter Lippman, copyright 1927 by The Macmillan Company.

Lewis Mumford and *Current History;* "The America of Sinclair Lewis," by Lewis Mumford, *Current History,* January 1931.

Rebecca West, The Viking Press, Inc., and A. D. Peters; "Sinclair Lewis Introduces Elmer Gantry," from *The Strange Necessity* by Rebecca West, copyright 1927, 1955 by Rebecca West. First appeared in New York *Herald Tribune Books,* March 13, 1927.

Rebecca West and *The Newstatesman;* "Babbitt," by Rebecca West, *The Newstatesman,* October 21, 1922, copyright 1922 by Rebecca West.

Edmund Wilson and The New Yorker Magazine, Inc.; "Salute to an Old Landmark: Sinclair Lewis," by Edmund Wilson, *The New Yorker,* October 13, 1945, copyright © 1945, The New Yorker Magazine, Inc.

Mrs. T. K. Whipple and Appleton-Century-Crofts, Inc.; "Sinclair Lewis," by T. K. Whipple, *Spokesmen,* copyright 1928 by D. Appleton and Company. Part of this appeared first in *The New Republic,* April 15, 1925.

Table of Contents

SINCLAIR LEWIS

Introduction

by Mark Schorer

Generally speaking, the writings of Sinclair Lewis have almost never been the subject of serious criticism. Most of our best critics, when they have not ignored his work entirely, have assailed it for certain philistine attitudes that infected it, but either they did not analyze it as art, or they have treated him as "a publicist in fiction" whose work cannot sustain that kind of analysis. Even the novels of the 1920's, which seemed to so many to mark Sinclair Lewis as the leading novelist in the United States, which aroused enormous controversy in their enormous audience and to which hundreds of thousands of lines of newsprint were devoted, suffered this fate.

The instance of Lewis's treatment in the pages of *Dial,* where the best American literary criticism was appearing in the 1920's, is instructive. *Main Street* (1920) and *Babbitt* (1922) were not regarded as important enough to deserve a full review and were dismissed peremptorily (even though the second was regarded as a better novel than the first) in one short paragraph under the heading "Briefer Comment." *Mantrap* (1926), one of the most absurd of Lewis's novels, received equal space. (Of this work the editors conjectured that Lewis had written it with one hand tied behind his back and they wished that his other hand might have been similarly incapacitated.) Only *Arrowsmith* (1925) received a full review, this by Robert Morss Lovett, who found the novel increasingly unbelievable once it had passed its middle. *Elmer Gantry* (1927) was ignored entirely. By the time that *Dodsworth* (1929) appeared, *Dial* was dead, but it may be assumed that the editors, so many of whom had themselves been expatriated aesthetes, could hardly have found anything to sympathize with in this novel that satirized American artists abroad and gave its blessing to an American businessman.

Book reviewers (as opposed to critics) were another matter; from the first, they took Sinclair Lewis with considerable seriousness. At least three of the five novels that he published before *Main Street* were given the most respectful attention (the other two were frank hack work for which Lewis himself expected no praise). These novels—*Our Mr. Wrenn*

(1914), *The Trail of the Hawk* (1915), and *The Job* (1917)—announced, for most reviewers, the appearance of a new and original talent on the American literary scene.

Sinclair Lewis had come to his maturity before 1914, the beginning of the first World War and the end of a period extending from the opening of the century when the prevailing intellectual view was committed to a critical but still happy optimism about the promise of American life, of democracy and the middle class. At the same time, the American novel seemed to be written in two sharply opposing ways—with the alarming naturalism of a man like Theodore Dreiser on the one hand and with the sentimental gentility of the "Hoosier school"—most prominently, Booth Tarkington and Meredith Nicholson—on the other. Lewis's early novels were seen as important because they seemed to bridge this gap.

What the reviewers remarked in them was the unusual blending of "realism" and "romance." Realism meant a faithful depiction of the details of ordinary life and a willingness to come to grips with all that is not genteel in experience. Romance meant precisely that happy optimism about American life that characterized the pre-war years, its adventurousness, its flexibility, its variety. It meant, too, the potentiality of adventure, even of heroism, in the lives of "little people"—an obscure clerk, a country boy, a village girl. So, each of Lewis's first three central characters illustrated the point: Mr. Wrenn, the timid little clerk who breaks out of his boresome routine for a European adventure and finds it with a cynical bohemian artist, Istra Nash, before he returns to New York and finds a more substantial woman for his wife; Carl Ericson, the country boy who becomes a famous aviator and marries a fashionable girl; Una Golden, the village girl who arrives in the city and, fighting all its hardships, becomes a successful career woman before she marries the bright young man of her dreams.

These novels are shot through with flashes of satire directed against certain American types and attitudes, but they are not primarily satirical. Yet, when these novels are viewed retrospectively, as they are by Maxwell Geismar in his essay on Sinclair Lewis in *The Last of the Provincials* (1947), they can be seen quite clearly to lay down not only the central themes of the later work, the chief pattern of action, and the ambiguous attitudes toward American culture, but also, in much of their detail, the satiric technique that was to make Lewis famous.

Nevertheless, *Main Street* broke in the literary atmosphere like an explosion, like something absolutely new and absolutely devastating, not only unlike anything that Sinclair Lewis had done before but unlike anything that anyone had done before. Neither of these assumptions was quite accurate. While the prevailing fictional view of the American village had presented it as friendly and good, there was a long if much less populous tradition in fiction that showed it as narrow and cruel.

The difference is chiefly that these earlier critical novels were not, like *Main Street,* predominantly satirical. But that is also the chief difference between *Main Street* and Lewis's earlier novels. The pattern is identical—of a young person who finds herself in a stultifying environment, tries to reform and then break out of that environment, succeeds for a time, and then makes a necessary compromise with it. The optimism may be less gentle now, but it is still there. When H. L. Mencken, in his laudatory review of the book, remarked like so many others on the apparent reversal in Lewis, he was misled in part by his misreading of Lewis's attitude toward his heroine, Carol Kennicott.

Lewis by no means thought of "her superior culture" as "chiefly bogus," although certainly any reader today must so regard it. If she had to yield in the end to the taste of Gopher Prairie and of her kind but stodgy husband, Will, that, for Lewis, was the pathos of the novel. Although Will has the last word in the novel, it in fact ends in an impasse, and this impasse represents precisely the cultural ambiguities that Lewis could not resolve in his earlier novels and that Mr. Geismar has observed: his rather embarrassed admiration for "Eastern" culture and manners, and his inherent faith in "Western" simplicity and downright substantiality.

Yet he had, it is true, found his *métier* in the satirical treatment of American provincial life, and this vein he would continue to exploit. The pitch of the satire in *Babbitt* is much intensified, and this enabled H. L. Mencken once more to misplace the emphasis in his review, where he found only the kind of Babbitt that he wanted, not the kind that Lewis had shown, or not the whole kind. It is Rebecca West, rather, in her review, who observes the continuing strain of optimism, Babbitt's discontents with his environment, his sense of the promise of something better, something more fulfilling for the individual, less suffocating. It is "that something extra and above the logical treatment of its subject . . . which makes the work of art." For Mencken *Babbitt* was "a social document of a high order"; for Miss West, it was more nearly a kind of poem. And so, when Constance Rourke came to write of these two Lewis novels in *American Humor* (1931), she could quite correctly write of him as not simply a realist but as a "fabulist"—the creator of figures of archetypal stature. Inversely, Sherwood Anderson, whose own prose was in a murky way so much more explicitly "poetical" than Lewis's, found that it was exactly this extra dimension that was missing. However that question may ultimately be settled, the fact is that both terms, "Main Street" and "Babbitt," had become part of the international vocabulary, the United States had been "created" for the international mind, and Sinclair Lewis had established an international reputation.

The next novel, *Arrowsmith,* thoroughly consolidated that reputation and it quieted even his harshest critics. For here at last Lewis had found a specific and realizable object in which to locate his idealism and beside which he could pose his satire in some sort of balance. Martin Arrowsmith, pursuing in his laboratory what are presented as his lonely truths, was a new kind of hero, scientific idealism a new subject, and scientific individualism a new (and rather unscientific) perspective. Sinclair Lewis was once again in the vanguard.

Reviewers and critics, English as well as American, were almost unanimous in asserting its superiority to *Main Street* and *Babbitt,* and in basing the claim on aesthetic grounds. *The Atlantic Monthly* announced that Lewis was "no longer the composer of superlative jazz. He has shown himself an artist, sincere, powerful, restrained." Joseph Wood Krutch, in *The Nation* found it "better" because it was "essentially truer," and T. K. Whipple, in *New Republic,* took the same view; the New York *Times,* in two different reviews, agreed, along with Stuart Pratt Sherman of the New York *Herald Tribune,* who none too lucidly found that the novel was "hot with the authentic fire in which art and science are purified." "The humanity of it outshines the science," declared the *Literary Review.* Other reviewers thought that in its very attention to science it had performed a tremendous "service." On these grounds, the *Dial* made its historic exception for a Lewis novel when Robert Morss Lovett declared that Sinclair Lewis had served "a public cause which gives largeness of view and significance to *Arrowsmith.*"

Almost perversely, after the foolish interlude of *Mantrap,* an adventure story, Lewis chose to fly in the face of all this praise by publishing *Elmer Gantry,* his novel about the corruption of the religious life in America. No novel in the history of American literature outraged its audience so completely, and very few novels in American literature had a larger immediate audience. The outrage was so intense that it extended to threats of personal assault upon the author. It was the rare critic, like Joseph Wood Krutch, who could see the novel in some perspective and could see that it had some virtue. "*Elmer Gantry* is as good as *Main Street* and *Babbitt,*" wrote Mr. Krutch with critical sense and moderation, "and it is good in exactly the same way." Extremes were more characteristic of the reception of this novel. At one side of Mr. Krutch is H. L. Mencken, predictably ecstatic and shouting, "Voltaire! Voltaire! Not since Voltaire!" And at the other is the disappointed Rebecca West, for whom this satire fails because its chief character is unworthy of satire, because it seems to have been written on the assumption that "Voltaire would have got anywhere if he had spent his emotions on the pietistic errors of washerwomen in Brittany." Because *Elmer Gantry* aroused such hot feelings, it is probably the only one of Lewis's better novels that has been critically underestimated. In my own essay I have tried to write as dispassionately as Mr. Krutch, but, I fear, at much greater length.

In 1927 Sinclair Lewis was at his zenith, and at about this time extended surveys of his work began to appear, attempts at assessment of the whole of his work thus far. V. F. Parrington in his essay, "Our Own Diogenes"

(1927), defines the nature of Lewis's satire, discusses his methods of gathering material, considers both his popularity and his unpopularity, and finds him rather harder on middle class America than Lewis in fact was and would presently make very clear in his defense of Dodsworth. T. K. Whipple, whose fine essay of 1928 is a clear exception to the generalization with which this introduction began, does not make Parrington's error: he sees the complexity, the self-division in Lewis, the man, as clearly as he sees them in Lewis's novels; he sees what is lucid and valuable in these novels as well as he sees their limitations; he recreates the imaginative world of Sinclair Lewis with an artist's effectiveness; and he arrives at a final judgment with which, I believe, any dispassionate reader must agree. Walter Lippmann's essay of 1927 is an impressive piece of rhetoric, but it is written with a good deal more personal bias, even a kind of vindictiveness, than is to be found in the Whipple essay, and so it is critically less impressive. This is true even if one is inclined to agree with Mr. Lippmann that Sinclair Lewis, the man, had never fully matured. The essay ends with speculations on what subject Lewis will turn to next.

> But what interests me is whether Mr. Lewis will reach maturity, or remain arrested in his adolescent rebellion. After *Arrowsmith* one would have said that he was beginning to be free of that shapeless irritation and yearning which Carol Kennicott typifies. But after *Elmer Gantry* one cannot be so sure. The hatreds are turned inward, as if the effort to escape had failed and become morbid. There is some sort of crisis in this astonishing career, which is not yet resolved.

Many readers of Lewis's next novel, *Dodsworth,* felt that this is precisely what had happened—Lewis had matured at last, mellowed. Here is a story that praised an American businessman and that saved its satire for cultural affectations and snobbery, for "Europeanized" corruptions of virtue and taste. The American middle class was vindicated! At last the errant Lewis had returned to his own! And while it is true enough that Lewis's approval of Babbitry had never been so explicit before, careful readers of Lewis's previous novels, even *Elmer Gantry,* would not have been so deceived.

H. L. Mencken was, of course, disappointed, and gave the novel only a kind of grudging praise, but most reviewers were delighted with the book. Ford Madox Ford, that extremely sensitive British novelist, friend of Henry James whose own work was so centrally concerned with the *Dodsworth* theme, the American abroad, wrote enthusiastically of the "poetic" quality of the novel and suggested that it might quite as well have been called *Europa, an Epic.* Another fine English novelist, E. M. Forster, thought less well of it. Acknowledging Lewis's superb photographic gift as he employed it in his novels earlier in the 1920's, Forster said, "I persist in exclaiming, for what Mr. Lewis has done for myself and thousands of others is to lodge a piece of a continent in our imagination." But with *Elmer Gantry,* the photographic method had begun to fail him, and with *Dodsworth,* the failure was complete. "What has happened? What has changed the Greek Confectionery Parlour at Gopher Prairie, where every decaying banana mattered, to this spiritless general catalogue?" Mr. Forster concluded that photography was the art of a fresh, young man; Mr. Lewis was no longer young and he had no other resources. In this view, then, if Lewis had indeed matured, maturity was his disaster.

Yet it was indeed the fact that for thousands of Europeans, Lewis had created the image of America, and he had created it in the terms in which they wanted to believe—of a grossly materialistic, money-mad, smugly hypocritical, provincial civilization. It was not really surprising that in 1930 Sinclair Lewis should have been the first American writer to receive the Nobel prize. And the outraged Americans who regarded the award not as praise for American literature but as an insult to American culture were probably not entirely wrong. Yet it was praise for American literature, too, and not only for Lewis's novels but for a whole body of work that had throughout the 1920's developed a capacity for self-criticism that was new and that demonstrated that our writers, at least, were not chauvinists. For Europeans, Lewis had all along been the most effective of our social critics in the novel, and not only because he was the noisiest of them. He loved his country all the time that he scolded it, and this quality the Swedes, at least, found endearing in him, and for this quality, together with his humor, they praised him.

It was the climax of his career, of course, and from that high point a long descent lay ahead. He was to publish ten more novels of uneven quality, some very bad indeed and none as good as the five big novels of the 1920's. The immediate concern in critical America was not with Lewis's future but rather with an assessment of his past, and all over the United States the question that was being asked was whether Lewis deserved the great prize. Lewis Mumford's essay of 1931 is characteristic. It gives its subject due praise for the qualities that his best work showed, and it asserts that "on his literary merits, he would undoubtedly be one of the six or seven names that would come to mind as candidates for this prize." But it concludes that if the Swedish Academy had been capable of recognizing the qualities that are "most precious and significant in contemporary American literature," it would have recognized Robert Frost.

A gap of a few years followed in Lewis's production. For some time he had worked at the preliminary materials for a novel about labor in the United States, and in the early 1930's he devoted himself most intensively to this project, but he felt that he could not yet write it, and even though he never quite relinquished the idea, he never did write it. He began then to write a whole series of novels about less complex (or at least, for him, more manageable) social areas. Having recently married Dorothy Thompson, a career woman, he now wrote *Ann Vickers* (1933), a novel about the career woman in the United States who yearns to be a mere woman as well. Then followed a poor novel about the hotel industry, *Work of Art* (1934), in which the satire is directed against art (poor art, to be sure) and the real art lies in the dream of a perfect hotel. Because of Dorothy Thompson's interest, as a newspaperwoman, in the developments in Hitler's Germany, Lewis next wrote *It Can't Happen Here* (1935), a sensational novel about fascism in the United States, and while the novel excited all readers of liberal mind (for the threat of fascism in the mid-thirties seemed very real), it in fact makes its appeal to the good old American middle-of-the-road virtues as these are embodied in its hero, Doremus Jessup, a small town newspaper editor. Then, seeming to reverse himself once more, Lewis published *The Prodigal Parents* (1938), which was meant as a satiric exposé of communist activity in the United States and which is unquestionably one of his feeblest efforts.

He was writing now with a kind of mechanical fury, and in 1936 it was this relentless grinding out of anything at all that most impressed Robert Cantwell in his survey for the *New Republic*. The famous Lewis "ear" is challenged in this essay—is this really the way that Americans talk? Lewis is beginning to seem old-fashioned—he who had always been out in front; and the essay already takes on the tone, as writing about Lewis increasingly would, of elegiac assessment. When Lewis found his substantial place in Alfred Kazin's brilliant history of modern American literature, *On Native Grounds* (1942), the extended analysis and the eminently fair judgment on the whole career and on Lewis's importance to American literature nearly suggest that the subject has already been dead for some time.

Bethel Merriday (1940), a novel about a young actress, had indeed suggested that at least the satiric novelist in Lewis was dead. While *Gideon Planish* (1943), a satiric attack on organized philanthropy and the activities of liberal "do-gooders," returned, in a crude way, to the old mode, it did little to support the old reputation. *Cass Timberlane* (1945), a novel about American marriage, is half-sentimental, half-splenetic, and one can understand why a lady like Diana Trilling, reviewing this book, should have found Lewis "The victim, so to speak, of his own divided heart." Most male reviewers felt rather differently. Edmund Wilson, for example, considering this novel, was impressed with the fact that Lewis was "one of the people in the literary field who do create interest and values, that he has still gone on working at this when many others have broken down or quit, and that he is, in fact, at his best—what I never quite believed before—one of the national poets." This judgment should be put beside the harsher view of Maxwell Geismar, who finds Lewis now writing in "the land of Faery"—out of all touch with American realities.

In *Kingsblood Royal* (1947) he made his last strenuous effort to reenter it by addressing himself to the problem of the negro minority in American life. The book aroused some excitement as a social document but none whatever as a literary performance, and even its social usefulness, it is now clear, is minimized by Lewis's mechanical oversimplification of what is, of course, one of the most complex, as well as one of the most pressing issues in our national life. From this attempt to deal with the immediate present, Lewis retreated into the historical past of Minnesota. *The God-Seeker* (1949) is apparently the first part of what was finally projected as a trilogy about labor in the United States, but it is a wooden performance about which even Lewis's faithful publishers despaired.

His last novel, *World So Wide* (1951), was published posthumously. A thin attempt to write another *Dodsworth,* it is the final self-parody. As Malcolm Cowley wrote, his characters sound now "like survivors from a vanished world, like people just emerging from orphanages and prisons where they had listened for thirty years to nothing but tape recordings of Lewis novels."

It was a long and sad decline and it complicates the problem of making any final judgment. The patent weaknesses of the poor books highlight weaknesses already present but not so obvious in the great books, and the dimness of the final vision somehow casts in shadow their portions of brilliance. Yet, following in the steps of the few good critics who risked writing seriously about him (and now, in retrospect, they do not seem quite so few, although the fact remains that there is nothing from Eliot, from Levin or Pritchett or Mattheissen, from Brooks or Warren, from Tate or Ransom or Trilling or Rahv, and certainly nothing from the bearded old-young)—following the few who risked judgments, one must take the risk oneself.

Unquestionably, he helped us into the imagination of ourselves as did no other writer of the 1920's. What he helped us to imagine is a part of ourselves that we do not greatly admire and that, in some of its grossest features, we may indeed by now have outgrown. It was the very worst of our gawky adolescence that he showed us, with the chin weaker than it would finally be, the nose larger, the hands still hanging out of the sleeves, pimples all over the flushed face. Interestingly enough, Sinclair Lewis himself, one of the gawkiest adolescents of all time, always aspired to become an elegant man of the world. So, his fiction, without much more subtlety, tried to whip the most barbarous kind of American into the Lewis conception of culture. When his personal ambition failed, his novels fell back into a defense of the very barbarousness that he had always held onto as an ace in the hole. If the strategy was mistaken, and only marked the long falling off of his powers, he had, nevertheless, in his great years, not only made a personal fortune remarkable for an American literary man but he had also made his contribution to the fortunes of

American literature. That treasure remains in our literary and cultural inheritance, remains both to enrich us and to remind us of our potential bankruptcy. At the very least, we must agree with T. K. Whipple's judgment that "Lewis is the most successful critic of American society because he is himself the best proof that his charges are just." In spite of all the bad writing, the lapses in taste and judgment, the sheer wilfulness of the whole career, we can only concur, too, with the observation of Joseph Wood Krutch that Lewis "recorded a reign of grotesque vulgarity which but for him would have left no record of itself because no one else could have adequately recorded it."

An involuntary achievement, perhaps, but not a small one. And if, besides, we can hope with Rebecca West that the very vitality that animates that vulgarity suggests the possibility of a more civilized future, we must thank Sinclair Lewis in large part among writers for pushing us into it.

Origins of a Dynasty

by Maxwell Geismar

The hero of *The Trail of the Hawk,* in 1915—in some respects the most ambitious of Lewis's early novels—comes from [the] prairie hamlets of the northern Middle West in the eighteen-nineties: "the straggly rows of unpainted frame shanties, the stores with tin-corniced false fronts that pretended to be two stories high."

But Carl Ericson, son of a Norwegian carpenter, brought up among the "New Yankees" of Wisconsin, Minnesota, and the Dakotas, who were, as Lewis says, a human breed that could grow, with a thousand miles to grow in—also knows the exhilaration of the western prairies: the pastures of wild clover, the creeks with minnows and perch, the hazelnut bushes around the sloughs, the quivering cry of the gophers. Here, along with the arc lights of the tiny farming settlements at night, are those provincial philosophers who figure so largely in the Ohio tales of Sherwood Anderson—indeed the "Bone" Stillman of *The Trail of the Hawk,* a familiar type of village atheist who "read Robert G. Ingersoll and said what he thought," is the dominant influence of Carl's earlier years.

"Son, son, for God's sake live in life," Bone Stillman tells the boy. "It's a thing I ain't big enough to follow up, but I know it's there. . . . You want to know that there's something ahead that's bigger and more beautiful than anything you've ever seen, and never stop till—well, till you can't follow the road any more." And during his years at Plato College in Minnesota, Carl does remember this precept. He reads Shelley, Keats, Ibsen, and Shaw; he becomes something of a rural intellectual, or —caught up by the earlier and touching vision of the brotherhood of man that marked our provincial thinking in the nineteen-hundreds—a sort of prairie radical. Rebelling against the academic conventions, he leaves college in protest and in disgrace, to become, as Lewis says, "utterly tough and reckless"—a day laborer in Chicago, a circus roustabout, a provincial wanderer and discoverer. "Out of this wholesome, democratic, and stuffy village life, Carl suddenly stepped into the great world."

Yet the "great world" of the early Lewis hero has a curious history—it starts out with Carl's equal passion for a horseless carriage and for the

Gertrude Cowles of his childhood. The Cowleses themselves, with their brick mansion, their hired maids, and their library—"the only parlor in Joralemon that was called a library, and the only one with a fireplace or a polished hardwood floor"—the Cowleses represent an early vision of luxury in the machine age. "Gertie," who has gone East for her education, remains fixed in Carl's mind as an image of grace and refinement, not only during his early adventures as a vagabond, but also during his more celebrated exploits as a pioneer aviator and stunt flyer. Unfortunately, these exploits occupy the entire middle section of *The Trail of the Hawk,* the earlier account of the western countryside fades into the "romantic and miraculous" story of aviation, while the account of Carl Ericson's own education and human development is subordinated to the glamorous adventures of "the best monoplane pilots America will ever see." [1]

Meanwhile, in 1914, Lewis had already written *Our Mr. Wrenn,* a different sort of novel with a different sort of hero—one who has had no childhood to speak of, whose entire horizon is contained in the disorganized files of the "Souvenir Company," and who would apparently regard a prairie hawk as he would a dodo. Unlike Carl Ericson, "Wrenny" is no adventurer. He has never had a drink or a woman, he is full of fears rather than recklessness, while even his animal instincts have been sublimated into a sort of vague yearning and anxiety. He dreams of becoming a rabbit. His single standard is "respectability"—respectability means his job with the Souvenir Company—and, adds Lewis, "his fear of losing the job was about equal to his desire to resign from the job." His only escape is the "Fairyland of Travel," into which he slips nightly by means of a large collection of steamship advertising brochures.

Yet *Our Mr. Wrenn* also deals with the emotional education and even the spiritual emancipation of the early Lewis hero. Through receiving a small legacy, Mr. Wrenn is released from his economic servitude. Through his European trip he meets both Harry Morton, a Socialist vagabond, and Istra Nash, an alluring and exotic bohemian. And through Istra and her contact with a wider world of art and culture, Mr. Wrenn begins his own revolt against respectability. He gains sophistication and self-confidence; he learns not only how to discuss "Yeats and the commutation of sex energy," but also how to play. In fact, he now wants to shout to Istra across all the city: "Let us be great lovers! Let us be mad! Let us stride over the hilltops!" Just as Harry Morton has given Mr. Wrenn a sense of that "fine flame of shared hope" that was the common heritage of the workers of the world in the nineteen-hundreds, so Istra (with her red hair and her savoir-faire, her lack of corsets and her knowledge of all the really "interesting" artistic people) seems to sum up, in Lewis's mind, a phase of the Aesthetic Revolt that followed hard on the heels of the

[1] In this connection it is interesting to notice that the first recorded [long] work of Lewis's, a juvenile by "Tom Graham," in 1912, is called *Hike and the Aeroplane.*

Progressive Movement in America. Moreover, with *The Job,* in 1917—a less whimsical and more fully realized novel—Lewis carries forward this pattern of his early development.[2]

For his new heroine, Una Golden—the first full-length portrait in the series of Lewis's American women that will extend from the Carol Kennicott of 1920 to the Bethel Merriday of 1940—is a sort of fusion of Mr. Wrenn and Istra Nash. She is both the white-collar office worker and the emancipated woman; she has both more of a past and more of a future. She comes from those lower-middle-class folk who believe that Panama, Pennsylvania, "is good enough for anybody"—and this village scene is viewed somewhat differently from that of Carl Ericson's western origins. "To Una there was no romance in the sick mansion, no kindly democracy in the village street, no bare freedom in the hills beyond."

So Una sets out on her own. "She *would* go to New York, become a stenographer, a secretary to a corporation president, a rich woman, free, responsible." New York, as Lewis says, which aspires to the heavens in her skyscrapers, and dreams a garden dream of Georgian days in Gramercy Park, and "bares her exquisite breast and wantons in beauty" on Riverside Drive. And the recurrent early dream of these Lewis characters—their belief in a rather hazy Utopian Socialism—blends into the vision of Scientific Business:

> For business, that one necessary field of activity to which the egotistic arts and sciences and theologies and military puerilities are but servants, that long-despised and always valiant effort to unify the labor of the world, is at last beginning to be something more than dirty smithing. No longer does the business man thank the better classes for permitting him to make and distribute bread and motorcars and books. No longer does he crawl to the church to buy pardon for usury. Business is being recognized—and is recognizing itself—as ruler of the world. With this consciousness of power it is reforming its old, petty, half-hearted ways; its ideas of manufacture as a filthy sort of tinkering; of distribution as chance peddling and squalid shop-keeping; it is feverishly seeking efficiency. . . .

And, Lewis adds, this vision of a business efficiency so broad that it can be kindly and sure, this search for systems and charts and new markets and the scientific mind, is growing everywhere—"is discernible at once in the scientific businessman and the courageous labor-unionist."

It is a vision of mercantile bliss, however, that isn't immediately discernible in the actual facts of Una Golden's life. New York is also the

[2] A sort of sub-realistic whimsicality also marks what is probably the worst novel of Lewis's first period, *The Innocents,* in 1917. The story concerns the adventures of an aged and rather pathetic lower middle-class couple. But the account of their exploits is so incredible, and their final "success" (financial and social) is so unattractive, that the novel can justly be called "a flagrant excursion," as Lewis admits, and a tale "for people who still read Dickens and clip out spring poetry and love old people and children."

city of boxlike apartments and unvaried streets, of the "loveless routine" of office jobs, of an unceasing round of unessentials against which Una bruises herself from hour to hour. It is the city of such "organisms" as Bessie Kraker, who has been modified by the Ghetto, Lewis says, to the life which still bewildered Una; of Walter Babson, the disillusioned poet who has turned into a cheap publicity man; of Phil Benson, the hall-room Lothario who would have been an excellent citizen "had the city not preferred to train him . . . to a sharp unscrupulousness"; and of the unsuccessful salesman, Eddie Schwirtz, whose "thwarted boyish soul" never can understand the reasons for his failure. Nor is Lewis's "Bewildered New Muse" of Scientific Business any more apparent in the high-pressure efficiency of that Pemberton's Cosmetic Supply Company, to which Una graduates and which operates on the principle "of giving the largest possible number of people the largest possible amount of nervous discomfort, to the end of producing the largest possible quantity of totally useless articles." In fact, as Lewis traces the course of Una Golden's business career—the succession of tedious and exhausting jobs, the series of unfulfilled and uneasy men whom she meets through these jobs, and then her own attempt to escape from the impending disaster of middle age through an even more disastrous marriage—this entire lower-middle-class office world of "respectability" and "success" is dissected and laid open.

In these sections of the novel, *The Job* is the best and solidest example of Lewis's early realism. Yet in some respects it is an odd realism. Is the Lewis heroine still haunted by that dim view of a better society? Does there still come, into her workaday mind, a low light from that fire that was just then kindling the world—"the dual belief that life is too sacred to be taken in war and filthy industries and dull education; and that most forms and organizations and inherited castes are not sacred at all"? But it is actually through her friendship with Miss Beatrice Joline, the aristocratic type of successful business woman—the New York "thoroughbred"—that Una Golden finds the chance to salvage her ruined life. And it is through her own successful operation of the "White Line Hotels" that she meets and marries the now successful Walter Babson, and simultaneously conquers Job and Home. "We can both work, keep our jobs, and have a real housekeeper—a crackajack maid at forty a month—to mind the cat."

It is interesting to remember that the earlier Mr. Wrenn follows a similar course of salvation. Was Istra Nash the epitome of Modern Sophistication—the Bohemian Revolt incarnate? Her sense of freedom is hardly matched by her sense of achievement—toward the close of *Our Mr. Wrenn,* indeed, the Sophisticate is more miserable than the Businessman. "For when a person is Free, you know," Lewis points out, "he is never free to be anything but Free." And just as Mr. Wrenn's European trip leads him to a new discovery of America, his experience with Istra's larger world of art and intellect brings him to a new recognition of the business world itself: to a determination to reform its manners if he can, but to advance his own status at all events. Even his earlier sense of isolation in the economic pattern is resolved through his success, as a more widely cultivated person, both in captivating his "business friends" and in developing the theme of "Friendship" as an advertising motif.

Similarly, the boldest and most rebellious of these early Lewis figures —the Carl Ericson of *The Trail of the Hawk*—becomes the most financially secure. In the midst of his exploits as an aviator—as one of Lewis's new heroes of the machine age—Carl dreams of becoming rich "as soon as he could," and Wrenn, in his wildest fantasies, cannot touch the twenty-five thousand dollars a year which Carl finally achieves through his masterpiece, the "Touri-Car." Indeed, if Carl conquers and then leaves the Gertie Cowles who was the tormenting symbol of eastern sophistication during the years of his midwestern youth, it is because he has found, in the later Ruth Winslow of *The Trail of the Hawk,* a more authentic representative of that sparkling and aristocratic New York society: of "the inside view, the sophisticated understanding of everything." And if Lewis opens his work with an evocation of that equalitarian frontier society which flourished with the arc light and the hired girl, one sees that he is really describing the impact of the machine and of wealth on this society—and the establishment, along with "servants," of rather rigid social classes. The human breed that could grow, and that had a thousand miles of prairie to grow in, is now chiefly concerned with getting ahead in society.

Perhaps this explains the curious emotional pattern of these early Lewis figures: their fear of expressing, or having, deeper feelings or strong convictions, and their retreat into whimsicality as a refuge from both emotion and ideas; their great desire to be young and have "fun" and their equal uncertainty as to what "fun" really is; their hurried excursions into a realm of defiance and revolt, and their swift return to the familiar security of their own economic and social routine—their "own folks."

And while they seem really to believe that a change of environment is equal to a change of personality, their uneasy view of their own geographical origins is matched only by their very definite sense of their economic destination. The closing pages of *The Trail of the Hawk,* at any rate, are devoted to an almost interminable discussion of this issue between Lewis's Ruth Winslow and the "Hawk" himself—"he remembering the fact that she was a result of city life; she the fact that he wasn't a product of city life." The real fact was, Lewis says, that Carl Ericson had come in a few years from Oscar Ericson's back yard to Ruth Winslow's library—"he had made the step naturally, as only an American could, but it was a step." It isn't definitely established, however, that Ruth Winslow uses her library, and meanwhile there is another interesting element in the early work of this novelist who is to become the outstanding satirist of the social patterns of the new American money society.

For the dominant characteristic of all these early Lewis novels is that they are not essentially satires at all, but "romances." [3] Just as the middle section of *The Trail of the Hawk* is devoted to the "romance of the machine," the main emphasis of *Our Mr. Wrenn* is on the "romance of culture," and the main emphasis of *The Job* is on the "romance of business," while the realistic elements of these novels—the earlier agrarian society of Carl Ericson or the white-collar office world of Mr. Wrenn and Una Golden—are in turn subordinated to the demands of the romance. Moreover, in the last of Lewis's early novels, *Free Air,* in 1919, the element of fantasy is almost completely released.

The story deals with an improbable automobile trip through the western states that is undertaken by a young society girl from Brooklyn Heights, and her father, a New York financier. In a sense the machine is still the central figure of Lewis's imagination. The title of the novel—the "Free Air" that Claire Boltwood first meets in the West—is taken from a sign in a local garage, while the novel is filled with observations on the erratic behavior of Claire's seventy-horsepower Gomez-Dep roadster, as against that of Milt Daggett's proletarian "Bug." For, just as Claire is again the aristocratic eastern heroine, Milt, who saves her at once from the foibles of the machine and the perils of the frontier, is also the western democratic hero. In fact, the basic theme of Lewis's literary apprenticeship emerges most clearly in the streamlined narrative of *Free Air.* The western countryside—the background of Gopher Prairie and of Zenith—is cruder now, with its dirty and littered farmyards, its ugly and run-down "hotels," its crossroads settlements like Schoenstrom, Minnesota, whose entire business district consists of

> Heinie Rauskukle's general store, which is brick; the Leipzig House, which is frame; the Old Home Poolroom and Restaurant, which is of old logs concealed by a frame sheathing; the farm-machinery agency, which is galvanized iron, its roof like an enlarged washboard; the church; the three saloons; and the signs . . . The Agency for Teal Car Best at the Test, Stonewall Tire Service Station, Sewing Machines and Binders Repaired. Dr. Hostrum the Veterinarian every Thursday, Gas Today 27c.

And, correspondingly, the eastern city life of Claire Boltwood, with its gracious talk and smart clothes and elaborate social distinctions, is, for the young Milt Daggett, even more rarefied.

[3] "One of the things interesting to the author," Lewis himself says, in the introduction to his *Selected Short Stories,* in 1935, "is the discovery that he, who has been labeled a 'satirist' and a 'realist,' is actually a romantic medievalist of the most incurable sort." But this new description of himself, as we shall see, is not altogether accurate either.

The machine is transforming the Western provinces also, to be sure. The "missionaries of business," who are instructing the rural merchants in how to build up trade and trim windows and "treat customers like human beings," are binding East and West together. "They," says Lewis, "as much as the local ministers and doctors and teachers and newspapermen, were the agents of spreading knowledge and justice. It was they . . . who encouraged villagers to rise from scandal and gossip to a perception of the Great World, of politics and sports, and some measure of art and science." And it is through these businessmen and drummers that Milt Daggett gets his first glimpse of the correct clothes and manners that go along with financial success, just as it is through his assiduous cultivation of the arts and sciences, as well as tennis, dancing, and bridge, that he finally becomes acceptable to the belle of Brooklyn Heights.

In the raw frontier towns of the early Sinclair Lewis, then, social position is even more desirable than it is in the drawing rooms of the eastern metropolis. How fervently, how studiously, in any case, these young Lewis heroes, reared on the immense empty western plains, seek to emulate an eastern sophistication: a sophistication which implies social poise, to be sure—and the effort "to be gracious and aphoristic and repartistic and everything," as Lewis's heroine admits—and also limousines and marble bathrooms and pâté de foie gras. How devoutly they aim to be, because of their native western heritage, better Easterners than the Easterners! Sometimes both the eastern girls and western boys of Lewis's first period appear to be so fundamentally similar in their approach to life that it is questionable whether their large sacrifices for the sake of each other are justified.

As a matter of fact, always proclaiming their desire for adventure and excitement and "New Horizons," these early Lewis figures as a group are probably the least well suited of all the restless young Americans in our letters to enjoy new horizons—or to recognize them. From Will Kennicott to Sam Dodsworth, too, this set of emotional responses is to remain dominant, fixed, and almost rigid in the work of Lewis's maturity. . . . Yet, for all that, there are ambiguous undertones in the novels of Lewis's age of innocence, while the conflict of cultural values that has been embodied in his "East" and his "West" will remain a persistent and disturbing theme in the next and most celebrated period of Lewis's work.

One might say that these cultural extremes are the true poles of Lewis's modern American world: that Middle-Class Empire and its House of Babbitt which we now approach.

Consolation

by H. L. Mencken

After all, Munyon was probably right: there is yet hope. Perhaps Emerson and Whitman were right too; maybe even Sandburg is right. What ails us all is a weakness for rash over-generalization, leading to shooting pains in the psyche and delusions of divine persecution. Observing the steady and precipitate descent of promising postulants in beautiful letters down the steep, greasy chutes of the *Saturday Evening Post,* the *Metropolitan,* the *Cosmopolitan* and the rest of the Hearst and Hearstoid magazines, we are too prone, ass-like, to throw up our hands and bawl that all is lost, including honor. But all the while a contrary movement is in progress, far less noted than it ought to be. Authors with their pockets full of best-seller money are bitten by high ambition, and strive heroically to scramble out of the literary Cloaca Maxima. Now and then one of them succeeds, bursting suddenly into the light of the good red sun with the foul liquors of the depths still streaming from him, like a prisoner loosed from some obscene dungeon. Is it so soon forgotten that Willa Cather used to be one of the editors of *McClure's*? That Dreiser wrote editorials for the *Delineator* and was an editor of dime novels for Street & Smith? That Huneker worked for the *Musical Courier*? That Amy Lowell imitated George E. Woodberry and Felicia Hemans? That E. W. Howe was born a Methodist? That Sandburg was once a Chautauqua orator? That Cabell's first stories were printed in *Harper's Magazine*? . . . As I say, they occasionally break out, strange as it may seem. A few months ago I recorded the case of Zona Gale, emerging from her stew of glad books with *Miss Lulu Bett.* Now comes another fugitive, his face blanched by years in the hulks, but his eyes alight with high purpose. His name is Sinclair Lewis, and the work he offers is a novel called *Main Street.*

This *Main Street* I commend to your polite attention. It is, in brief, good stuff. It presents characters that are genuinely human, and not only genuinely human but also authentically American; it carries them through a series of transactions that are all interesting and plausible; it exhibits those transactions thoughtfully and acutely, in the light of the social and cultural forces underlying them; it is well written, and full of a sharp sense of comedy, and rich in observation, and competently designed. Superficially, the story of a man and his wife in a small Minnesota town, it is actually the typical story of the American family—that is, of the family in its first stage, before husband and wife have become lost in father and mother. The average American wife, I daresay, does not come quite so close to downright revolt as Carol Kennicott, but that is the only exaggeration, and we may well overlook it. Otherwise, she and her Will are triumphs of the national normalcy—she with her vague stirrings, her unintelligible yearnings, her clumsy gropings, and he with his magnificent obtuseness, his childish belief in meaningless phrases, his intellectual deafness and near-sightedness, his pathetic inability to comprehend the turmoil that goes on within her. Here is the essential tragedy of American life, and if not the tragedy, then at least the sardonic farce; the disparate cultural development of male and female, the great strangeness that lies between husband and wife when they begin to function as members of society. The men, sweating at their sordid concerns, have given the women leisure, and out of that leisure the women have fashioned disquieting discontents. To Will Kennicott, as to most other normal American males, life remains simple; do your work, care for your family, buy your Liberty Bonds, root for your home team, help to build up your lodge, venerate the flag. But to Carol it is far more complex and challenging. She has become aware of forces that her husband is wholly unable to comprehend, and that she herself can comprehend only in a dim and muddled way. The ideas of the great world press upon her, confusing her and making her uneasy. She is flustered by strange heresies, by romantic personalities, by exotic images of beauty. To Kennicott she is flighty, illogical, ungrateful for the benefits that he and God have heaped upon her. To her he is dull, narrow, ignoble.

Mr. Lewis depicts the resultant struggle with great penetration. He is far too intelligent to take sides—to turn the thing into a mere harangue against one or the other. Above all, he is too intelligent to take the side of Carol, as nine novelists out of ten would have done. He sees clearly what is too often not seen—that her superior culture is, after all, chiefly bogus—that the oafish Kennicott, in more ways than one, is actually better than she is. Her war upon his Philistinism is carried on with essentially Philistine weapons. Her dream of converting a Minnesota prairie town into a sort of Long Island suburb, with overtones of Greenwich Village and the Harvard campus, is quite as absurd as his dream of converting it into a second Minneapolis, with overtones of Gary, Ind., and Paterson, N. J. When their conflict is made concrete and dramatic by the entrance of a *tertium quid,* the hollowness of her whole case is at once made apparent, for this *tertium quid* is a Swedish trousers-presser who becomes a moving-picture actor. It seems to me that the irony here is delicate and delicious. This, then, is the end-product of the Maeterlinck complex! Needless to say, Carol lacks the courage to decamp with her Scandinavian.

Instead, she descends to sheer banality. That is, she departs for Washington, becomes a war-worker, and rubs noses with the suffragettes. In the end, it goes without saying, she returns to Gopher Prairie and the hearthstone of her Will. The fellow is at least honest. He offers her no ignominious compromise. She comes back under the old rules, and is presently nursing a baby. Thus the true idealism of the Republic, the idealism of its Chambers of Commerce, its Knights of Pythias, its Rotary Clubs and its National Defense Leagues, for which Washington froze at Valley Forge and Our Boys died at Chateau Thierry—thus this genuine and unpolluted article conquers the phoney idealism of Nietzsche, Edward W. Bok, Dunsany, George Bernard Shaw, Margaret Anderson, Mrs. Margaret Sanger, Percy Mackaye and the I.W.W.

But the mere story, after all, is nothing; the virtue of the book lies in its packed and brilliant detail. It is an attempt, not to solve the American cultural problem, but simply to depict with great care a group of typical Americans. This attempt is extraordinarily successful. The figures often remain in the flat; the author is quite unable to get that poignancy into them which Dreiser manages so superbly; one seldom sees into them very deeply or feels with them very keenly. But in their externals, at all events, they are done with uncommon skill. In particular, Mr. Lewis represents their speech vividly and accurately. It would be hard to find a false note in the dialogue, and it would be impossible to exceed the verisimilitude of the various extracts from the Gopher Prairie paper, or of the sermon by a Methodist dervish in the Gopher Prairie Wesleyan cathedral, or of a speech by a boomer at a banquet of the Chamber of Commerce. Here Mr. Lewis lays on with obvious malice, but always he keeps within the bounds of probability, always his realism holds up. It is, as I have said, good stuff. I have read no more genuinely amusing novel for a long while. The man who did it deserves a hearty welcome. His apprenticeship in the cellars of the tabernacle was not wasted. . . .

Portrait of an American Citizen

by H. L. Mencken

The theory lately held in Greenwich Village that the merit and success of *Main Street* constituted a sort of double-headed accident, probably to be ascribed to a case of mistaken identity on the part of God—this theory blows up with a frightful roar toward the middle of *Babbitt*. The plain truth is, indeed, that *Babbitt* is at least twice as good a novel as *Main Street* was—that it avoids all the more obvious faults of that celebrated work, and shows a number of virtues that are quite new. It is better designed than *Main Street;* the action is more logical and coherent; there is more imagination in it and less bald journalism; above all, there is a better grip upon the characters. If Carol Kennicott, at one leap, became as real a figure to most literate Americans as Jane Addams or Nan Patterson; then George F. Babbitt should become as real as Jack Dempsey or Charlie Schwab. The fellow simply drips with human juices. Every one of his joints is movable in all directions. Real freckles are upon his neck and real sweat stands out upon his forehead. I have personally known him since my earliest days as a newspaper reporter, back in the last century. I have heard him make such speeches as Cicero never dreamed of at banquets of the Chamber of Commerce. I have seen him marching in parades. I have observed him advancing upon his Presbyterian tabernacle of a Sunday morning, his somewhat stoutish lady upon his arm. I have watched and heard him crank his Buick. I have noted the effect of alcohol upon him, both before and after Prohibition. And I have seen him, when some convention of Good Fellows was in town, at his innocent sports in the parlors of brothels, grandly ordering wine at $10 a round and bidding the professor play "White Wings."

To me his saga, as Sinclair Lewis has set it down, is fiction only by a sort of courtesy. All the usual fittings of the prose fable seem to be absent. There is no plot whatever, and very little of the hocus-pocus commonly called development of character. Babbitt simply grows two years older as the tale unfolds; otherwise he doesn't change at all—any more than you or I have changed since 1920. Every customary device of the novelist is absent. When Babbitt, revolting against the irksome happiness of his home, takes to a series of low affairs with manicure girls, grass-widows and ladies even more complaisant, nothing overt and melodramatic happens to him. He never meets his young son Teddy in a dubious cabaret; his wife never discovers incriminating correspondence in his pockets; no one tries to blackmail him; he is never present when a joint is raided. The worst punishment that falls upon him is that his old friends at the Athletic Club—cheats exactly like himself—gossip about him a bit. Even so, that gossip goes no further; Mrs. Babbitt does not hear it. When she accuses him of adultery, it is simply the formal accusation of a loving wife: she herself has absolutely no belief in it. Moreover, it does not cause Babbitt to break down, confess and promise to sin no more. Instead, he lies like a major-general, denounces his wife for her evil imagination, and returns forthwith to his carnalities. If, in the end, he abandons them, it is not because they torture his conscience, but because they seem likely to hurt his business. This prospect gives him pause, and the pause saves him. He is, beside, growing old. He is 48, and more than a little bald. A night out leaves his tongue coated in the morning. As the curtain falls upon him he is back upon the track of rectitude—a sound business man, a faithful Booster, an assiduous Elk, a trustworthy Presbyterian, a good husband, a loving father, a successful and unchallenged fraud.

Let me confess at once that this story has given me vast delight. I know the Babbitt type, I believe, as well as most; for twenty years I have devoted myself to the exploration of its peculiarities. Lewis depicts it with complete and absolute fidelity. There is irony in the picture; irony that is unflagging and unfailing, but nowhere is there any important departure from the essential truth. Babbitt has a great clownishness in him, but he never becomes a mere clown. In the midst of his most extravagant imbecilities he keeps both feet upon the ground. One not only sees him brilliantly; one also understands him; he is made plausible and natural. As an old professor of Babbittry I welcome him as an almost perfect specimen—a genuine museum piece. Every American city swarms with his brothers. They run things in the Republic, East, West, North, South. They are the originators and propagators of the national delusions—all, that is, save those which spring from the farms. They are the palladiums of 100% Americanism; the apostles of the Harding politics; the guardians of the Only True Christianity. They constitute the Chambers of Commerce, the Rotary Clubs, the Kiwanis Clubs, the Watch and Ward Societies, the Men and Religion Forward Movements, the Y. M. C. A. directorates, the Good Citizen Leagues. They are the advertisers who determine what is to go into the American newspapers and what is to stay out. They are the Leading Citizens, the speakers at banquets, the profiteers, the corruptors of politics, the supporters of evangelical Christianity, the peers of the realm. Babbitt is their archetype. He is no worse than most, and no better; he is the average American of the ruling minority in this hundred and forty-sixth year of the Republic. He is

America incarnate, exuberant and exquisite. Study him well and you will know better what is the matter with the land we live in than you would know after plowing through a thousand such volumes as Walter Lippmann's *Public Opinion*. What Lippmann tried to do as a professor, laboriously and without imagination, Lewis has here done as an artist with a few vivid strokes. It is a very fine piece of work indeed.

Nor is all its merit in the central figure. It is not Babbitt that shines forth most gaudily, but the whole complex of Babbittry, Babbittism, Babbittismus. In brief, Babbitt is seen as no more than a single member of the society he lives in—a matter far more difficult to handle, obviously, than any mere character sketch. His every act is related to the phenomena of that society. It is not what he feels and aspires to that moves him primarily; it is what the folks about him will think of him. His politics is communal politics, mob politics, herd politics; his religion is a public rite wholly without subjective significance; his relations to his wife and his children are formalized and standardized; even his debaucheries are the orthodox debaucheries of a sound business man. The salient thing about him, in truth, is his complete lack of originality—and that is precisely the salient mark of every American of his class. What he feels and thinks is what it is currently proper to feel and think. Only once, during the two years that we have him under view, does he venture upon an idea that is even remotely original—and that time the heresy almost ruins him. The lesson, you may be sure, is not lost upon him. If he lives, he will not offend again. No thought will ever get a lodgment in his mind, even in the wildest deliriums following bootleg gin, that will offer offense to the pruderies of Vergil Gunch, president of the Boosters' Club, or to those of old Mr. Eathorne, president of the First State Bank, or to those of the Rev. Dr. John Jennison Drew, pastor of the Chatham Road Presbyterian Church, or to those of Prof. Pumphrey, head of the Zenith Business College, or even to those of Miss McGoun, the virtuous stenographer. He has been rolled through the mill. He emerges the very model and pattern of a forward-looking, right-thinking Americano.

As I say, this *Babbitt* gives me great delight. It is shrewdly devised; it is adeptly managed; it is well written. The details, as in *Main Street*, are extraordinarily vivid—the speech of Babbitt before the Zenith Real Estate Board, the meeting to consider ways and means of bulging the Chatham Road Sunday-school, the annual convention of the real-estate men, Babbitt's amour with the manicure-girl, the episode of Sir Gerald Doak, the warning visit when Babbitt is suspected of Liberalism, the New Thought meeting, the elopement of young Theodore Roosevelt Babbitt and Eunice Littlefield at the end. In all these scenes there is more than mere humor; there is searching truth. They reveal something; they mean something. I know of no American novel that more accurately presents the real America. It is a social document of a high order.

Babbitt

by Rebecca West

Main Street was a good book. One was as glad that it attained the incredibly tremendous triumph of being an American best-seller as one might be when a thoroughly nice girl wins the Calcutta Sweepstake. But on reading *Main Street* one did not in the least feel as if one were dancing round a bonfire. Heat and light and exhilaration were foreign to the hour. It was a sincere, competent, informative, even occasionally passionate piece of writing, but it had not that something extra and above the logical treatment of its subject—that "peacock's feather in the cap," as Yeats has called it—which makes the work of art. Moreover, it had not much in it of its author's own quality, and that was felt as a serious deprivation by those who were acquainted with Mr. Lewis and his literary past, by those who knew, for example, of the entertaining investigation into spiritualism he conducted on behalf of one of the American magazines. (During the course of this, swathing with seriousness a remarkable personal appearance which bears a strong resemblance to that of Mr. George Grossmith, but made more glorious with red hair, he sat down beside many mediums and asked chokingly for a message from his "dear friend, Mr. H. G. Wells, the English novelist, who recently passed over"; and usually got one.) But these deficiencies are rectified in *Babbitt*. It has that something extra, over and above, which makes the work of art, and it is signed in every line with the unique personality of the writer. It is saturated with America's vitality which makes one obey the rhythms of its dance music, which gives unlimited power over audiences to their actresses whether they be artistically dog-lazy like Ethel Levey, or negligible like Peggy O'Neill. And combined with this, Mr. Lewis has an individual gift of humour, a curiously sage devotion to craftsmanship, and a poetic passion for his own, new country.

To write satire is to perform a miracle. One must hate the world so much that one's hatred strikes sparks, but one must hate it only because it disappoints one's invincible love of it; one must write in denunciation of ugliness and put the thing down in unmistakable black and white, yet keep this, as all written things, within the sphere of beauty. But Mr.

Lewis has been equal to these things. He writes of vulgar Zenith City and its vulgar children, yet never writes a vulgar line. He is merciless to George F. Babbitt, that standardised child of that standardised city, with his pad-cheeks and his puffy hands, his hypocrisy and his ignorance, his dishonesty and his timid sensualities; and he reveals him lovable and pitiable, a strayed soul disconsolate through frustrated desires for honour and beauty. He can flame into transports of exasperation with the religion of business and its paunchy priesthood—marvellous transports these are, for what we have here is the Celt getting angry with the Englishman. For Zenith City and Babbitt are amazingly English. They represent that section of America which seems the least affected by the Latin and Jewish and Celtic leavens; the resemblance of kinship is patent, even blatant. Oh, never star was lost here but it rose afar! Look West where whole new thousands are! In Zenith City what Leverhulme! And the Celt in the person of Mr. Lewis cannot bear it. Vindictively he reports their flat, endlessly repetitive, excessively and simultaneously ignorant and sophisticated conversation at dinner parties and in smoking-cars. He snatches out of the paper enraged parodies of the *Poemulations* they read instead of poetry—by T. Cholmondeley Frink, who was not only the author of *Poemulations,* which, syndicated daily in sixty-seven leading newspapers, gave him one of the largest audiences of any poet in the world, but also an optimistic lecturer and the creator of "Ads. that Add."

> I sat alone and groused and thunk, and scratched my head and sighed and wunk and groaned. There still are boobs, alack, who'd like the old time gin-mill back; that den, that makes a sage a loon, the vile and smelly old saloon! I'll never miss their poison booze, whilst I the bubbling spring can use, that leaves my head at merry morn as clear as any babe new-born!

He describes with deadly malice the proceedings at the lunch of the Zenith Boosters' Club. "The International Organisation of Boosters' Clubs has become a world-force for optimism, manly pleasantry, and good business." Its members all wore a button marked "Boosters—Pep!" At each place at the lunch-table, on the famous day when George F. Babbitt was elected Vice-President, was laid a present, a card printed in artistic red and black:

> SERVICE AND BOOSTERISM.
>
> Service finds its finest opportunity and development only in its broadest and deepest application and the consideration of its perpetual action upon reaction. I believe the highest type of Service, like the most progressive tenets of ethics, senses unceasingly and is motived by active adherence and loyalty to that which is the essential principle of Boosterism—Good Citizenship in all its factors and aspects.
>
> DAD PETERSEN.
>
> Compliments of Dadbury Petersen Advertising Corp.
> "Ads not Fads at Dads."

"The Boosters all read Mr. Petersen's aphorism and said they understood it perfectly."

Yet behind all this is a truth. There is something happening in among these hustling congregations of fat and absurd men. The present condition of George F. Babbitt may be discomfortable. Loathing at the smooth surface of his standardised life, destitute of interstices that might admit romance, may move him to vain and painful flights towards the promise of light; to his comical attempts to find spiritual comfort in the Chatham Street Presbyterian Church; to his efforts to make a synthetic substitute for love out of the kittenish contacts of Mrs. Tanis Judique. ("And shall I call you George? Don't you think it's awfully nice when two people have so much—what shall I say?—analysis that they can discard all these conventions and understand each other and become acquainted right away, like ships that pass in the night?") Little as he has, he yet possesses a promise. The value of that possession can be estimated by comparing Babbitt with his English analogue, Sir Gerald Doak, whom Mr. Lewis shows, touring the States in a state of panic because a title bought by the accumulations of industry in Nottingham brings on him the attentions of earnest hostesses who (misled by their conception of the British aristocracy) talk to him about polo and the galleries of Florence. Paunch for paunch these two sound business men seem much the same. But there is for Babbitt a certain advantage; or perhaps, in the transitional and blundering state of affairs revealed in this book, it should be called a certain opportunity. He moves in a setting so vast and so magnificent that surely it must ultimately dictate vastness and magnificence to the action it contains. There are in this volume a few pages, which must be counted among the masterpieces of satire; they profess to give a verbatim report of the speech delivered by Mr. George F. Babbitt at the Annual Dinner of The Zenith Real Estate Board. In it Mr. Lewis' exasperation rises to the pitch of genius. It dances on the chest of Babbitt's silly standardised self and his silly standardised world. There is one absurd passage, when Babbitt cries:

> "With all modesty, I want to stand up here as a representative business-man and gently whisper, 'Here's our kind of folks! Here's the specifications of the standardised American Citizen! Here's the new generation of Americans: fellows with hair on their chests and smiles in their eyes and adding machines in their offices. . . . So! In my clumsy way I have tried to sketch the Real He-man, the fellow with Zep and Bang! And it's because Zenith has so large a proportion of such men, that it's the most stable, the greatest of our cities. New York also has its thousands of Real Folks, but New York is cursed with unnumbered foreigners. So are Chicago and San Francisco. Oh, we have a golden roster of cities—Detroit and Cleveland with their renowned factories. Cincinnati with its great machine-tool and soap products, Pittsburgh and Birmingham with their steel, Kansas City and Minneapolis and Omaha that open their bountiful gates on the bosom of the ocean-like

> wheatlands, and countless other magnificent sister-cities, for by the last census, there were no less than sixty-eight glorious American burgs with a population of over one hundred thousand! And all these cities stand together for power and purity, and against foreign ideas and communism. Atlanta with Hartford, Rochester with Denver, Milwaukee with Indianapolis, Los Angeles with Scranton, Portland, Maine, with Portland, Oregon. A good live-wire from Baltimore, or Seattle or Duluth is the twin brother of every like fellow booster from Buffalo or Akron, Fort Worth or Oskaloosa!"

It is a bonehead Walt Whitman speaking. Stuffed like a Christmas goose as Babbitt is, with silly films, silly newspapers, silly talk, silly oratory, there has yet struck him the majestic creativeness of his own country, its miraculous power to bear and nourish without end countless multitudes of men and women. He is so silly, so ill-educated (though as he says, "the State University is my own Alma Mater, and I am proud to be known as an alumni") that he prefers to think of it bearing and nourishing countless multitudes of featureless standardised Regular Guys. But there is in these people a vitality so intense that it must eventually bolt with them and land them willy-nilly into the sphere of intelligence; and this immense commercial machine will become the instrument of their aspiration.

> Before he followed his wife, Babbitt stood at the westernmost window of their room. This residential settlement, Floral Heights, was on a rise; and though the centre of the city was three miles away—Zenith had between three and four hundred thousand inhabitants now—he could see the top of the Second National Tower, an Indiana limestone building of thirty-five storeys.
>
> Its shining wall rose against April sky to a simple cornice like a streak of white fire. Integrity was in the tower, and decision. It bore its strength lightly as a tall soldier. As Babbitt stared, the nervousness was soothed from his face, his slack chin lifted in reverence. All he articulated was, "That's one lovely sight!" but he was inspired by the rhythm of the city; his love of it renewed. He beheld the tower as a temple-spire of the religion of business, a faith passionate, exalted, surpassing common men; and as he clumped down to breakfast he whistled the ballad, "Oh, by gee, by gosh, by jingo," as though it were a hymn melancholy and noble.

Sinclair Lewis

by Sherwood Anderson

Of the four American writers concerning whose handling of our speech I have had the temerity to express my own feeling there is left Mr. Sinclair Lewis.

The texture of the prose written by Mr. Lewis gives me but faint joy and I cannot escape the conviction that for some reason Lewis has himself found but little joy, either in life among us or in his own effort to channel his reactions to our life into prose. There can be no doubt that this man, with his sharp journalistic nose for news of the outer surface of our lives, has found out a lot of things about us and the way we live in our towns and cities, but I am very sure that in the life of every man, woman and child in the country there are forces at work that seem to have escaped the notice of Mr. Lewis. Mr. Ring Lardner has seen them and in his writing there is sometimes real laughter, but one has the feeling that Lewis never laughs at all, that he is in an odd way too serious about something to laugh.

For after all, even in Gopher Prairie or in Indianapolis, Indiana, boys go swimming in the creeks on summer afternoons, shadows play at evening on factory walls, old men dig angleworms and go fishing together, love comes to at least a few men and women, and everything else failing, the baseball club comes from a neighboring town and Tom Robinson gets a home run. That's something. There is an outlook on life across which even the cry of a child, choked to death by its own mother, would be something. Life in our American towns and cities is barren enough and there are enough people saying that with the growth of industrialism it has become continually more and more ugly, but Mr. Paul Rosenfeld and Mr. Ring Lardner apparently do not find it altogether barren and ugly. For them and for a growing number of men and women in America there is something like a dawn that Mr. Lewis has apparently sensed but little, for there is so little sense of it in the texture of his prose. Reading Mr. Sinclair Lewis, one comes inevitably to the conclusion that here is a man writing who, wanting passionately to love the life about him, cannot bring himself to do so, and who, wanting perhaps to see beauty descend upon our lives like a rainstorm, has become blind to the minor beauties our lives hold.

And is it not just this sense of dreary spiritual death in the man's work that is making it so widely read? To one who is himself afraid to live there is, I am sure, a kind of joy in seeing other men as dead. In my own feeling for the man from whose pen has come all of this prose over which there are so few lights and shades, I have come at last to sense, most of all, the man fighting terrifically and ineffectually for a thing about which he really does care. There is a kind of fighter living inside Mr. Sinclair Lewis and there is, even in this dull, unlighted prose of his, a kind of dawn coming. In the dreary ocean of this prose, islands begin to appear. In *Babbitt* there are moments when the people of whom he writes, with such amazing attention to the outer details of lives, begin to think and feel a little, and with the coming of life into his people a kind of nervous, hurried beauty and life flits, like a lantern carried by a night watchman past the window of a factory as one stands waiting and watching in a grim street on a night of December.

Round Up

by Constance Rourke

Retrospect has deepened in these narratives,[1] spreading over a wider area than in the '70's and '80's, finding closer human values; fancy has taken new forms. The comic is no longer the single prevailing impulse, but has receded to a simpler and more casual, perhaps a more natural place, as in the later poetry; the harsh emotions of an early day are mingled with others of more varied character. But even with the widening range, which might seem to permit the easier and more direct view, the immediate scene has not been penetrated with imaginative force and fullness. With one exception none of those definitive novelists have appeared who make an aspect of contemporary life their own and leave it with the color of their imagination upon it forever afterward.

The exception of course is Sinclair Lewis; he possesses the copious touch; and people of the present day fill his pages. Yet with all his grasp of an immediate life, Lewis remains within the older American tradition; he is primarily a fabulist. In *Main Street* he stresses his intention at the outset.

> On a hill by the Mississippi where Chippewas had camped two generations ago, a girl stood in relief against the cornflower blue of Northern sky. She saw no Indians now; she saw flour-mills and the blinking windows of skyscrapers in Minneapolis and St. Paul. . . . A breeze which had crossed a thousand miles of wheatlands bellied her taffeta skirt in a line so graceful, so full of animation and moving beauty, that the heart of a chance watcher on the lower road tightened to wistfulness over her quality of suspended freedom. . . . The days of pioneering, of lassies in sunbonnets, and bears killed with axes in piney clearings, are deader now than Camelot; and a rebellious girl is the spirit of that bewildered empire called the American Middlewest.

[1] Not only the novels of Willa Cather, but many novels of the first three decades of this century whose "purpose is to recover if possible the essence of the past, some lost quality, a vanished stream." [M.S.]

Even occasional digressions from immediate circumstance in *Main Street* have the fabulous touch, like the wind that blows a thousand miles, or the eras of history brought to bear upon the Kennicott's courtship. Later in the book Lewis changes his definition of the pioneer, declaring that the farmers—"those sweaty wayfarers"—whose lands surround Gopher Prairie and stretch into the farther distance, are pioneers, "for all their telephones and bank-accounts and automatic pianos and co-operative leagues." In the end Gopher Prairie itself takes on aspects of a pioneer existence, half shaped, inarticulate, pressed against an uncertain void. Then once again the theme enlarges, and Main Street becomes a national street, its existence a pervasive American existence.

This is that highly circumstantial fable-making which had been a characteristic American gift; and the prevailing tone is one which had appeared within the whole line of American fabulists, particularly those of the frontier. The material is prosaic, the mood at bottom romantic; gusto infuses the whole, with an air of discovery. Even the derision is not a new note; this had appeared again and again in American attitudes toward American life, and is part of the enduring native self-consciousness; it is seen here, as before, in a close tie with the comic. Lewis uses homely metaphors that might have been spoken by Yankee Hill, describing "an old farmer, solid, wholesome, but not clean—his face like a potato fresh from the earth." The familiar biting understatement appears, and the inflation; the western strain is as strong in Lewis as the Yankee. "She sat down as though it were a gymnasium exercise." "He was always consulting John Flickerbaugh, who handled more real estate than law, and more law than justice." The American gift for comic mimicry seems concentrated in Lewis, and his people seem to possess the unfailing native passion for the monologue: flood-gates of their talk are opened at a touch. Sights, sounds, the look of things and of people, as well as speech, are crowded against one another with tireless fluency. Nothing halts this movement in *Main Street;* nothing halts the cumulative intention; episode is piled on episode. The movement lengthens, and finally becomes in the large flow sagalike. The outcome is to portray the generic; the human situation steadily diminishes in force. At the beginning it is clear that the division between Carol and Kennicott is emotional, not civic: but the human circumstance is pushed aside by an urgent intention to reveal a comprehensive aspect of American life. The preoccupation is the familiar social preoccupation.

Lewis displays a detachment which never belonged to the early fabulists. Babbitt's shrewd traction dealings are seen with an appraising eye instead of with that exhilaration by which earlier artists had been carried away, viewing similar triumphs. An unmitigated nationalism is slit by the same penetrative view; and that primitive desire for cohesion which had risen strongly through early comedy is shown to have become the crudest of mass instincts. Lewis turns his abundant fables into critiques and challenges, but the transcendent effect is the traditional effect: the American portrait, a comic portrait once more, has been drawn in amplitude. Babbitt takes a place beside the archetypal Yankee; and for the first time an archetypal native scene is drawn in Main Street. The response too has been the habitual response. Bitterly as the direct seizure of American life has been resented, it has offered the portrait; the mirror was upheld, and the American with his invincible curiosity about himself could not fail to gaze therein.

There is a sense in which Lewis may be considered the first American novelist. In his unflagging absorption of detail and his grasp of the life about him he suggests Defoe; and it may be that like Defoe in England he will prove to have opened a way for the development of the novel in America. The impact of his scrutiny lies all about; the American scene and the American character can never slide back into the undifferentiated state of an earlier view. Yet the novel may not develop at all in America in the older sense. In England it arose out of an immensely long preparation even before Defoe; for a century its growth was gradual; in the Victorian period it came to a great completion. If the word Victorian means anything on the English side it is a rich and settled stability within which traditions, long rooted, could come into bloom; the outlines of the Victorian period were not straitened but hospitable, so that the most divergent motives and movements found comfortable quarters there. No mere spatial invitation of a continent could offer the same breadth or depth. No such accumulation of effort and tradition has been possible in the short and broken cycle of American life; traditions are even now only beginning to take a coherent shape. Part of the vexing judgment of American literature has come from the expectation on the American side, born of an exhilarated fancy, that American literature could match English literature.

An Interpreter of American Life

by Robert Morss Lovett

Mr. Sinclair Lewis, like Mr. H. L. Mencken, is a paradox in the United States of to-day. A leading trait of the American people is a youthful self-consciousness amounting to an inferiority complex, which makes us impatient of all criticism. Everything which we have done is right because we did it. All our wars were just; all our statesmen are pure; all our business is honest. Ours is the land of liberty, of tolerance, of opportunity, of righteousness. Our favourite prophets are the sayers of smooth things in Zion, those who speak comfortably to Jerusalem of her ideals and performances—Wilson, Harding, Coolidge. And yet by some sort of saving grace, in the midst of this complacency appear Mr. Lewis and Mr. Mencken, to tear the hoods and sheets off our moral and civic Ku Klux Klan, to show the cringing forms and the false, cowardly, cruel faces beneath the mask—and Mr. Mencken and Mr. Lewis as critic and novelist are, in this day and generation, the most read and considered interpreters of American life. They are constantly telling truths about their country for which less fortunate devils are being hounded out of pulpits and college chairs, losing business and social standing, and occasionally suffering physical punishment at the hands of court or clan, and yet they flourish like two green bay trees.

One explanation of this phenomenon is to be found in the fact that both Mr. Mencken and Mr. Lewis write the American language. It is a natural impulse when one hears one's own tongue in the midst of foreign speech—and most of his literature is foreign to the ordinary sensual American—to turn and listen, even if the meaning is unpleasant. And a second explanation lies in the fact that both Mr. Mencken and Mr. Lewis are good-natured and affable. They find the spectacle one tending to amusement rather than indignation. Humour is the form in which the American takes his cathartic—*The Biglow Papers,* Josh Billings, Artemus Ward, and Mark Twain, for examples. Even so there is still an unexplainable residuum, especially in the case of Mr. Lewis who is undoubtedly long and, in the opinion of many readers whose devotion is the more remarkable, dull. If Mr. Lewis attracts his great audience by the sense of reality which his pages convey, and the careless humour of his approach, he holds it by a sense of the importance of what he has to say.

In *Main Street* Mr. Lewis employed the inclusive formula of the naturalists, setting down as much of the visual and audible stuff of life in Gopher Prairie as his vehicle could carry, the motive power being furnished by the ambitions of Carol Kennicott, wife of the local physician. In *Babbitt* he adopted a much more rapid and impressionistic method. The life of Zenith is merely the background for the hero, who in his egregious vulgarity and pitiful self-conceit, is accepted everywhere along with General Dawes as the typical American business man, booster, and patrioteer. If *Main Street* looks back to Zola, *Babbitt* is in the more humorous, highly coloured, exaggerated manner of Daudet. George F. Babbitt is an American Tartarin. In *Arrowsmith,* Mr. Lewis returns to his earlier method. There is much of life as it is lived in a Mid-Western university town, a Dakota village, an Iowa city, and finally in New York; but the background is chiefly occupational as in the classics of the Rougon-Macquart series. Martin Arrowsmith is a physician and a medical scientist, and the experience of his disillusionment with that high calling is the core of the book. We first meet Arrowsmith as a medical student at the University of Winnemac; he gives up his scientific passion for a wife and general practice in the village of Wheatsylvania; he is stirred by the pretentious programme of public health, and becomes assistant and finally successor to Dr. Pickerbaugh, Director of Public Health of Nautilus, Iowa. Driven forth by a citizenry justly indignant at his interference with business as usual, he turns to the McGurk Institute for medical research in New York. After fighting the bubonic plague in one of the Lesser Antilles where his wife, Leora, dies, he returns to find the disinterested pursuit of truth as remote to the patrons and directors of McGurk as to the politicians of Nautilus, and takes refuge in a sort of hermitage of research among the Vermont hills.

In all this there is something of the conscientious thoroughness of Zola. Mr. Lewis is determined to leave no stone of the medical edifice unturned, and under each he finds human nature in reptilian form. Indeed, to reach the fraud of the commercial drug firm he is obliged to cut loose from the hero and follow the story of his teacher, Professor Gottlieb, on his way from Winnemac to McGurk. Undoubtedly in this occupational interest we miss something of the regional unity of *Main Street* and *Babbitt.* We do not know Mohalis, Wheatsylvania, and Nautilus as we do Gopher Prairie and Zenith. Toward the end of the book the social background of New York is hardly realized at all, and this is the chief reason why its entrance into Arrowsmith's life with his second marriage seems mere fiction. The essential truth of Arrowsmith's experience as medical student, country doctor, and director of public health, no physician will question. Even the preposterous Pickerbaugh, Director of Public Health of Nautilus, Iowa, is plausible enough to readers in New York and Chicago. Pickerbaugh revives the exuberant caricature of Babbitt. Besides his titular office he is "founder of the first Rotary Club in Iowa; superintendent of the Jonathan Edwards Congregational Sunday School of Nautilus; president of the Moccasin Ski and Hiking Club, of the West Side Bowling Club, and the 1912 Bull Moose and Roosevelt Club; organizer and cheer-leader of a Joint Picnic of the Woodmen, Moose, Elks, Masons, Oddfellows, Turnverein, Knights of Columbus, B'nai B'rith, and the Y.M.C.A.; and winner of the prizes both for reciting the largest number of biblical texts and for dancing the best Irish jig at the Harvest Moon Soirée of the Jonathan Edwards Bible Class for the Grown-ups," and author of such rhyming roads to health as

> Boil the milk bottles, or by gum
> You better buy your ticket to Kingdom Come.

All this is in Mr. Lewis's best vein. When he conducts Arrowsmith to the McGurk laboratory we feel that he is on less firm ground. Here he is indebted to Mr. Paul H. DeKruif for the inside stuff. The bacteriological detail is, of course, sound. Never before in fiction has the psychology of the scientist, the passion for research, been rendered with such penetration and justice. When, however, Arrowsmith in fighting the plague in St. Hubert is bidden by his scientific conscience to divide the population into two parts, one half to be inoculated with his phage, the other to be refused in order absolutely to control the results of the experiment, we have either an example of scientific fanaticism or a piece of pure fiction. The phenomena of the plague have been sufficiently observed to make it practically certain that, if all who were inoculated under favourable circumstances survived, the remedy had been found—and probably half the population would have resisted inoculation anyway. This air of unreality hangs over the latter part of the book as Mr. Lewis becomes more absorbed in his purpose. Leora's death, from smoking in the laboratory a half finished cigarette on which a maid had spilt a test-tude of germs, at the time when Martin is caressing another woman, is necessary to Mr. Lewis's programme. This other woman, Joyce Lanyon, the symbol of the intrusion of the social world into the privacies of science, would be obnoxious were she not quite inconceivable. We suspect her, along with Capitola McGurk, Rippleton Holabird, and other inmates of the McGurk Institute, of being aimed at the people who have been annoying Dr. DeKruif. As such they do not reach their mark.

Arrowsmith is an important step in the campaign to de-bamboozle the American public and relieve its institutions of bunk. Mr. Lewis has attacked this old enemy in one of its highest places. In all phases of medicine—education, private and public practice, and finally research—

he has revealed its pretensions and exposed its perpetrators. If he has sacrificed the reality of fiction, it is in the interest of the reality of a public cause which gives largeness of view and significance to *Arrowsmith.*

Mr. Babbitt's Spiritual Guide

by Joseph Wood Krutch

With *Elmer Gantry* Mr. Lewis returns to the practice of his own particular trade. In *Arrowsmith* he turned aside in an effort to achieve certain qualities, characteristic of the conventional novel, which his detractors had declared outside his range, and in *Mantrap* he demonstrated that he had not forgotten the requirements of merely popular fiction. The new book is in every way a companion volume to *Main Street* and *Babbitt*. In it the author, sure of the tested effectiveness of a certain technique, and with a zeal undiminished by success, turns his attention to Mr. Babbitt's spiritual guide and adds the third member to his impressive trilogy devoted to the most grotesque aspects of American life. What *Main Street* was to the small town and *Babbitt* to the business man that, neither more nor less, is *Elmer Gantry* to the vulgarest contemporary type of pulpit-thumping materialist.

The book begins with its hero, a coarse young giant, happily engaged in a street fight and in that most blissful condition to which a powerful young man can attain—"unrighteous violence in a righteous cause"; it carries him through his muddled conversion in a denominational college, through the ups and downs of his checkered career as pastor and evangelist; and it ends with his triumphant vindication at the hands of an enthusiastic congregation from the latest of the many near-scandals which threatened his career. Too unreflective ever to know himself, too incapable of thought ever to be really a hypocrite, Elmer is honored and beloved of most of those with whom he comes in contact because he is made of the same coarse clay as they, because no learning, no integrity, and no spirituality sets him apart from those to whom he is paid to minister. He is the type most fit to occupy the pulpits supported by materialists like himself to whom the church is half the defender of petty privileges against subversive forces and half the instrument through which a nominal respect may be paid to virtues inconvenient to practice; and to Elmer himself the pulpit is quite as useful as he is to it since, by virtue of the license which permits him to mount it, he is enabled not only to taste the intoxication of an orator's power but to enjoy as well an income and a position which the mediocrity of his will, the fundamental meanness of his character, and the shallowness of his brain could not have earned for him by any other means.

Mr. Lewis is careful not to leave his picture unrelieved. He does take pains to indicate that every one of the few civilizing influences which the boy Elmer ever received—the most rudimentary forms of art, music, literacy, learning, and ethical idealism—had been, in his experience, connected with the church, and he allows to appear momentarily upon the scene certain ministers of a higher type. But in the book it is everywhere darkness that prevails. Elmer himself has not a single quality which goes to the making of a decent man. He is heartless, treacherous, and cruel; he has nothing resembling even the puritan virtues except the vices of vindictiveness, phariseeism, and hypocrisy into which they can turn; and his career is an indictment of the church as a whole at least in so far as it shows how the mechanism of the church permits the rise of such a man and demands of its servants no qualities which viciousness cannot convincingly imitate. *Elmer Gantry* is as good as *Main Street* and *Babbitt* and it is good in exactly the same way. Here again, as in the two books which made Mr. Lewis's the best-known name among contemporary American novelists, is a completeness of documentation not less than amazing, a power of mimicry which, so far as I know, no living author can equal, and a gusto which, considering the meanness of the material, is all but inexplicable. No mere study, however painstaking and devoted, could make possible the intimate ease with which Mr. Lewis handles the material or the completeness with which he fills in the details of every picture. He seems to know the life he is describing with a thoroughness which could only come from his having in a real sense lived in it; the contagious rapture with which he pours out his scenes is the only thing which can keep one from entertaining a profound pity for a writer compelled to do anything so dreadful. Some strange twist in Mr. Lewis's character has enabled him to take a joy in examining, almost participating in, mediocrity at its most grotesquely intolerable moments, and has enabled him, miraculously, to make it interesting to others too.

In one respect at least *Elmer Gantry* is superior even to its companion pieces, for up to the last seventy-five pages (which are distinctly less interesting than the rest) it has a greater variety of incident and a more sustained interest than either of the other two. In both *Babbitt* and *Main Street* there was a certain static, descriptive quality. The picture unfolded without developing new interest, and there was no continuous, steady march of incident, while in the new book there is a progressive plot which never, until it has almost reached its conclusion, shows any signs of flagging. There is, besides, an exposure of Elmer's character which goes further, perhaps, than anything else to justify Mr. Lewis's method—an exposure which seems detached, unhurried, relentless; too calm and too sure to seem to spring from hatred or malice, but inspired by a rage which a confidence in his power to describe has calmed.

Elmer Gantry, with its innumerable incidents and its many ramifications, is indeed a structure far more impressive than most satires, a sort of cathedral in which every stone is a gargoyle; and though there will be many who will not be able to read it without the Devil's question, "But what is art?" it is not likely that any review will answer that question definitively. At least it can be said that Mr. Lewis has done something that no one else is capable of doing. In a manner that seems to be merely the almost too literal truth but which manages nevertheless to contain its own criticism he has, in three books, recorded a reign of grotesque vulgarity which but for him would have left no record of itself because no one else could have adequately recorded it.

Sinclair Lewis Introduces Elmer Gantry

by Rebecca West

This sequence of sermons and seductions—two forms of human activity which Mr. Lewis, contrary to the opinion of mankind from pole to pole, represents as on a common plane of tedium—is probably one of the most disappointing books that a man of genius has ever produced. It is full of wilful abnegations of fine qualities. Why should Mr. Lewis, who used to tread the sward of our language as daintily as a cat, use the word *amour?* Not *an amour,* which is good eighteenth-century English, but *amour.* "When Elmer as a freshman just arrived from the pool halls and frame high school of Paris, Kansas, had begun to learn the decorum of amour. . . ." In 1917 he ceased, we are told, "to educate his wife in his ideals of amour." A loathsome usage. It makes one see a pimpled male child smoking a cheap cigar outside a place marked "Eats," sustaining his soul against the drabness of Main Street by turning over in his mind a nickelodeon conception of Europe. So need not Mr. Lewis be, unless he chooses.

Mr. Lewis has also thrown away his sound engineering capacity for handling incident, such as he showed, for example, in contriving the death of Leora in *Arrowsmith.* In the course of this novel it becomes necessary for him in a manner of speaking to incinerate Aimée Semple McPherson, and a poor job he makes of it. Elmer Gantry meets and preaches and is entwined with a woman evangelist named Sharon Falconer, who is a sufficiently curious and interesting conception. She is a play-acting hussy, little Katie Jonas of the Utica brickyards, who flows above reality on the tides of her own ecstasy, being God's right hand in a flowing white robe among lilies and roses in a shell-shaped pulpit in a mission tent, being a member of "an old Virginian family" in correct sports clothes in "her old home" (acquired from an authentic Virginian family bearing the name of Sprugg by a series of financial transactions ultimately unsatisfactory to the Spruggs), being a pure and holy woman in circumstances that would make most of us withdraw the claim, because of her conviction that whatever happens to her is sanctified: A new expression of Madame Guyon in terms of Lulu Belle. She has all the charm of the fantasy builder, who combines the fascination of the talented liar capable at any moment of arranging the phenomena of reality into a wilder pattern than that into which life has cast them; and she has also the lovability of the perfectly sincere person who believes every word she is saying and will be as hideously disappointed as anybody if it is brought home to her that it is not true. She would be a remarkable creation if, oddly enough, she had not absorbed her creator. When she stages a preposterous scene for her first amorous encounter with Elmer, in a shrine which had apparently been prised out of the Paramount Picture Theatre, with chanted prayers in the Los Angeles free-liturgical style, one has an uneasy feeling that Mr. Lewis himself is as impressed as Elmer Gantry was; that, for a minute, he has sunk from his own high level to that where little Katie Jonas of the Utica brickyard put it over on him.

It seems good to Mr. Lewis that Sharon should die a violent death, that Gantry may be bereft and free to find his way to the orthodox pastorate where we leave him; though these surely are the aniline dyes of the fancy rather than the sunset colours of the imagination. Surely the way of life would have been that she would have passed into a fantasy where he was not, and looked at him with a lack of knowledge of him which would have been as integral and true to itself as her lying, as her sincerity, as her purity, as her voluptuousness. But Mr. Lewis insists on grilling her to a cinder in a pier hall that goes on fire during a big meeting, and his preparations for this climax are unbelievably, disgracefully crude. Preliminary hints concerning the layout of the hall, explanations during the crisis of exactly where the flames broke out so that the platform party would not get away, remind one of the maps people used to make during the war on the dinner-table with forks and spoons and glasses. One has the same conviction that there are times when clarity ought to be sacrificed to the preservation of even a superficial harmony.

Now, Mr. Lewis is a very considerable person. He has mimetic genius to an extent that has hardly ever been transcended. *Babbitt* as a book was planless; its end arrived apparently because its author had come to the end of the writing-pad, or rather, one might suspect from its length, to the end of all writing-pads then on the market. But George Babbitt was a triumph of impersonation. It was a bit of character-exhibition comparable to Mr. Micawber; and if it be recalled to Mr. Lewis's disadvantage that Dickens invented a host of characters as vivid, it can also be recalled that never did Dickens make so complete an inventory of a human being as Mr. Lewis does in George Babbitt. We know the poor fatuous being in his standing up and his lying down. And so, too, we know Elmer Gantry, this snorting, cringing creature, this offspring of the hippopotamus and the skunk, between whose coarse lips the texts sound as if he were munching sappy vegetation, under whose coarse hands sex becomes a series of gross acts of the body ending in grosser acts of the spirit, such as deceit and cruelty. There are one or two conversations in the book—the scene where he refuses to marry a frightened girl who pretends she is going to have his child, the scene where he rushes like a charging pachyderm on his moneyed and insipid bride—when one can hear in one's ears the alternate whine and snarl of the creature, its blind bellow, its canoodling softer tones. How exquisite, too, is his response to Mr. North, the vice-crusader, when that gentleman at last comes across with the long-sought invitation to speak on behalf of the National Association for the Purification of Art and the Press. "Do you suppose you could address the Detroit Y. M. C. A. on October 4?" "Well, it's my wife's birthday, and we've always made rather a holiday of it—we're proud of being an old-fashioned homey family—but I know Cleo wouldn't want that to stand in the way of my doing anything I can to further the Kingdom." How exquisite also are his notes for a sermon:

Love:
a rainbow
AM and PM star
from cradle to tomb
inspires art etc. music voice of love
slam atheists etc. who do not appreciate love.

Since Mr. Lewis has not lost this power of impersonation, since he has on certain pages exercised it even more successfully than he has ever done before, there must be some flaw in the central conception of the book which explains why the effect of the whole is tedious, and why he falls into these tricks of flat writing and lethargic handling of incidents. The sense of tedium must be the result of one's feeling that all these sermons and seductions are leading nowhere. The incompetence must be the result of the author's feeling that the enterprise on which he has embarked is not worth while. The trouble is that the book is not merely the life of a particular individual named Elmer Gantry, it is a satire on organized religion; and Mr. Lewis has neglected a very necessary condition which the satirist must fulfil before he starts working.

What that condition is has probably never been more neatly illustrated than by Yvonne Printemps in the vaudeville prelude of *L'Illusioniste.* She comes forth as the singer and dancer who practises under the *nom de guerre* of—is it Miss Hopkins or Miss Tompkins? It is ten years since I saw the play and I can remember only its essence. It is at any rate an English *nom de guerre,* for she is a second-rater and needs every adventitious aid she can find, and an English singer has an aroma of romance; since all the peoples of the world suspect that their neighbours have been endowed with an intenser life than themselves, and in peace are more alluring, as in war they are more hateful. Assuming this meagre personality, Yvonne Printemps gives a performance that is a satire on nearly all bad singing and dancing; on nearly all bad art of every kind. She cannot let her personality speak for itself. She has to point her youth and prettiness by assuming a baby beauty expression which is superimposed on the real expression into which her innate characteristics and her embarrassment at the present situation have moulded her young flesh, so that the result is confused and ineffective. She lifts up her little voice and it is strangled to a weak pretty pipe in her throat, because she has no clear idea of what sounds she wishes to produce. She importunes the audience, "Listen! Listen! I am being tender! Listen! Listen! In a minute I am going to be even more tender!" Even so her dancing creates no definite effect because she has not previously imagined a pattern woven through the air which she must follow, and her movements are retarded and qualified by this doubt of her enterprise.

Yvonne Printemps is able to do all this because she knows how not to do all this. She is an artist. She paints her personality not by assuming airs and graces, but by eliminating everything that is irrelevant to its effective characteristics. She has so clear a conception of what she wants to do before she does it that her voice and her movements flow in an unimpeded stream of grace towards their goal. Having known from the beginning that she was going to encounter certain crises in her theme, she is able to treat them with absolute justice, not dragging them on before their turn, not intervening between them and the audience by explanatory overemphasis. It is because she has habitually practised perfection that she is able to anatomize imperfection and imitate it.

That is the first necessary condition which the satirist must fulfil. He must fully possess, at least in the world of the imagination, the quality the lack of which he is deriding in others.

Mr. Lewis does not fulfil that necessary condition of the satirist. He has not entered into imaginative possession of those qualities the lack of which he derides in others. He pillories Elmer Gantry and those who follow him because they are obviously misusing the force that makes men want to speak and to hear speech of religion; but he has no vision of the use they ought to be making of it. The passages in the book which present to one what Mr. Lewis regards as the proper attitude to religion are disconcertingly jejune—are disconcertingly on the same mental plane as Elmer Gantry. There is a St. Francis of Assisi type of good man who worries not at all about theology because of the comfort he can draw for himself and for others from God the Father. But he is perfunctorily described. One seems to hear a flushed and disorderly introduction, "Wancha to meet Father Pengilly. One of the best friens I have." . . . Mr. Lewis's enthusiasm over him is as glib and rootless and meaningless as the getting together of the salesmen of the Pequot Farm Implement Company, which he so masterfully records ("My name's Ad Locust—Jesus, think of it! The folks named me Adney. Can you beat that? Ain't that one hell of a name for a fellow that likes to get out with the boys and have a good time! But you can just call me Ad") and from which he so properly recoils.

There is—and this is far more painful—a sincere seeker after truth named Frank Shallard, a minister who is troubled by doubts, who against all his worldly interests gives up his ministry because he is not satisfied of the validity of the Christian religion. But, he turns out to be an albino Babbitt; and those doubts are represented as taking place on a mental plane lower than is conceivable.

Listen, for example, to his remarks on Jesus:

". . . I'm appalled to say I don't find Jesus an especially admirable character!

"He is picturesque. He tells splendid stories. He's a good fellow, fond of low company. . . . But He's vain. He praises himself outrageously, He's fond of astonishing people by little magical tricks which we've been taught to revere as 'miracles.' He is furious as a child in a tantrum when people don't recognize Him as a great leader. He loses His temper. He blasts the poor barren fig-tree when it doesn't feed Him . . . Far from the Christian religion—or any other religion—being a blessing to humanity, it's produced such confusion in all thinking, such second-hand viewing of actualities, that only now are we beginning to ask what and why we are and what we can do with life!

"Just what are the teachings of Christ? Does He come to bring peace or more war? He says both. Did He approve earthly monarchies or rebel against them? He says both. Did He ever—think of it, God Himself, taking on human form to help the earth—did He ever suggest sanitation, which would have saved millions from plagues? . . .

"What *did* He teach? One place in the Sermon on the Mount He advises—let me get my Bible—here it is: 'Let your light so shine before men that they may see your good works and glorify your Father which is in heaven,' and then five minutes later, 'Take heed that ye do not your alms before men, to be seen of them, otherwise ye have no reward of your Father which is in heaven.' That's an absolute contradiction. Oh, I know you can reconcile them. . . . That's the whole aim of ministerial training. . . ."

Now, is this not reverse English for Babbittry? Remember, Mr. Lewis is not exhibiting this stuff for our pity; he is not tearfully demonstrating that the texture of life in the American hinterland is so miserably poor that even the best of it is far less than good; he is holding it up for our admiration. Actually he admires this clodhopping comment on that tale of a Son of God who comes down and partakes of life and death along with man, which is so near to some fantasy that lies at the heart of all created men that, no matter whether we believe in its actual truth and whether it comforts us or not, we know it as something as much a part of us as our flesh and blood, as something intensely relevant to being. He can tolerate re-entrance into that mood of scorn for the past which makes *A Yankee at the Court of King Arthur* one of the most painful books in the world. Mark Twain looked at medieval Europe and said in astonishment: "My, weren't they dumb?" because he was so uninstructed that he believed the philosophical assumptions of his age had always existed for the intelligent to lay hold of when they wanted, and was unaware that they had been slowly and courageously snatched out of chaos by the past he was despising. Even so, Mr. Lewis talks of the Church as something apart from human thought and a brake on it, whereas the Church happened to be a channel, and for centuries the main channel of human thought. "It's produced such confusion in all thinking" . . . Zip! Bam! Zowie! It was St. Thomas Aquinas who went that time. As for that suggestion that Christ should have halted on the way to the Cross to recommend the American bathroom, no doubt performing a really useful miracle by placing the requisite metallurgical resources at the disposal of the population of Palestine slightly ahead of time, it ought to go into the Americana section of the *American Mercury*.

Is it not curiously below Mr. Lewis's form? Is not that comparison between the two tests strange in one who wrote such a fervent plea that George F. Babbitt should let the light of his real character shine before men instead of darkening it by insincere standardized speech and behaviour, and who should know better than to regard an ordinary rule of good manners as contradiction to that plea?

The trouble is that Mr. Lewis is possessed by an idea that in order to combat Babbittry it is necessary to enter into argument with Babbitt; to disprove what he says; to reverse his opinions. This is a profound error which if persisted in would sterilize all radicalism. Babbitt receives pernicious ideas because he is arguing on a plane of thought where it is pretended that life is simpler and coarser than it is, so that our conclusions reached there can be valid in reality. Merely to contradict him is to take up another position in a futile world of fantasy. It is no effective repartee to prohibition to get drunk on Scotch. That is merely to match one crudity with another. But to educate one's perceptions in the direction of ecstasy by taking exactly the right amount of Napoleon brandy, that is an assertion of all that prohibition denies. In the practical world one may have to fight Babbitt when he does something foolish and tyrannous, and it may be the duty of the artist to turn journalist for a second or two and explain to the general public exactly what the silly old fool has been up to. But in the world of art, in the world of intellect, the artist must first raise himself above Babbitt by practising a finer and more complicated mode of thought and feeling. That Mr. Lewis has failed to do. Just as he ends by consorting with little Katie Jonas of the brickyards as an equal, so he approaches Elmer Gantry on his own level. The result of that is that this book will not start any great movement towards enhanced sensitiveness of life, which might make people reject fake religion. It will start a purely factual controversy as to whether parsons do in any large numbers get drunk and toy with their stenographers, which is really a matter of very little importance. Because hypocrisy stinks in the nostrils one is likely to rate it as a more powerful agent for destruction than it is. It is the creatures, with longings so largely and vaguely evil, that they cannot disappoint them by realizing them in the terms afforded by this wholesome world who make the dangerous opposition; as all those must realize who have heard the most famous vice-crusader preach and marked how he got more lustful pleasure out of saying the word *brothel* than any sinner ever got by going to one.

Why has Mr. Lewis produced a book that in spite of its humour, its research, its bravery, has not succeeded in being the satire he has the wit to plan? It is because he has not left himself enough energy to make that ultimate vigorous contraction of the muscles of the soul which is necessary for a work of genius. He has dissipated his forces in going about making the effect of a hand grenade, in throwing up his hat and cheering at floridities of existence that anybody over fourteen ought to take calmly. He has committed himself to pettiness by imitating the futile school of radicalism which finds no game too small and will on occasion waste powder and shot on a silly old woman in Iowa who announces her intention of reading the Bible for the three hundredth time in her life, as if Voltaire would have got anywhere if he had spent his emotions on the pietistic errors of washerwomen in Brittany. If he would sit still so that life could make any deep impression on him, if he would attach himself to the human tradition by occasionally reading a book which would set him a standard of profundity, he could give his genius a chance.

Sinclair Lewis and the Method of Half-Truths

by Mark Schorer

Let us begin with a pair of quotations that are concerned with the conception of the novel as a social instrument. The two conceptions are opposed, but the author of each is led by his conception to conclude that because of it the novel is the most important literary form in the modern world, and *for* the modern world. The first is from D. H. Lawrence, and it is, I believe, a unique conception:

> It is the way our sympathy flows and recoils that really determines our lives. And here lies the vast importance of the novel, properly handled. It can inform and lead into new places the flow of our sympathetic consciousness, and it can lead our sympathy away in recoil from things gone dead. Therefore, the novel, properly handled, can reveal the most secret places of life: for it is in the *passional* secret places of life, above all, that the tide of sensitive awareness needs to ebb and flow, cleansing and freshening.
>
> But the novel, like gossip, can also excite spurious sympathies and recoils, mechanical and deadening to the psyche. The novel can glorify the most corrupt feelings, so long as they are *conventionally* "pure." Then the novel, like gossip, becomes at last vicious, and, like gossip, all the more vicious because it is always ostensibly on the side of the angels.[1]

Lawrence's conception implies a novel that will admit us directly into the life-affirming activities of the integrated consciousness of his own ideal man; a novel that, concerned with the formed individual consciousness, reforms ours; a novel that is not about society or the social character but that is ultimately indispensable to the health of both. We know whose fiction he has in mind; we know, too, with what exasperation he achieved the first term of his exalted ambition, the writing itself, and how impossible it is to achieve the second, the therapy.

Our second quotation is a commonplace in the annals of American naturalism, and we could find it, in substance, in any of a dozen writers. Frank Norris will serve. I quote first from his essay, "The Responsibilities

[1] *Lady Chatterley's Lover* (Florence, 1928), p. 118.

of the Novelist," an attack on what he calls "lying novels," novels of sentiment and romance.

> Today is the day of the novel. In no other day and by no other vehicle is contemporaneous life so adequately expressed; and the critics of the twenty-second century, reviewing our times, striving to reconstruct our civilization, will look not to the painters, not to the architects nor dramatists, but to the novelists to find our idiosyncrasy. . . . If the novel . . . is popular it is popular with a reason, a vital, inherent reason; that is to say, it is essential . . . it is an instrument, a tool, a weapon, a vehicle. Public opinion is made no one can say how, by infinitesimal accretions, by a multitude of minutest elements. Lying novels, surely in this day and age of indiscriminate reading, contribute to this more than all other influences of present-day activity . . . The People have a right to the Truth as they have a right to life, liberty and the pursuit of happiness. It is *not* right that they be exploited and deceived with false views of life, false characters, false sentiment, false morality, false history, false philosophy, false emotions, false heroism, false notions of self-sacrifice, false views of religion, of duty, of conduct and of manners.[2]

And where do we find the truth-telling novel? In the novel with a "purpose," as it is discussed in the essay of that name.

> Every novel must do one of three things—it must (1) tell something, (2) show something, or (3) prove something. Some novels do all three of these. . . . The third, and what we hold to be the best class, proves something, draws conclusions from a whole congeries of forces, social tendencies, race impulses, devotes itself not to a study of men but of man. . . . Take this element from fiction, take from it the power and opportunity to prove that injustice, crime and inequality do exist, and what is left? Just the amusing novels, the novels that entertain. . . . the modern novel . . . may be a flippant paper-covered thing of swords and cloaks, to be carried on a railway journey and to be thrown out the window when read, together with the sucked oranges and peanut shells. Or it may be a great force, that works together with the pulpit and the universities for the good of the people, fearlessly proving that power is abused, that the strong grind the faces of the weak, that an evil tree is still growing in the midst of the garden, that undoing follows hard upon righteousness, that the course of Empire is not yet finished, and that the races of men have yet to work out their destiny in those great and terrible movements that crush and grind and rend asunder the pillars of the houses of the nation.[3]

It is within this somewhat crude conception of "the novel with a purpose" that we are accustomed to place the novels that brought Sinclair Lewis his fame. Lewis himself was not content to have his work thus

[2] *"The Responsibilities of the Novelist" and Other Literary Essays* (New York, 1903), pp. 5-11.

[3] "The Novel with a Purpose," *ibid.*, pp. 25-32.

located. In a heavily playful refutation of the charge that he was "a raging reformer, an embittered satirist, a realist dreary as cold gravy," he said:

> I should have thought Brother Lewis was essentially a story-teller—just as naive, excited, unselfconscious as the Arab story-tellers about the caravan fires seven hundred years ago, or as O. Henry in a hotel room on Twenty-third Street furiously turning out tales for dinner and red-ink money. In his stories Lewis does not happen to be amused only by the sea or by midnight encounters on the Avenue, but oftener by the adventure of the soul in religion and patriotism and social climbing. But they are essentially stories just the same.[4]

The fact is that the novels we have in mind are not "essentially stories," that the "story" element is secondary and quite feebly managed; and that if they are not quite the "novel with a purpose" as Norris conceived it —motivated by an outraged sense of justice and executed with naturalistic fulness—their impulse is plainly the exposition of social folly. H. L. Mencken, some years after he had ceased to be a well-known literary critic, takes us to the center of Lewis's imaginative uniqueness when, in 1945, he congratulates him on a poor novel called *Cass Timberlane,* an exposure of the corruptions of marriage in the middle class:

> I am not going to tell you that "Cass Timberlane" is comparable to "Babbitt" or "Elmer Gantry" (all except the last 30,000 words, which you wrote in a state of liquor), but it seems to me to be the best thing you have done, and by long odds, since "Dodsworth." . . . In brief, a well-planned and well-executed book, with a fine surface. . . . The country swarms with subjects for your future researches. You did the vermin of the Coolidge era, but those of the Roosevelt and post-Roosevelt eras are still open—the rich radical, the bogus expert, the numskull newspaper proprietor (or editor), the career-jobholder, the lady publicist, the crooked (or, more usually, idiotic) labor leader, the press-agent, and so on. This, I believe, is your job, and you have been neglecting it long enough. There are plenty of writers of love stories and Freudian documents, though not many as good at it as you are, but there is only one real anatomist of the American Kultur. I think it stinks, but whether it stinks or not is immaterial. It deserves to be done as you alone can do it.[5]

The catalogue of social types is the significant item in this letter. Each of these, with its implied section of social life in the United States, could

[4] From an unpublished "self-portrait," perhaps intended as a publicity release, apparently written in about 1935, among the Lewis papers, Yale University. All quotations from Sinclair Lewis's writings are used here with the permission of Melville H. Cane and Pincus Berner as Executors under the will of Sinclair Lewis, and the quotations from *Dodsworth, Main Street,* and *Elmer Gantry* are used with the further permission of the publishers, Harcourt, Brace and World, Inc.

[5] From an unpublished letter, printed here by permission of August Mencken, literary executor of the late H. L. Mencken.

have become a Lewis novel. Some already had. With Lewis, the subject, the social section, always came first; systematic research, sometimes conducted by research assistants and carrying Lewis himself into "the field" like any cultural anthropologist, followed; the story came last, devised to carry home and usually limping under the burden of data. If the result in some ways filled the Norris prescription for a novel of the contemporary social character, it was still by no means a naturalistic product; at the same time, precisely what was "new" in it was what D. H. Lawrence called "dead," and he would have howled in outrage at the complacency with which Lewis asserted that his stories described "the adventure of the soul in religion and patriotism." For in the world of Sinclair Lewis there is no soul, and if a soul were introduced into it, it would die on the instant.

The world of Sinclair Lewis rests upon two observations: the standardization of manners in a business culture, and the stultification of morals under middle-class convention. All his critical observations are marshalled in support of these propositions, and his portrait of the middle class rests entirely upon them. The proliferation of detail within these observations gives them an apparent breadth, and his easy familiarity with the manners—in Robert Cantwell's catalogue—of "the small towns and square cities, the real-estate developments and restricted residential areas, the small business men, the country doctors, the religious fakers, the clubwomen, the county officeholders, the village atheists and single-taxers, the schoolteachers, librarians, the windbags of the lower income groups, the crazy professors and the maddened, hyperthyroid, high-pressure salesmen—the main types of middle-class and lower-middle-class provincial society, conspicuous now because he has identified them so thoroughly" [6]—all this gives his observations an apparent richness and variety; yet in fact it is all there in support of the extremely limited program. Similarly, his world is broken into many social sections—the small town, business ethics, medical science, evangelical religion, marriage, the career woman, professional philanthropy—and this is to name only those that come most immediately to mind; but every section rests, again, on one or both of the two primary principles. This is an extremely narrow and intellectually feeble perspective, but given the particular character of Lewis's achievement, its force paradoxically rests upon its narrowness.

For its narrowness projects a very sharply defined image. "Life dehumanized by indifference or enmity to all human values—that is the keynote of both Gopher Prairie and Zenith," wrote T. K. Whipple nearly thirty years ago in what remains one of the very few critical essays on Lewis, and one to which my own essay is much indebted.

[6] "Sinclair Lewis," *After the Genteel Tradition,* ed. Malcolm Cowley (New York, 1937), p. 115.

> . . . nowhere does this animosity show itself more plainly than in hostility to truth and art. The creed of both towns is the philosophy of boosting, a hollow optimism and false cheeriness which leads directly to hypocrisy, as in making believe that business knavery is social service. Toward ideas likely to break this bubble of pretense the people are bitterly opposed; toward new ideas they are lazily contemptuous; toward other ideas they are apathetic . . . intellectually both are cities of the dead, and in both, the dead are resolved that no one shall live.[7]

Dead in the senses as they are in intellect and the affections, these people are horrible ciphers, empty of personality or individual consciousness, rigidly controlled by set social responses; and yet, being dead, together they do not form a society in any real sense, but only a group, a group which at once controls them and protects them from the horrors of their own emptiness. Their group activities, whether as families, as clubs, as friends, are travesties of that human interchange that makes for meaningful social activities: conversation is buffoonery, affection is noise, gaiety is pretense, business is brutal rush, religion is blasphemy. The end result is vacant social types in a nonsocial world. Quite brilliantly T. K. Whipple made and Maxwell Geismar developed the observation that *Babbitt* is set in Hell: "it is almost a perfectly conceived poetic vision of a perfectly . . . standardized hinterland." [8]

Poetic, that is to say, in the sense that it *is* visionary, *not* documentary, so that nothing is either a lie or the truth. These are categories that have no relevance. Collecting his massive accumulations of social data with the naturalist's compulsiveness, Lewis creates a visual world and a world of manners that appear to be absolutely solid, absolutely concrete; but all that accumulation of data has from the outset been made to submit so severely to the selective strictures of two highly limited and limiting observations that what emerges in fact is an image and a criticism of middle-class society and not in the least a representation of it. A fragment blown into the proportions of the whole, it is a fantastic world dominated by monstrous parodies of human nature. Elmer Gantry, in his hypocrisy and self-deception, his brutal cruelty and fearful faith, his shallow optimism and wretched betrayals, his almost automatic identification of salvation and economic success, his loathing of all thought, his hatred of all human difference, his incapacity for any feelings but lust and fear and self-interest: in all this he carries to its extreme Sinclair Lewis's conception of the middle-class character. Both the paradox and the secret of such a creation lie in the fact that, except for the power of observation, the sensibility of the creator has few resources beyond those of the thing created, that Lewis's own intellectual and moral framework, and the

[7] "Sinclair Lewis," *Spokesmen* (New York, 1928), pp. 210-11.

[8] Geismar, *The Last of the Provincials: The American Novel, 1915-1925* (Boston, 1947), p. 96.

framework of feeling, is extremely narrow, hardly wider than the material it contains. And the power of the creation, I would insist, lies in these limitations.

The limitations are so apparent that we need do little more than name them. As his conception of middle-class society is fragmentary, so his sense of history is vestigial. The characteristic widening of his shutter over social space does not qualify or alter the narrow social conception:

> Eight thousand radio-owners listening to Elmer Gantry—A bootlegger in his flat, coat off, exposing his pink silk shirt, his feet up on the table. . . . The house of a small-town doctor, with the neighbors come in to listen—the drugstore man, his fat wife, the bearded superintendent of schools. . . . Mrs. Sherman Reeves of Royal Ridge, wife of one of the richest young men in Zenith, listening in a black-and-gold dressing-gown, while she smoked a cigarette. . . . The captain of a schooner, out on Lake Michigan, hundreds of miles away, listening in his cabin. . . . The wife of a farmer in an Indiana valley, listening while her husband read the Sears-Roebuck catalogue and sniffed. . . . A retired railway conductor, very feeble, very religious. . . . A Catholic priest, in a hospital, chuckling a little. . . . A spinster school-teacher, mad with loneliness, worshiping Dr. Gantry's virile voice. . . . Forty people gathered in a country church too poor to have a pastor. . . . A stock actor in his dressing-room, fagged with an all-night rehearsal.
>
> All of them listening to the Rev. Dr. Elmer Gantry as he shouted . . . (pp. 399-400).

Similarly, the characteristic extensions into time do not enrich the sense of history but merely provide broadly ironic contrasts that are analogically meaningless, both in the drama and in the intellectual framework:

> So Elmer came, though tardily, to the Great Idea which was to revolutionize his life and bring him eternal and splendid fame.
>
> That shabby Corsican artillery lieutenant and author, Bonaparte, first conceiving that he might be the ruler of Europe—Darwin seeing dimly the scheme of evolution—Paolo realizing that all of life was nothing but an irradiation of Francesca—Newton pondering on the falling apple—Paul of Tarsus comprehending that a certain small Jewish sect might be the new religion of the doubting Greeks and Romans—Keats beginning to write "The Eve of St. Agnes"—none of these men, transformed by a Great Idea from mediocrity to genius, was more remarkable than Elmer Gantry of Paris, Kansas, when he beheld the purpose for which the heavenly powers had been training him (p. 409).

The characters of this world are aware of no tradition within which their lives are located; behind them lies no history except for the faintly heroic figure of a pioneer whose sacrifice their lives have made meaningless. And if the seat of this deficiency is in the imagination of the author, its result is the captive blankness of their existence, which is a large element in the egregious parody.

From an early if not very forcibly held socialist position, Sinclair Lewis, in his best novels, swung round to the antidemocratic views of H. L. Mencken; yet paradoxically, he had no values of his own (not even Mencken's vague Nietzscheanism) except those of the middle-class that both were lampooning. The ambition to find in the East what is not available in the Midwest is always exposed as false; and when "the East" is pushed on to mean Europe, the same evaluation is made. The Midwest is shown as hopelessly narrow, yet somehow it is shown finally as the only sensible place to choose. Aristocrats are suspect if not phony; workmen tend to become shiftless mongrels; intellectuals and artists are irresponsible bohemians. The picture of middle-class provincialism is framed by a middle-class provincial view. "Russian Jews in London clothes," Lewis writes in *Dodsworth,* "going to Italian restaurants with Greek waiters and African music." And again, if the deficiency in a sense of tradition and of history is the author's own, it contributes to the force of his image, for it permits his characters no escape. Always excepting the figures of Doctors Gottlieb and Arrowsmith, with their dedication to pure science, the dissident figures in Lewis's novels, the critics of this society, are permitted no realizable values toward which they or that society may aspire.

The feeblest characters in *Main Street,* and those most quickly routed, are the discontented. Carol Kennicott's vaporous values are the equivalent of that deeply sentimental strain in the author that led him as a young man to write in imitation of the early Tennyson and, as a man of over fifty, to say that "he, who has been labeled a 'satirist' and a 'realist,' is actually a romantic medievalist of the most incurable sort." Thus Carol:

> . . . a volume of Yeats on her knees. . . . Instantly she was released from the homely comfort of a prairie town. She was in the world of lonely things —the flutter of twilight linnets, the aching call of gulls along a shore to which the netted foam crept out of darkness, the island of Aengus and the elder gods and the eternal glories that never were, tall kings and women girdled with crusted gold, the woeful incessant chanting . . . (p. 120).

Thus the Babbitt who momentarily challenges Zenith does not so much present us with a scale of humane values that we can oppose to the inhumanity of the environment, as he presents us with all the insecurity on which Babbittry, or the environment, rests. The fact that there is never any real opposition of substantial values to "convention," or false values (as there is never any truly individual character to resist the social types), is what makes Lewis's world so blank and limits so drastically his social realism. In *Elmer Gantry* we do not have even these fitful glimmerings in the realm of reverie. This is a world of total death, of social monsters without shadow. It is, in my view and on re-reading, the purest Lewis.

The publication of *Elmer Gantry* early in 1927 was not so much a literary event as it was a public scandal, and from the beginning, therefore, excitement took the place of criticism. Preceded by the well-publicized "Strike me dead" episode, it called forth remarks like this from William Allen White: "Sinclair Lewis stood in the pulpit of a Kansas City church last spring and defied God to strike him dead. So far as Sinclair Lewis, the artist, is concerned in the book 'Elmer Gantry,' God took him at his word." Municipal bans extended from Kansas City to Camden; from Boston to Glasgow. Its initial printing of 140,000 copies was probably the largest to that date of any book in history, and the whole emphasis of the promotion campaign was on the *size* of the enterprise: the book was advertised on billboards; a publicity release from the publishers was headed "What it Means to Manufacture the First Edition of *Elmer Gantry*," and provided statistics on amounts of paper, thread, glue, board, cloth, and ink, both black and orange—black for the text, orange for the cover. (But then, as Lewis tells us in the novel, "Elmer was ever a lover of quantity.") In April of 1927, in a resolution supporting the Anti-Saloon League of New York State, the Rev. Dr. Otho F. Bartholow declared at the annual session of the New York East Conference, "The Methodist Church is cordially hated, not only by the class represented by Mr. Sinclair Lewis and the rum organizations, but also by every evil organization of every kind whatsoever," while, two weeks later, the graduating class of New York University voted Sinclair Lewis its favorite author. A news item in an Ohio newspaper ran as follows:

> Trouble in the home of Leo Roberts, general manager of the Roberts Coal and Supply Company, began when his wife brought home a copy of "Elmer Gantry" and he burned it as undesirable reading matter, according to Mrs. Roberts at a hearing Wednesday before Judge Bostwick of Probate Court, when Roberts was ordered to a private sanitarium for a short rest, after his wife, Mrs. Margaret Roberts, 1671 Franklin Park South, charged him with lunacy.

Literary appraisal seems to have been a quite secondary matter. Yet, if only because the images that Lewis projected came to play such a powerful role in the imagination both of America and of Europe, it is worth our time to analyze the method or lack of method that established them. Leslie Fiedler recently wrote as follows:

> . . . no one has succeeded since the age of Sinclair Lewis and Sherwood Anderson in seeing an actual American small town or a living member of the Kiwanis club. The gross pathos of Anderson or the journalistic thinness of Lewis is beside the point; for all of us, the real facts of experience have

> been replaced by Winesburg, Ohio and by Babbitt; myth or platitude, we have invented nothing to replace them.[9]

How, then, did *he* invent them? What props up and holds in place that terrifying buffoon, Elmer Gantry—that "gladiator laughing at the comic distortion of his wounded opponent," as he sees himself; that "barytone solo turned into portly flesh," as Lewis shows him to us?

The primary fact in Lewis's method is the absence of conflict between genuine orders of value, and in *Elmer Gantry* this fact emerges most starkly.

In *Elmer Gantry,* any drama exists in the immediate victory of the worst over the weakest (who are the best), or in the struggle of the bad to survive among the worst: all is corrupt. In this extraordinarily full account of every form of religious decay, nothing is missing except all religion and all humanity. As there are no impediments to Elmer's barbarous rise from country boob to influential preacher, so there are no qualifications of the image of barbarity. On the very fringes of the narrative, among his scores of characters, Lewis permits a few shadowy figures of good to appear—Bruno Zechlin and Jim Lefferts, the amiable skeptics who are routed before they are permitted to enter the action; Andrew Pengilly, a humane preacher who asks the most striking question in the novel ("Mr. Gantry, why don't you believe in God?") but who himself no more enters the story than his question enters the intellectual context; and finally, Frank Shallard, who does come and go in the story, an honest human being, but one so weak that he presents no challenge to Elmer, serves only to illustrate the ruthlessness of Elmer's power.

In the novel, values can be realized only in action, and the action of *Elmer Gantry* is an entirely one-way affair. This is the inevitable consequence in structure of Lewis's method. Like most of Lewis's novels, *Elmer Gantry* is a loosely episodic chronicle, which suggests at once that there will be no sustained pressure of plot, no primary conflict about which all the action is organized and in which value will achieve a complex definition or in which that dramatization of at least two orders of value that conflict implies will be brought about. The chronicle breaks down into three large parts, each pretty nearly independent of the others. In each event Elmer's progress is colored and in two of them threatened by his relation with a woman, but from each Elmer emerges triumphant. The first part takes us through his Baptist education, his ordination, his first pulpit, and his escape from Lulu; the second takes us through his career as an evangelist with the fantastic Sharon Falconer; the third takes us through his experience of New Thought and his rise in Methodism, together with the decline of his marriage to Cleo and his es-

[9] "The Ant on the Grasshopper," *Partisan Review* (Summer, 1955), p. 414.

cape from Hettie, who threatens to bring him to public ruin but who is herself routed as, in the final sentence, Elmer promises that "We shall yet make these United States a moral nation."

It should not be supposed that the frank prominence in *Elmer Gantry* of sexual appetite—a rare enough element in a Lewis novel—or the fact that it several times seems to threaten Elmer's otherwise unimpeded success, in any way provides the kind of dramatized counterpoint on the absence of which we are remarking, or that it in any way serves to introduce an element of human tenderness that qualifies Elmer's brutal nakedness. On the contrary, it is an integral part of his inhumanity and an integral part of the inhumanity of the religious environment within which he exists. Indeed, of all the forms of relationship that the novel presents, the sexual relation is most undilutedly brutish, and it is perhaps the chief element in that animus of revulsion that motivates the creation of this cloacal world and upon which I shall presently comment. Finally, its identification with the quality of Elmer's religious activity is made explicit in the climactically phantasmagoric scene in which Sharon capitulates to Elmer before an altar where she associates herself, in a ritual invocation, with all goddesses of fertility.

> "It is the hour! Blessed Virgin, Mother Hera, Mother Frigga, Mother Ishtar, Mother Isis, dread Mother Astarte of the weaving arms, it is thy priestess, it is she who after the blind centuries and the groping years shall make it known to the world that ye are one, and that in me are ye all revealed, and that in this revelation shall come peace and wisdom universal, the secret of the spheres and the pit of understanding. Ye who have leaned over me and on my lips pressed your immortal fingers, take this my brother to your bosoms, open his eyes, release his pinioned spirit, make him as the gods, that with me he may carry the revelation for which a thousand thousand grievous years the world has panted. . . .
>
> "Ye veiled ones and ye bright ones—from caves forgotten, the peaks of the future, the clanging today—join in me, lift up, receive him, dread nameless ones; yea, lift us then, mystery on mystery, sphere above sphere, dominion on dominion, to the very throne!
>
> ". . . O mystical rose, O lily most admirable, O wondrous union; O St. Anna, Mother Immaculate, Demeter, Mother Beneficient, Lakshmi, Mother Most Shining; behold, I am his and he is yours and ye are mine!" (pp. 186-87).

The extravagant absurdity of this scene is underlined by the absence in it of any candid recognition of human need or of human fulfillment. The travesty that it makes of both the sexual and the religious experience is of course to be associated with the temper of orgiastic evangelism with which the book is full. Dramatically, however, it must be associated with such an earlier scene, as homely as this one is horrendous, in which a deaf old retired preacher and his wife are going to bed after fifty years of marriage, and the whole of that experience of fifty years is equated with an "old hoss."

They were nodding on either side of a radiator unheated for months.

"All right, Emmy," piped the ancient.

"Say, Papa— Tell me: I've been thinking: If you were just a young man today would you go into the ministry?"

"Course I would! What an idea! Most glorious vocation young man could have. Idea! G'night, Emmy!"

But as his ancient wife sighingly removed her corsets, she complained, "Don't know as you would or not—if *I* was married to you—which ain't any too certain, a second time—and if I had anything to say about it!"

"Which *is* certain! Don't be foolish. Course I would."

"I don't know. Fifty years I had of it, and I never did get so I wa'n't just mad clear through when the ladies of the church came poking around, criticizing me for every little tidy I put on the chairs, and talking something terrible if I had a bonnet or a shawl that was the least mite tasty. ''Twant suitable for a minister's wife.' Drat 'em! And I always did like a bonnet with some nice bright colors. Oh, I've done a right smart of thinking about it. You always were a powerful preacher, but's I've told you—"

"You have!"

"—I never could make out how, if when you were in the pulpit you really knew so much about all these high and mighty and mysterious things, how it was when you got home you never knew enough, and you never could learn enough, to find the hammer or make a nice piece of cornbread or add up a column of figures twice alike or find Oberammergau on the map of Austria!"

"Germany, woman! I'm sleepy!"

"And all these years of having to pretend to be so good when we were just common folks all the time! Ain't you glad you can just be simple folks now?"

"Maybe it is restful. But that's not saying I wouldn't do it over again." The old man ruminated a long while. "I think I would. Anyway, no use discouraging these young people from entering the ministry. Somebody got to preach the gospel truth, ain't they?"

"I suppose so. Oh, dear. Fifty years since I married a preacher! And if I could still only be sure about the virgin birth! Now don't you go explaining! Laws, the number of times you've explained! I know it's true—it's in the Bible. If I could only *believe* it! But—

"I would of liked to had you try your hand at politics. If I could of been, just once, to a senator's house, to a banquet or something, just once, in a nice bright red dress with gold slippers, I'd of been willing to go back to alpaca and scrubbing floors and listening to you rehearsing your sermons, out in the stable, to that old mare we had for so many years—oh, laws, how long is it she's been dead now? Must be—yes, it's twenty-seven years—

"Why is it that it's only in religion that the things you got to believe are agin all experience? Now drat it, don't you go and quote that 'I believe because it *is* impossible' thing at me again! Believe because it's impossible! Huh! Just like a minister!

"Oh, dear, I hope I don't live long enough to lose my faith. Seems like the older I get, the less I'm excited over all these preachers that talk about hell only they never saw it.

"Twenty-seven years! And we had that old hoss so long before that. My how she could kick— Busted that buggy—"

They were both asleep (pp. 70-71).

The two scenes, the extravagantly repulsive and the devastatingly barren, supplement one another; they represent the extremes of the nightmare image of a world that, totally empty of human value, monstrously, and without relief, parodies the reality.

If the narrative method of loose chronicle, without sustained dramatic conflict, is the primary means to this end, certain orders of technical detail contribute no less and seem entirely consistent with the imagination that is working through the narrative method. It has been complained, for example, that there is a coarsening of Lewis's style in this novel, and that his view of the hinterland threatens to fall into a kind of crackerbarrel stereotype. Both charges are true, but it can be argued that both qualities make possible the kind of effect we are trying to describe. *Elmer Gantry* is the noisiest novel in American literature, the most *braying, guffawing, belching* novel that we have, and it is its prose that sets this uproar going; if we are to have a novel filled with jackasses and jackals, let them, by all means, bray and guffaw. On the same grounds, I would defend the "By crackee, by jiminy" crudities of the physical environment within which this noise goes on, this imbecilic articulateness, only pointing out in addition that Lewis's old ability to invoke a concrete world—the smell of Pullman car dust, the food at a church picnic, the contents of the library of a small Methodist bishop—is still sufficiently in force to cram full the outlines of his stereotypes. One can go further. At each of his three climaxes, Lewis abdicates such sense of the dramatic scene as he may have had and retreats into melodrama: once to an inversion of the farmer's daughter situation, once to a catastrophic fire, finally to a cops-and-robbers treatment of some petty criminals who have attempted to play the badger game on old Elmer. In each situation, through bad timing, through a refusal to develop even a suggestion of suspense, any potential human elements in the situation are sacrificed to the melodramatic stereotype. And yet, out of this very weakness, cumulatively, arises again the whole impression of bare brutality which is, after all, the essential social observation. As the drama is only half realized, so the social observation is only half true, but in its partiality resides such force of which it is capable.

Most novels operate through a conflict, dramatized in a plot, of social and individual interest, and the more sustained the pressures of the plot, the more likely is the individual to be forced into a position of new self-awareness, which prominently contains an awareness of his relation to his society. A certain dynamic interchange has been at work, and the result is that the historical forces which contain the individual's experience have been personalized in his awareness. What is most characteristic of the novels of Sinclair Lewis, and above all of *Elmer Gantry,* is the fact that there are no such dynamics of social action, that we are presented with a static, unpersonalized image—and that *there* lies its horror.

Elmer Gantry has perhaps one brief moment of honesty. He has come to Sharon's fantastic home, he is looking out upon the river, he fancies himself in love:

> "Shen-an-doah!" he crooned.
>
> Suddenly he was kneeling at the window, and for the first time since he had forsaken Jim Lefferts and football and joyous ribaldry, his soul was free of all the wickedness which had daubed it—oratorical ambitions, emotional orgasm, dead sayings of dull seers, dogmas, and piety. The golden winding river drew him, the sky uplifted him, and with outflung arms he prayed for deliverance from prayer.
>
> "I've found her. Sharon. Oh, I'm not going on with this evangelistic bunk. Trapping idiots into holy monkey-shines! No, by God, I'll be honest! I'll tuck her under my arm and go out and fight. Business. Put it over. Build something big. And laugh, not snivel and shake hands with church-members! I'll do it!" (pp. 180-81).

Then and there his rebellion against himself ends, and after that he knows nothing of self-recognition. This is about as close to it as he can come:

> "I'll have a good time with those folks," he reflected, in the luxury of a taxicab. "Only, better be careful with old Rigg. He's a shrewd bird, and he's onto me. . . . Now what do you mean?" indignantly. "What do you mean by 'onto me'? There's nothing to be onto! I refused a drink and a cigar, didn't I? I never cuss except when I lose my temper, do I? I'm leading an absolutely Christian life. And I'm bringing a whale of a lot more souls into churches than any of these pussy-footing tin saints that're afraid to laugh and jolly people. 'Onto me' nothing!" (p. 315).

A character so open to self-deception is not in a position to estimate the forces that have made him so: to him, society is given, accepted, used. Elmer Gantry was raised in an important if stultifying American tradition: the protestantism of the hinterland; and Sinclair Lewis gives us a complete and devastating account of it that extends over four pages and from which I now draw fragments, reluctantly omitting Lewis's substantiating body of detail:

> The church and Sunday School at Elmer's village . . . had nurtured in him a fear of religious machinery which he could never lose. . . . That small pasty-white Baptist church had been the center of all his emotions, aside from hell-raising, hunger, sleepiness, and love. And even these emotions were represented in the House of the Lord . . . the arts and the sentiments

> and the sentimentalities—they were for Elmer perpetually associated only with the church . . . all the music which the boy Elmer had ever heard was in church . . . it provided all his painting and sculpture. . . . From the church came all his profounder philosophy . . . literary inspiration . . . here too the church had guided him. In Bible stories, in the words of the great hymns, in the anecdotes which the various preachers quoted, he had his only knowledge of literature. . . . The church, the Sunday School, the evangelistic orgy, choir-practise, raising the mortgage, the delights of funerals, the snickers in back pews or in the other room at weddings—they were . . . a mold of manners to Elmer. . . . Sunday School text cards . . . they gave him a taste for gaudy robes, for marble columns and the purple-broidered palaces of kings, which was later to be of value in quickly habituating himself to the more decorative homes of vice. . . . And always the three chairs that stood behind the pulpit, the intimidating stiff chairs of yellow plush and carved oak borders, which, he was uneasily sure, were waiting for the Father, the Son, and the Holy Ghost.
>
> He had, in fact, got everything from the church and Sunday School, except, perhaps, any longing whatever for decency and kindness and reason (pp. 25-28).

And having neither decency nor kindness nor reason (as the novel contains no animated examples of these humane virtues), Elmer is necessarily unaware of the history in which he is involved.

That history, perhaps no larger than it is beautiful in our tradition, is nevertheless considerable, and Sinclair Lewis was aware of it even if, because he had no alternatives, he could not let his characters become so. (The tradition survives, of course: a Madison Avenue patina, extending from Washington, D. C., to Whittier, California, does not alter the motives of cynically opportunistic politicians; it merely moves boorish Elmer into gray flannel and the seat of power.) The whole brutally accurate conception of R. H. Tawney, which coupled business success and salvation, and then, in popular culture, began to pay dividends on the "saved" soul; the obvious connection between the Puritan repressions (I use Lewis's terms, not mine) and the orgiastic outbursts of middle-border evangelism; the Gospel of Service (made in Zenith) becoming the equivalent of the Gospels—all this is in the author's mind as he creates his characters, but the very nature of his creation prohibits it from in any way sharing his knowledge. The result is that the Lewis character cannot separate itself from the Lewis society; and this, in the dynamics of fiction, means that the Lewis character *has* no character apart from the society in which it is embedded, and that therefore the Lewis society is not a society at all, but a machine. And this is the moral, for criticism as for life today, of Lewis's novels, and especially of this one.

"All vital truth," said D. H. Lawrence, "contains the memory of all that for which it is not true." And Frank Norris, that infinitely simpler man, said, "You must be something more than a novelist if you can, something more than just a writer. There must be that nameless sixth sense or sensibility . . . the thing that does not enter into the work, but that is back of it. . . ." Here these two unlikely companions become companionable: both are asking for a certain reverberating largeness behind any concretely conceived situation if that situation is to echo back into the great caverns of the human condition. This quality, I think, even a partisan could not claim that Sinclair Lewis had. Almost justly, Robert Cantwell described him as one "who thought of his writing, not in terms of its momentary inspirations and the . . . pressure of living that played through him and upon him, but in terms of the accomplishment of a foreknown task";[10] and almost plausibly, Maxwell Geismar wrote that "Just as there is really no sense of vice in Lewis's literary world, there is no true sense of virtue. Just as there is practically no sense of human love in the whole range of Lewis's psychological values, and no sense of real hatred—there is no genuine sense of human freedom." [11] Most of this indictment one may allow, but if we are speaking specifically of *Elmer Gantry,* we would wish to insist on two of the items that these descriptions deny him: "the pressure of living that played through him and upon him," and the "hatred."

Elmer Gantry is a work of almost pure revulsion. It seems to shudder and to shake with loathing of that which it describes. The very fact that the novelist must create the image of the thing he loathes, in order to express his loathing, points to the peculiar imaginative animus that motivates this novel. We can speculate about its sources: Lewis's own early evangelistic impulse, his dedication to the missionary field now turning in upon itself; the lonely, goofy boy at Oberlin, himself pushing the handles of a handcar (as Elmer Gantry does) to get to a rural Sunday School where, without conspicuous success, he doled out Bible stories; the poor fool of the hinterland at New Haven, who had never been given more by the hinterland than the dubious gift of deriding it, and therefore of having to love it. Perhaps such speculations are not much to the point. The point is only that in no novel does Sinclair Lewis more clearly announce his loathing of the social environment with which he is concerned, and in no novel does he make it more mandatory that we remain within the terrifying limits of that environment.

Sinclair Lewis is not unlike Elmer Gantry. The vicious circle in this picture exists, of course, in the fact that Elmer remakes society in precisely the terms that society has already made him. No one can break out; everyone, including the novelist, spins more madly in the mechanical orbit.

The novelist trapped in his own hallucination of the world as a trap: this seems to be the final observation that we can make. But it is not quite final. Finally, we are left with the hallucination of the novels them-

[10] Cantwell, *Genteel Tradition,* p. 117.
[11] Geismar, *Last of the Provincials,* p. 108.

selves, with their monstrous images of what we both are and are not, their nearly fabulous counter-icons in our culture. They stand somewhere between the two conceptions of the novel with which we began: they tell us too much of why we are dead and not enough of how we can live to satisfy the prescription either of Lawrence or of Norris, deprived as they are of all that psychic affirmation that would meet the demands of the first, and of most of that social realism that would meet those of the second. But they have—for this very reason—their *own* quality. If that quality is of the half-truth, and the half-truth has moved back into our way of estimating our society, the judgment falls on us, on our own failure of observation and imagination. If we accept the half-truth for the fact, then the novel is indeed the most important literary instrument in and for our world; and we can only lament the inability, not of our novelists to provide the stimulus, but of ourselves to repel it, of our failure, in the sympathetic consciousness, to recoil from it. *Elmer Gantry* reminds us that we continue to embrace as fervently as we deny this horror that at least in part we are.

Sinclair Lewis: Our Own Diogenes

by Vernon L. Parrington

As the row of his pudgy orange-backed volumes lengthens on the shelf, it becomes evident that Sinclair Lewis is the bad boy of American letters whose thoughts are on bent-pins while the deacon is laboring in prayer. His irrepressible satire belongs to a new and irritatingly effective school. He has studied the technique of the realists, and under the beguiling pretense of telling the truth objectively and dispassionately, he insists on revealing to us unaccommodated man as a poor, bare, forked animal, who like Jurgen[1] persists in thinking himself a monstrous clever fellow. He is maliciously severe on all respectable dignities. In his hands the noble *homo sapiens* of common repute is translated into an ignoble *homo libidinus et ventosissimus*—an unattractive animal that runs in herds, serves its belly, and has a taking way with the dams. The free-born American citizen, master of the earth and its destiny, is little flattered by the portrait he draws, and Mr. Lewis finds himself, in consequence, *persona non grata* in any convention of Elks or Rotarians.

The method he has chosen to adopt is a clever advance over the technique of the eighteenth century, when pricking balloons was the business of every wit. Those older satirists—nagging souls like Pope and bold bad fellows like Churchill—were mainly concerned to annoy their victims with pin-pricks. They were too completely the gentleman to grow chummy with base fellows whom they frankly despised; and in consequence they never discovered half the possibilities of the gentle art of satire. Sinclair Lewis is wiser than they were. He has learned that before one can effectively impale one's victim, one must know all his weaknesses and take him off his guard. So he ingratiatingly makes up to George F. Babbitt of Zenith, drinks chummily with him, swaps greasy jokes, learns all the hidden vanities and secret obscenities that slip out in the confidences of the cups, beguiles him into painting his own portrait in the manly midnight hours; and when the last garment that covers his naked-

[1] The hero of a novel by James Branch Cabell, a notorious novelist of the twenties. [M.S.]

ness is stripped off, the flashlight explodes and the camera has caught the victim in every feature of his mean and vacuous reality.

No doubt it is an ungentlemanly thing to do—a calculating betrayal of trusting human nature done in the sacred name of art; and it is certain that the unhappy victim will hate the artist when he sees the developed print next morning. Yet the picture is extraordinarily lifelike. All the unlovely details of fat stomach and flabby muscles are sharply revealed. It is too late to put on one's clothes, and *homo sapiens* in the person of George F. Babbitt is revealed as a shambling, two-legged animal, for the world to laugh at. The method is immensely clever; it is the last word in the technique of despoiling one's victim of adventitious dignity, without which life becomes a mean, bleak affair; but it is scarcely charitable. To think well of oneself and to wish to impose that good opinion upon others, are common human weaknesses that every tailor blesses. Without clothes man is only a caricature of the godlike, and the artist who betrays our nakedness to our enemies is very far from a gentleman. The confidences of the cups must be held sacred, for if we cannot drink without fear of our babbling being reported, what becomes of goodfellowship?

But the charge of betraying goodfellowship leaves Sinclair Lewis unconcerned. His satire knows no compunctions. An irreverent soul, he dares the wrath not only of George F. Babbitt, but of the innumerable clubs to which Babbitt belongs. A buoyant scoffer, he does not permit even the organized wrath of the Chamber of Commerce to disturb his equanimity. He provokes respectable people on principle, and he has laid a devilish plan to work systematically through our sacred American decalogue, smashing one commandment after another. Already behind him is strewn a sorry wreckage of established creeds and authoritative slogans—a wreckage that delights the wicked and gives aid and comfort to all evil-wishers in our comfortable and excellent society. Not even a banker is sacred to him. Rotarians and Kiwanians, Billy Sundays and Billy Bryans,[2] voluble Congressmen and silent Presidents, even our venerable Constitution itself, he scoffs at and makes merry over. And to add insult to injury, he prospers in his sins. His calculating wickedness returns him a fattening bank account. His impudent satires sell like bargain-counter silk stockings. We pay handsomely to see ourselves most unhandsomely depicted. If we would only take a lesson from the strategy of the heathen Chinese, we might boycott Mr. Lewis's wares and reduce him to the beggary that is more becoming to wickedness than a wanton prosperity. But a Christian people will not go to school to the heathen, and so Mr. Lewis prospers in his wickedness and waxes vulgarly rich.

Now what is the tremendous discovery that Sinclair Lewis makes so much of, and that we pay so great a price to learn? It is no other than this: that the goodly United States of America are peopled by a mighty

[2] William Jennings Bryan, "The great commoner, politician, and Fundamentalist" 1860-1925). [M.S.]

herd, which like those earlier herds that rumbled about the plains, drives foolishly in whatever direction their noses point—a herd endowed with tremendous blind power, with big bull leaders, but with minds rarely above their bellies and their dams. In the mass and at their own romantic rating they are distinctly imposing—big-necked, red-blooded, lusty, with glossy coats got from rich feeding-grounds, and with a herd power that sweeps majestically onward in a cloud of dust of its own raising, veritable lords and masters of a continent. But considered more critically and resolved into individual members, they appear to the realist somewhat stupid, feeble in brain and will, stuffed with conceit of their own excellence, esteeming themselves the great end for which creation has been in travail, the finest handiwork of the Most High who spread the plains for their feeding-grounds: with a vast respect for totems and fetishes; purveyors and victims of the mysterious thing called Bunk, who valiantly horn to death any audacious heretic who may suggest that rumbling about the plains, filling their bellies, bellowing sacred slogans, and cornering the lushest grass, are scarcely adequate objectives for such immense power: a vast middleman herd, that dominates the continent, but cannot reduce it to order or decency.

Consider, suggests Mr. Lewis, what this rumbling herd signifies in the light of rational and humane ideals. What sort of custodians of civilization are these lumbering mobsters with their back-slappings and bellowings? What becomes of the good life in a society that flowers in Rotarian conventions? The banker has reduced America to the level of a banker's Utopia, and now bids us admire his handiwork. Other societies, aristocratic and feudal, honored the priest and knight and artist above the usurer and tradesman; other generations professed to serve truth and beauty and godliness in their daily lives; but the great American herd cares nothing for such things. In the name of democracy priest and knight and artist are turned lackeys to merchants and realtors, to men who would not recognize faith or chivalry or imagination if they met them on the golf course, and who understand democracy as little as they understand Christianity. In this land of material abundance the good life is reduced to being measured in commissions and percentages; civilization comes to flower in the broker; the mahogany desk is the altar at which we sacrifice in a land of triumphant materialism. "God help the country," said Fenimore Cooper, years ago when the herd was small, "that has only commercial towns for its capitals." "Such a country is past helping," retorts Sinclair Lewis. "God cannot help it, or the Devil. In the name of George F. Babbitt and Dr. Almus Pickerbaugh and the Reverend Elmer Gantry, what can be expected of such a country? A people that worships the great god Bunk shall have its reward!"

To prove his amiable thesis Mr. Lewis has been at enormous pains to gather his materials at their sources. He has taken upon himself to become a specialist in depicting the *genus Americanus*. He has loafed along Main

Street, played poker in back rooms with wicked young men, drunk in respectable clubs, and exchanged hearty back-slappings with the sons of Rotary. He has devoted days to the smoking-compartments of Pullmans, garnering the ripest wisdom and choicest stories of traveling salesmen. He has listened to philosophic brokers discourse on ethics, studied political and constitutional theory with realtors, learned all about Bolshevism from presidents of Chambers of Commerce, been instructed in the elements of economics by Republican Congressmen, discovered the fallacies in Darwinian evolution from clerical fundamentalists and the superiority of Fascism over democracy from the greatest captains of industry. No field of American experience has escaped his minute investigation, no authority has eluded his catechizing. In the course of his studies he has come to master the lusty American language in its subtlest shades and manliest *nuances,* from the comic supplement to Dunn and Bradstreet, and he talks easily with Main Street in its own vernacular. His rich and copious vocabulary fills a commonplace scholar with envy, and his ebullient slang, his easy slovenliness of enunciation, inflict on the simple-minded user of the King's English a hopeless inferiority complex.

Thus amply equipped with all the resources of scholarship, he has written four learned treatises in exemplification of the thesis that the *genus Americanus* is cousin-german to the scoffing Mr. Mencken's lately discovered *boobus Americanus.* The introductory study, *Main Street,* provided a comprehensive background and setting for the full-length portraits he was to draw later. Gopher Prairie, situated in the heart of agricultural America—in Meredith Nicholson's Valley of Democracy where the old-fashioned, kindly, neighborly, wholesome, democratic virtues are presumed to thrive in a congenial habitat—becomes in his unsympathetic analysis a place that William Allen White[3] would not recognize as his home town. Here, he tells us, is respectability made sluggish and sterile. Here is "slavery self-sought and self-defended." Here is "dullness made God." Here, diluted and spread over a vast territory, the spirit of Babbitt has erupted in cheap and pretentious county-seats, parasites on the producing hinterland over whose politics and credit and morals Main Street tradesmen have set up a strict custodianship—futile and complacent and drab, mere echoes of the greater cities that lie on the horizon and to which the sons of Main Street turn for light and guidance.

It is these greater cities that constitute the true capitals of our red-blooded Americans who proclaim themselves "the greatest race in the world"—fruitful centers from which radiates the philosophy of pep, punch, and progress for the upbuilding and enlightenment of the world. Of these centers the hustling and mighty Zenith is the wonder and admiration of all right-minded citizens; it is the brightest and bloomiest sunflower of the great American garden. And in Zenith dwells George F.

[3] Editor of the Emporia (Kansas) *Gazette* (1868-1944. [M.S.]

Babbitt, realtor, Sinclair Lewis's full-length portrait of a hero sprung from the loins of America, the completest embodiment of the triumphant American genius that is conquering the earth. Babbitt as an upstanding he-member of the great herd is a marvel, the apotheosis of the regnant middle class, the finished product of our snappy civilization. Other lands, no doubt, have produced men accounted great. Plato and Saul of Tarsus, St. Francis and Leonardo, Pascal and Galileo and Hegel, were no doubt esteemed in their own times and by their own cities; but Zenith does not go in for out-of-date merchandise; it is up-to-the-minute and it specializes in George F. Babbitts. And so when the Reverend Elmer Gantry rises to influence in Gopher Prairie, he is called to Zenith as its spiritual counselor, and becomes the custodian of the Zenith moralities, the apostle of Zenith Bunk, the devotee of the Zenith Mumbo Jumbo. And through Zenith passes also Martin Arrowsmith the rebel, the perverse outlandish scientist who refuses to worship Mumbo Jumbo, on his solitary way to discover reality in a world of Zenith chicanery. Babbitt, Gantry, Arrowsmith—these are the figures that Sinclair Lewis comes upon in his exploration of the land of the free and the home of the brave. A somewhat curious showing at the best.

So slashing an attack upon our common creed and practice has naturally aroused vigorous protest. Human nature does not like to have its idols assailed; even the devotees of Mumbo Jumbo will defend their god against the heretics; and Sinclair Lewis has become the target for many a shaft. The critics have pressed home their counter attack with ardor. They insist that he is suffering from an aggravated case of astigmatism, and that in consequence he does not see eye to eye with those of normal vision. The world is out of focus to him—askew in all its structural lines; and this distorted vision prompts those jaundiced opinions and malicious judgments in regard to the ideals cherished by our best citizens. He has deliberately cultivated a spleen that makes him dislike his neighbors because they are comfortable and contented. Diogenes railing at mankind gained a vast reputation, but it is a nice question if Diogenes was a useful citizen. What did he do to further the well-being of his community? How much time and money did he give to charity and the upbuilding of his city? For all his talking Mr. Lewis does not seem to know what the good life is. He rails at Babbitt for not being Plato, but does he understand the A B C of service? To take a homely figure: the family cow, standing knee-deep in June and chewing the cud of contentment, would excite his Diogenic scorn. As a fault-finder and knocker, Brindle is not the equal of Diogenes; but to criticize her mentality and manners, forgetful of the fact that from the contented chewing of a plentiful cud will come a plentiful supply of milk and cream and butter to sweeten the bread of life, is a somewhat sorry business. In her modest, democratic sphere she is devoted to service, and if there is a nobler function, Rotary humbly confesses it has not discovered it. One must not, of course, press too far the analogy between Brindle and Babbitt; the figure is useful only to suggest that even in the lowliest spheres Mr. Lewis completely fails to understand the fine ethical values that underlie and animate the common American life at which he rails. How, then, shall he understand them in the higher? Comfort and service are excellent things in themselves, and if they can be merged in everyday experience, surely the good life is in the way of achievement.

The point is of vast importance, for it is here that Diogenes Lewis, his critics assert, has totally misread the meaning and faith of America. Here in this prosperous land the union between comfort and service—or to put it in more dignified phrase, the synthesis of Hellenism and Hebraism—has been achieved in practice. A rich and abundant life, motivated by a fine sense of ethical responsibility and disciplined by a democratic public school, is, in sober fact, the distinguishing characteristic of America that sets our country apart from all other lands in western civilization. Call it a Babbitt warren[4] if you will, nevertheless where else has the industrial revolution been brought so completely and happily under dominion to the democratic ideal, or been so ennobled by ethical values? Here it has scattered its wealth amongst the plain people with a bountiful hand, until the poorest family enjoys its nickel-plated plumbing, its flivver, its telephone, its radio, its movies, its funnies, and all the thousand aids to comfort and intelligence which a few generations ago were denied kings—the result of all which is a standard of living that our forefathers would have envied. Our Hellenism is, happily, not Greek. That, as every schoolboy in America knows, was established in slavery; whereas our modern Hellenism is established in democracy and ennobled by a sensitive social conscience. Here the master serves. The richest and greatest amongst us—our Judge Garys and Andrew Mellons—are servants of the nameless public, and dedicate their creative genius to the common democratic prosperity. Our Hellenism, in short, is engrafted on a sturdy Hebraic root and flowers in righteousness—in charity, in education, in free clinics and hospitals, in scientific foundations, in great public libraries, in all the vast gifts that wealth freely offers to the cause of social amelioration. The Puritan strain is fortunately still the American strain, and we owe much to those excellent origins that Mr. Lewis scoffs at without understanding. Comfort and service—Hellenism and Hebraism: if this is not the good life, where shall one find it? In Bolshevik Russia? After all Diogenes Lewis is no more important—or useful—than the gad-fly that Brindle brushes from her glossy sides as she chews her cud. What gad-fly ever produced butter?

If Sinclair Lewis is unimpressed by such arguments it is because he is quite disillusioned with the current ideal of material progress. His dreams do not find their satisfaction in good roads and cheap gasoline. He would

[4] *The Babbitt Warren,* a book published in 1926, by C. E. M. Joad, was a journalistic attack on civilization in the United States. [M.S.]

seem to be an incorrigible idealist who has been bred up on the vigorous Utopianisms of the late nineteenth century. In the golden days before the deluge he had gone blithely to school to all the current idealisms that flourished in the land—to Jeffersonian democracy and to Marxian socialism; and in the well-stocked pharmacopoeias of hopeful young liberals he professed to discover specifics for all our social ills. But the war destroyed his faith in nostrums and removed his Utopia to a dim and foggy future. He has not yet traveled so far in disillusion as Mr. Cabell, who has seen fit to dwarf man to the compass of a flea on the epidermis of earth; nor has he achieved the irony—or the technique—of Clarence Darrow,[5] who suggests casually: "Of course I know that Confucius was as great a philosopher as Billy Sunday, and that as a thinker Buddha was the equal of Billy Bryan. But still all orthodox people know that Confucius and Buddha were spurious and the Billy brothers genuine." He has not even achieved the smug satisfaction of the psychologists who impose their preposterous intelligence tests on simple folk and triumphantly discover morons in respectable neighbors. Some lingering faith in our poor human nature he still clings to. In the great American mass that human nature is certainly foolish and unlovely enough. It is too often blown up with flatulence, corroded with lust, on familiar terms with chicanery and lying; it openly delights in hocus-pocus and discovers its miracle-workers in its Comstocks and Aimée Semple McPhersons. But for all its pitiful flabbiness human nature is not wholly bad, nor is man so helpless a creature of circumstance as the cynics would have us believe. There are other and greater gods than Mumbo Jumbo worshiped in America, worthier things than hocus-pocus; and in rare moments even Babbitt dimly perceives that the feet of his idol are clay. There are Martin Arrowsmiths as well as Elmer Gantrys, and human nature, if it will, can pull itself out of the trap. Bad social machinery makes bad men. Put the banker in the scullery instead of the drawing-room; exalt the test-tube and deflate the cash register; rid society of the dictatorship of the middle class; and the artist and the scientist will erect in America a civilization that may become what civilization was in earlier days, a thing to be respected. For all his modernity and the disillusion learned from Pullman-car philosophers, Sinclair Lewis is still an echo of Jean Jacques[6] and the golden hopes of the Enlightenment—thin and far off, no doubt, but still an authentic echo.

Whether we like Mr. Lewis's technique or not, whether we agree with his indictment of middle-class ideals or dissent from it, his writings are suggestive documents symptomatic of a dissatisfied generation given over to disillusion. The optimistic dreams of middle-class capitalism are not so golden as they seemed to us before the war; and these pudgy novels are

[5] Famous labor and criminal lawyer (1857-1938). [M.S.]

[6] Jean Jacques Rousseau (1712-1778), eighteenth-century libertarian philosopher. [M.S.]

slashing attacks on a world that in mouthing empty shibboleths is only whistling to keep up its courage. The faith of America is dead. These brisk pages are filled with the doings of automata—not living men but the simulacra of men, done with astonishing verisimilitude, speaking an amazingly realistic language, professing a surprising lifelikeness; yet nevertheless only shells from which the life has departed, without faith or hope or creative energy, not even aware that they are dead.

It is this consciousness of sketching in a morgue that differentiates Mr. Lewis from the earlier satirists of middle-class America, who in the hopeful years before the war were busily engaged in rebuilding the American temple. The preceding generation—earnest souls like Robert Herrick and Jack London and Upton Sinclair—were as well aware of the shortcomings of our industrial order as Sinclair Lewis, and hated them as vigorously. From the days of Emerson and George Ripley, of Carlyle and Ruskin, capitalistic society had been persistently subjected to sharp and devastating analysis; its drabness and regimentation, its sterility and emptiness and joylessness, had been pointed out by many pens. The Victorians long ago discovered that no generous or humane civilization was to be expected from the hands of Plugson of Undershot[7]—that the banker conceiving of human felicity in terms of eight per cent. is a mean and shabby fellow in comparison with St. Francis or Michelangelo. Long before Sherwood Anderson, William Morris had observed that the workman no longer sings in the factory as in other days he sang over his tool, and concluded that the creation of beauty is more important for human happiness than figuring profits from mass production.

But those earlier analysts were dealing with causes of which they could only forecast the ultimate consequences, whereas Sinclair Lewis is dealing with effects. Plugson of Undershot is now the universal dictator. Before the war there was still life and hope in western civilization; it was not yet reduced to being a common Babbitt warren, with its Billy Sundays and Almus Pickerbaughs, its artists and editors and scientists, on the Plugson pay-roll. What emerges from the drab pages of Sinclair Lewis that is suggestive is the authoritative pronouncement that the effects forecast by the earlier critics have become in our day the regnant order of things. Babbitt is the son of Plugson of Undershot, and Babbitt is a walking corpse who refuses to be put decently away to make room for living men. An empty soul, he is the symbol of our common emptiness. Historically he marks the final passing in America of the civilization that came from the fruitful loins of the eighteenth century. For a hundred and fifty years western civilization had sustained its hopes on the rich nourishment provided by the great age of the Enlightenment. Faith in the excellence of man, in the law of progress, in the ultimate reign of justice, in the

[7] Thomas Carlyle's typical commercial radical, who in the middle of the nineteenth century finds that no decent Tory will shake hands with him, but at the close of the century shares a free-competition company with latter-day Tories. [M.S.]

conquest of nature, in the finality and sufficiency of democracy, faith in short in the excellence of life, was the great driving force in those earlier, simpler days. It was a noble dream—that dream of the Enlightenment—but it was slowly dissipated by an encompassing materialism that came likewise out of the eighteenth century. Faith in machinery came to supersede faith in man; the Industrial Revolution submerged the hopes of the French Revolution. And now we have fallen so low that our faith in justice, progress, the potentialities of human nature, the excellence of democracy, is stricken with pernicious anemia, and even faith in the machine is dying. Only science remains to take the place of the old romantic creed, and science with its psychology and physics is fast reducing man to a complex bundle of glands, at the mercy of a mechanistic universe. Babbitt, to be sure, has not yet discovered the predicament he is in, but Martin Arrowsmith knows; and while Babbitt is whistling somewhat futilely, Arrowsmith is hard at work in the laboratory seeking a new philosophy to take the place of the old. The outlook is not promising, but until a new faith emerges from the test-tube Sinclair Lewis will wander in the fogs of disillusion.

But enough of such crape-hanging at a time when our best minds are engaged in the great work of stabilizing prosperity. What are test-tubes in comparison with the infallible statistics patriotically disseminated by the National City Bank? To parade such heresies in the face of the progressive American public is enough to damn any man, genius or not. We want no carpers or cynics in our congenial membership. We must all get together to put across the drive for a bigger and richer and better America; and so, reluctantly, despite the fact that in many ways he is a good fellow, we blackball Sinclair Lewis.

Sinclair Lewis

by T. K. Whipple

Sinclair Lewis has said of himself: "He has only one illusion: that he is not a journalist and 'photographic realist' but a stylist whose chief concerns in writing are warmth and lucidity." Such illusions are not uncommon: the scientist who prides himself on his violin-playing, the statesman who would like to be known as a poet—most men would rather think of themselves as excelling in another activity than that in which they are eminent. Lewis's wish need not prevent us from adopting the general view of him, namely, that though he is a "photographic realist" and also, at times, something of a novelist or creative artist, yet after all he is primarily a satirist—unless indeed he is even more interesting as a product than as a critic of American society. Surely no one else serves so well as he to illustrate the relation between literature and a practical world: in such a world he has himself lived all his life, and such a world he portrays and holds up to ridicule and obloquy.

No small part of his effectiveness is due to the amazing skill with which he reproduces his world. His knack for mimicry is unsurpassed. He is a master of that species of art to which belong glass flowers, imitation fruit, Mme. Tussaud's waxworks, and barnyard symphonies, which aims at deceiving the spectator into thinking that the work in question is not an artificial product but the real thing. Of this art Zeuxis, who painted grapes so truly that birds came and pecked at them, is the most eminent practitioner; but Lewis's standard is often little short of the Zeuxine. Dyer's Drug Store, with its "greasy marble soda-fountain with an electric lamp of red and green and curdled-yellow mosaic," Babbitt's Dutch Colonial house in Floral Heights, with its bathroom in which "the towel rack was a rod of clear glass set in nickel," and its bedroom in which were "the bureau with its great clear mirror, Mrs. Babbitt's dressing-table with toilet articles of almost solid silver, the plain twin beds, between them a small table holding a standard electric bedside lamp, a glass of water, and a standard bedside book with colored illustrations"—thus thoroughly are the houses and stores and office buildings in Gopher Prairie and in Zenith represented for us down to the last minute particular. The inhabitants also are portrayed in corresponding fashion, as to their looks, their habits, their talk, their thoughts. Nothing could be more lifelike than Lewis's counterfeit world in all its accurate and unbearable detail. His novels are triumphant feats of memory and observation.

Not of course that they are not also much else besides; for one thing, his mimicry is all charged with hostile criticism and all edged with a satirical intent which little or nothing escapes. His is a world ruled by the desire of each individual for his own self-aggrandizement, and it shows the effects of such a rule plainly in its appearance. Viewed externally, Gopher Prairie is most conspicuous for its hit-or-miss ugliness, its lack of attraction for the eye or any other organ of sense. It looks as if its inhabitants were more or less permanently camping out, not as if they had built themselves a lasting habitation. It is dreary, haphazard, uncared for—only one degree better than the boom towns of the last century, thrown together by pioneers just to "do" for a while, and betraying essentially much the same spirit. Yet Gopher Prairie has passed the stage of pioneering; it is established and prosperous, but the people do not know what to do with their prosperity, as witness the interiors of their houses, with their shiny golden-oak furniture and their hideous carpets. Not a room in any of the dwellings nor a structure in the village—still less the village as a whole—was made with the design of its being well fitted to human life. All of it cries aloud an indifference to humane living. It is an accurate index to the attitude of the people.

Zenith, on the other hand, has attained a real beauty in its grouped towering skyscrapers, yet wholly by luck and accident, not purpose. And this beauty is only in the large; a closer inspection, though it shows comfort and luxury and even a kind of æsthetic striving, reveals this effort at beauty as spurious: from the Old English dining room of the Athletic Club to the sepia photographs on the living-room walls in Floral Heights, the taste for art is affected and unreal. The material showiness of Zenith is no improvement over the ugliness of Gopher Prairie, for it is conventional only, and the inhabitants find their truest pleasure in the accumulation of ingenious mechanical contrivances and conveniences. Zenith has arrived at the perfection of a mechanical luxury in which the only flaw is that it is altogether inhuman.

Life dehumanized by indifference or enmity to all human values—that is the keynote of both Gopher Prairie and Zenith. And nowhere does this animosity show itself more plainly than in hostility to truth and art. The creed of both towns is the philosophy of boasting, a hollow optimism and false cheeriness which leads directly to hypocrisy, as in making believe that business knavery is social service. Toward ideas likely to break this bubble of pretense the people are bitterly opposed; toward new ideas they are lazily contemptuous; toward other ideas they are apathetic. In both places, to be sure, there is a conventional gesture at the pursuit of culture: in Gopher Prairie the Thanatopsis Club listens to papers on the English Poets, and in Zenith a symphony orchestra is advocated as a means of civic advertisement. Yet intellectually both are cities of the dead, and in both the dead are resolved that no one shall live.

In *Main Street* and in *Babbitt,* the life of the mind is noticeable only because of the void left unfilled; in *Arrowsmith,* however, Lewis has devoted all of a long book to the tribulations of a seeker for truth in the United States, and his handling of the theme is masterly. The hero is a physician who becomes a bacteriologist. Before he finally takes refuge in the wilds of Vermont where he can pursue his researches undisturbed, he encounters all the difficulties which the United States puts in the way of a doctor and an investigator who would like to be honest; he struggles with the commercialism of the medical school, the quackery which thrives in the country, the politics and fraud of a Department of Public Health in a small city, the more refined commercialism of a metropolitan clinic, and the social and financial temptations of a great institute for research. He is offered every possible inducement to prostitute himself to an easy success—manifest, worldly success. Nor is he indifferent to the pressures which are brought to bear on him; on the contrary, being a scientist by instinct rather than by reasoned conviction, he wins out only in spite of himself. He would like to succeed, he has been contaminated by the success-worship with which he is surrounded, but he is unable to cope with an ineluctable honesty and stubborn drive in himself. In the end, he succumbs to his own integrity. When one reflects that of all thinkers the scientist is among us much the most favored, and that among scientists none is more encouraged than the medical man, one realizes that Lewis has wisely taken for his theme the form of intellectual life in which it appears at its best. Martin's troubles would have been still more serious had he been a chemist, economist, historian, philosopher, or artist.

The intellectual life, however, is not the worst sufferer in the society Lewis deals with. The other humane activities fare no better; and of them all probably none is so debased as religion. In Gopher Prairie religion takes the form of repressive puritanism and prurient espionage. In Zenith it is only one form of boosting, with a go-getter in the pulpit and the best of hustlers in the Sunday school. Nothing in Lewis's work reads so like outrageous burlesque as his account of Babbitt's campaign to increase attendance at the Sunday school; yet no student of Mencken's *Americana* will dare to say that Lewis has not been scrupulously truthful. There is nothing unusual in "the good time the Sacred Trinity class of girls had at their wieniewurst party," nor in the publicity given "the value of the Prayer-life in attaining financial success." If Lewis goes so far as to fall into low farce, it is only in pursuit of absolute verisimilitude.

No doubt every detail of *Elmer Gantry* is faithfully accurate, and one ought to be grateful to Lewis for so detailed a clinical report on the morbid symptoms which attack religion in a land where the religious spirit is dead. Nothing is omitted, no possible fraud or quackery or hypocrisy or iniquity—nothing is missing but religion. And that perhaps is why one is less grateful than one ought to be. In the other books, there is always in some form or other some norm for comparison, some principle of protest—as there is in Carol Kennicott's aspirations, in Babbitt's sense of defeat, and most conspicuously in Arrowsmith's stubborn loyalty to science. The absence of relief—even comic relief—in *Elmer Gantry* may account for the fact that the book is so difficult to read and therefore, unfortunately, so much less effective as satire than its predecessors. It is too bad, for never has Lewis had so good a subject or such wealth of material. But perhaps I do *Elmer Gantry* an injustice; possibly the very qualities which make it inferior to *Arrowsmith* and the rest adapt it all the better to the audience at which it is aimed. However that may be, it can be studied with profit as a sociological survey—even if it cannot be read with pleasure as a work of literature—for as a report on the status of what passes as religion in most of the nation it has the virtue of completeness.

Furthermore, since Lewis's folk are not alive in senses, mind, or spirit, they could scarcely be expected to have a social life. They carry on, of course, a group existence, for solitude is terrifying to them. Yet when they have gathered together, they have nothing to say to one another. They tell stories, they talk about business and the weather and housekeeping and automobiles, they gossip endlessly and often maliciously. Their curiosity as to each other's doings, which is equalled only by their indifference to each other as persons, is not a friendly and welcoming curiosity. They do not really care to get acquainted with one another; they have, and are capable of having, no true personal relations. Sometimes they seek distraction in noise and artificial gaiety. Constantly they simulate goodfellowship and practise a forced and humorless jocularity, raucous and mechanical. Their sociability is ghastly as any lifeless imitation of a living thing must be ghastly. It is a dance of galvanized dead. Lewis's world is a social desert, and for the best of reasons, that it is a human desert. It is a social void because each of its members is personally a human emptiness.

The central vacuum at the core of these people is the secret which explains their manifestations. Having no substance in themselves, they are incapable of being genuine. They are not individual persons; they have never developed personality. A search for the real Babbitt reveals simply that there is no "real" Babbitt. There are several Babbitts who have never been integrated. And so with the others: in their inner vacancy, they necessarily have no integrity, and therefore they are insecure and uncertain. Having no guide, no standard, in themselves, they are driven to adopting the standards and the ideas of the herd. Their only existence is in the pack—naturally they fight for their tribal taboos with the ferocity of savages. It is impossible that they should be anything but standardized and uniform, since the wellsprings of individuality have gone dry in them; and it is inevitable that their uneasiness should make them defend themselves by assuming a blatant self-satisfaction and a bloodthirsty intolerance. Being unsure, they are self-conscious and snobbish and cruel. Their ignorance leads to bigotry and to scornful and uncomfortable ridicule of what they do not understand—which is everything unlike themselves. The women are devoted to a conception derived from without, an inherited convention, of what constitutes gentility, refinement, "niceness." The men, after their own fashion, are equally fanatical in behalf of their own notions of respectability and propriety in behavior. To both men and women, life is a hollow shell of deportment, and of course they hate any one who threatens to crack the shell.

If in the land which Lewis depicts "life at its most passionate is but a low-grade infection," the explanation is not far to seek. This society from the beginning has been developed under the dominance of one motive: the self-advancement of its separate members. The men are ruled mainly by the desire to get rich, the women by the desire to rise socially, but the two are ultimately the same. Both, in order to get up in the world, have denied themselves all other interests and experiences. They have starved themselves, until in the midst of the utmost material profusion they are dying of inanition. An unspoiled peasantry is rich in life in comparison with them, for they do not even live and grow like good vegetables, having cut themselves off from the source of nourishment. The instincts which cannot be entirely killed, such as sex, take on queer distorted forms among them. They are famine-sufferers who alienate sympathy by their own pride in their misshapenness and by their fierce determination that every one else shall be as deformed as themselves. Were it not for their complacency and contemptuousness, they would be pathetic—and at times, in spite of everything, they are pathetic. For these folk, who enjoy ample opportunity to do whatever they like and who do not know what to do with themselves, suffer from an obscure but acute dissatisfaction. After all, the impulse to live cannot be altogether extinguished; it can only be frustrated. The victim, though self-sacrificed, realizes that he has missed something. Mrs. Babbitt turns for succor to vaporous forms of New Thought; Zilla Riesling finds an outlet in a degraded and vindictive religiosity.

But the spiritual malady which afflicts Zenith is most fully analyzed in the person of Babbitt himself. He feels vague longings which cannot be satisfied by the mechanical toys which are his "substitutes for joy and passion and wisdom," his "symbols of truth and beauty"; there is in him a wish for something beyond even electric cigar-lighters. When illness gives him an opportunity to stop and reflect, he is conscious that something is wrong:

> He lay on the sleeping-porch and watched the winter sun slide along the taut curtains, turning their ruddy khaki to pale blood red. The shadow of

> the draw-rope was dense black, in an enticing ripple on the canvas. He found pleasure in the curve of it, sighed as the fading light blurred it. He was conscious of life, and a little sad. With no Vergil Gunches before whom to set his face in resolute optimism, he beheld, and half admitted that he beheld, his way of life as incredibly mechanical. Mechanical business—a brisk selling of badly built houses. Mechanical religion—a dry, hard church, shut off from the real life of the streets, inhumanly respectable as a top-hat. Mechanical golf and dinner-parties and bridge and conversation. Save with Paul Riesling, mechanical friendships—back-slapping and jocular, never daring to essay the test of quietness. . . .
>
> It was coming to him that perhaps all life as he knew it and vigorously practiced it was futile; that heaven as portrayed by the Reverend Dr. John Jennison Drew was neither very probable nor very interesting; that he hadn't much pleasure out of making money; that it was of doubtful worth to rear children merely that they might rear children who would rear children. What was it all about? What did he want?

Babbitt seeks relief in philandering and in drink, but finds hardly even a momentary distraction. He attempts a timid excursion into liberal thought—liberal for Zenith—but is frightened and cajoled back into orthodoxy. His only real happiness he finds in a few days' vacation with Paul Riesling in the Maine woods.

The discontent which is common among the pillars of Zenith's civilization flares at times into open rebellion among the less compliant members of the community. Paul Riesling, who should have been a violinist and who instead went into the tar-roofing business, is in complete revolt and is finally reduced to committing murder. Chump Frink, the syndicated poet, gets drunk and lets out the secret of his thwarted aspirations. Gopher Prairie likewise has many malcontents: Guy Pollock, the lawyer, the one civilized man in the town, a victim to what he calls "the village virus"; Raymie Wutherspoon, the shoe clerk, with his futile yearnings toward sweetness and light; Erik Valborg, the tailor's assistant, with a spark, but only a spark, of the true fire. Not the least tragic aspect of both city and country is the effect they have on such as these, denying them possibility of healthy growth, condemning them to ineffectuality if not to freakishness. The rebels are as badly off as the conformists; for in a society in which the bread of life is nowhere to be found, the few isolated seekers for it are in a hopeless situation, foredoomed to being stunted and distorted both by lack of nourishment and by the hostility of their environment.

In short, in *Main Street, Babbitt, Arrowsmith,* and *Elmer Gantry,* Sinclair Lewis has rendered in minute detail a vast panorama of an almost ideal practical society. To be sure, in my account of his work I have exaggerated the effect by omitting the shades and qualifications which are frequent in his books; nor does he himself analyze or explain the phenomena he depicts. Furthermore, Lewis himself, in spite of his fullness, has perforce selected and emphasized certain aspects of American life, so that his work cannot be taken as a complete portrait of the United States. His achievement is to have rendered more effectively than any one else several of the most conspicuous phases of our civilization. I hardly think that any one will deny that the United States recognized itself in Lewis's portrait, which therefore, though unflattering, may be accepted as on the whole a good likeness. We are all certain to find our neighbors in the picture, and likely, somewhere or other, if we try, to find ourselves. Nor is the author himself absent. No special discernment is needed to detect a self-delineation in Lewis's novels, for after all the world he deals with is no more the world of Carol Kennicott, George F. Babbitt, Martin Arrowsmith, and Elmer Gantry than it is the world of Sinclair Lewis. He belongs to it as completely as do any of his creatures. He too was bred and born in the briar patch, and he has not escaped unscratched.

As a novelist Lewis has several peculiarities and limitations all of which point to a poverty of invention or imagination. One of these, his fondness and aptitude for mimicry, has already been discussed. Closely allied to this trait is his extreme dependence on his own experience and on his power of observation. Another indication of the same weakness is the care with which he gets up his subjects, as he got up aviation for *The Trail of the Hawk,* or medicine and bacteriology for *Arrowsmith.* Furthermore, it is significant that his interest is in social types and classes rather than in individuals as human beings. With few exceptions, his treatment of his characters is external only; he confines himself largely to the socially representative surface, rarely exercising much insight or sympathy. He is above all a collector of specimens. May the explanation of this clinging to actuality and to externals not be that his imagination has failed to find adequate nutriment in his experience, especially in his social experience?

However that may be, of one thing there can be no doubt: that he has hated his environment, with a cordial and malignant hatred. That detestation has made him a satirist, and has barbed his satire and tipped it with venom. But his satire is no plainer a sign of his hatred than is his observation: he is as watchful as a wild animal on the lookout for its foes, or as a Red Indian in the enemy's country. His eye is always alert and keen for inconsistencies or weaknesses in his prey—and how quickly he pounces! Years of malicious scrutiny have gone to the making of his last four volumes. Such observation is but one sign of a defensive attitude. Undoubtedly, his hostility is only a reply to the hostility which he has had himself to encounter from his environment, such as every artist has to encounter in a practical society. But for the artist to adopt an answering unfriendliness is disastrous, because it prevents him from receiving and welcoming experience. From such a defensive shield, experience, which ought to be soaked up, rattles off like hail from a tin roof. I should judge that Lewis had been irritated rather than absorbed by his experience. His observation seems at the other extreme from realization; it seems vigilant and wary, whereas realization demands self-surrender and self-forgetfulness, and is possible only in friendly surroundings. If it be true that his imaginative power is somewhat lean and scanty, the fact would be in part accounted for by the enmity between him and his surroundings.

But to have evoked this enmity is not the only unfortunate effect which his environment has had on Lewis. Although he has changed not at all in essentials, some of his characteristics are disclosed more plainly in his early than in his later novels. *Our Mr. Wrenn, The Trail of the Hawk, The Job,* and *Free Air* assist materially toward an understanding of the author of *Main Street* and *Elmer Gantry.* In the former, for example, he betrays his defensive attitude in the extraordinary precautions he takes lest his readers misjudge him. He makes greater use of irony as a defensive weapon than any other writer I know of; he early made the discovery that if only he were ironical and showed that he knew better, he could be as romantic and sentimental and playful as he pleased. He writes as if always conscious of a hostile audience. He takes needless pains to make clear that he is more sophisticated than his characters, as if there were danger of our identifying him with them. He makes fun of their ingenuous enthusiasms, even when these enthusiasms have the best of causes. The result of it all is that he often seems unduly afraid of giving himself away.

In this respect he resembles his characters; nothing in them is more striking than their morbid self-consciousness. Only Will Kennicott and Leora are free from it. The others, especially those in the early books, are always wondering what people will think, always suspecting that they are the objects of observation and comment—and in Lewis's novels they are generally right. They are constantly posing and pretending, for the benefit even of waiters and elevator-boys. They do not dare to be natural; they are self-distrustful, uncertain, and insecure. They are self-analytical and self-contemptuous for their lack of sincerity; yet they continue to pose to themselves, adopting one attitude after another. That is to say, they conceive the object of life to be to pass themselves off as something they are not. This idea the author himself seems to share; he seems to think that the solution of all problems and difficulties is to find the one right pose, the one correct attitude.

Just as his people have no inner standards of their own, because they are not integral personalities, because they have not, in fact, developed any real personality at all, so Lewis himself shifts his point of view so often that finally we come to wonder whether he has any. One of the great advantages of *Arrowsmith* over its forerunners and its successor is that in it there seemed to emerge an almost established point of view. Otherwise, one would be inclined to call Lewis a man of multiple personality—

save that all these personalities have a look of being assumed for effect. All the Lewises are disdainful of one another. When he has been romantic, he throws in a jibe at sentiment lest we think him sentimental; when he has been cynical, he grows tender lest he be thought hard; when he has been severe with a member of the Babbittry, he emphasizes the virtues of the common people and the absurdities of highbrows and social leaders. All his manifold attitudes, however, may be resolved into four: most conspicuously, he is the satirist who has flayed American society; least obviously, he is the artist whom one feels sure nature intended him to be; in addition, and above all in the early novels, he is a romanticist, and he is a philistine—these two bitterly abusive of each other. That is, besides his other reactions, he has tried to escape from his environment, and he has tried, with more success, to conform to it.

His romanticism is of two kinds. In the first place, there is in him much of the conventional romanticist and even of the sentimentalist. He has said of himself that he is "known publicly as a scolding corn-belt realist, but actually (as betrayed by the samite-yclad, Tennyson-and-water verse which he wrote when he was in college) a yearner over what in private he probably calls 'quaint ivied cottages.' " This is the Lewis who flees from reality to fantasy, who sympathizes with Carol in her dislike of Gopher Prairie and in her longing for "a reed hut on fantastic piles above the mud of a jungle river," and who invents for Babbitt a dream of a fairy child playmate, "more romantic than scarlet pagodas by a silver sea." Then there is the second sort of romanticist, who has taken a tip from Arnold Bennett and gone in for the romance of the commonplace, who records the Swede farm-girl Bea's glamorous impressions of Main Street, who dilates on the excitement, adventure, and beauty of life in Zenith and who has no use for "Lloyd Mallam, the poet, owner of the Hafiz Book Shop," who wrote "a rondeau to show how diverting was life amid the feuds of medieval Florence, but how dull it was in so obvious a place as Zenith." To establishing the strangeness and beauty of humdrum life Lewis devoted his first four books; he undertakes to prove in *Our Mr. Wrenn* that a clerk's life in a Harlem flat is more romantic than travel in foreign lands, and in *The Job* that a stenographer is more romantic than Clytemnestra. This process is really no less an escape from reality than is the old-fashioned romance, for it consists, not in bringing out the essential quality and verity of ordinary life, but in casting a glamour over it and falsifying and sentimentalizing and prettifying it. Although romanticist the second is always highly contemptuous of romanticist the first, there is no essential difference between them.

Closely akin to the romanticist of the second sort is the Lewis who speaks as a man of the soil, one of the common herd, a Rotarian; he points out the essential goodness of small towns and their inhabitants and of boosters; he is homey and folksy, and strongly opposed to people whom he suspects of thinking that they are superior. This side of Lewis, plain enough in all his writing, is especially pronounced in the novels which preceded *Main Street;* in the first of them, the account of Wrenn's marketing the Dixieland Inkwell, a glorification of the romance of business, is sheer Babbittry, and the account of Mrs. Arty's boarding-house, a glorification of folks who are just folks, is sheer Main-Streetism. In *Free Air,* an extravaganza on the theme of "Out Where the West Begins," the heroine learns during her transcontinental journey that "what had seemed rudeness in garage men and hotel clerks was often a resentful reflection of her own Eastern attitude that she was necessarily superior to a race she had been trained to call 'common people.'" According to Lewis the superiority is all the other way: people who have enjoyed the hereditary advantages of wealth, social position, and education are ridiculous and contemptible—unless, like Claire, they have the good luck to be regenerated by the Great West. His whole tendency in his first four stories is to bring a warm glow of self-satisfaction to the heart of the great American majority, to strengthen and entrench the folk of Zenith and of Gopher Prairie in their complacency and also in their intolerance of every one unlike themselves. In short, he has not escaped contamination, but has partially conformed to his environment. One of the Lewises is a philistine.

Wonder has often been expressed at Lewis's popularity—that attacks such as his on American life and the American gods should meet a reception so enthusiastic. Yet I think his vogue is easily understood. For one thing, no doubt all the Zeniths enjoyed *Main Street* and all the Gopher Prairies *Babbitt,* and all who live on farms or in big cities liked both books. Moreover, Lewis caters to all tastes because he shares all points of view. For instance, I happened to see the play *Main Street* acted by a provincial stock company, and was amazed to find how readily the animus of the book had been shifted: a slight change had turned it into a traditional hick comedy—the rustics humorous but lovable and even admirable—and directed all the satire against Carol, Erik Valborg, and the other highbrows. Probably many readers took the novel so in the first place. In any case, whatever one's likes and dislikes, whether boosters, malcontents, romantics, radicals, social leaders, villagers, bohemians, or conventional people, one can find aid and comfort in the work of Sinclair Lewis.

Furthermore, Lewis's style must have contributed enormously to his success. It is of just the sort to please the people of whom he writes. His technique of raillery he has learned from Sam Clark and Vergil Gunch; he merely turns their type of wit and humor back upon themselves. All his satire is a long *tu quoque.* His crusade against the shortcomings of the clergy is conducted in the same spirit as Elmer Gantry's crusade against vice. His irony and sarcasm are of the cheap and showy variety popular on Main Street and in the Zenith Athletic Club:

> Babbitt's preparations for leaving the office to its feeble self during the hour and a half of his lunch-period were somewhat less elaborate than the plans for a general European war. . . .

> . . . the lithograph of a smirking young woman with cherry cheeks who proclaimed in the exalted poetry of advertising, "My tootsies never got hep to what pedal perfection was till I got a pair of clever classy Cleopatra Shoes."

Surely the point of these jibes would be plain even to Uncle Whittier or the Widow Bogart. Moreover, Lewis must think that his imitations or quotations of the speeches, advertisements, and conversation in *Babbitt* are amusing—that it is funny, that is, that the speakers should think themselves funny—and not merely dreary and faintly obscene. One comes finally to suspect, from his asperity, that not long ago the writer himself enjoyed such mispronunciations as *animiles, intellekschool, bacheldore, Heavings*. The reviewer who said that in *Elmer Gantry* Lewis had sent the preachers a comic valentine hit off Lewis's style to perfection. Lewis seems to aim at much the same stage of mental development as the movies, which is said to be the average age of fourteen. His manner is founded on the best uses of salesmanship, publicity, and advertising. It is heavily playful and vivacious, highly and crudely colored, brisk and snappy. He avails himself of all the stock tricks of a reporter to give a fillip to jaded attention. His people do not run, they "gallop"; instead of speaking, they "warble" or "gurgle" or "carol"; commonplace folk are "vanilla-flavored"; interior decorators are "daffodilic young men," "achingly well-dressed"; dancing becomes "the refined titillations of communal embracing." No wonder Lewis has sold satire to the nation—he has made it attractive with a coat of brilliant if inexpensive varnish. The excellence of his rare intervals of real writing is lost in the general glare.

For, though no one unaided could have guessed that Lewis thought himself "a stylist whose chief concerns in writing are warmth and lucidity," there are such intervals, and they serve to remind us from time to time of Lewis the artist, by no means insensible to beauty or devoid of the tragic sense of life. The account of Carl Ericson's boyhood in *The Trail of the Hawk* is full of poetry, and there are bits in the story of his *Wanderjahre* that make one wish Lewis had seen fit to develop the picaresque possibilities more fully. In *The Job,* the death of Una Golden's mother is powerfully felt and strongly written. And, although Carol Kennicott is mainly a medium and an object of satire, she is also a created character, as is Babbitt likewise. But Will Kennicott, who is little analyzed or dissected, is the best evidence before *Arrowsmith* that Lewis has the ability to create people. *Arrowsmith* itself, however, is the final proof of his creative power. Leora, Martin's first wife, is by general consent Lewis's masterpiece in the creation of character. Not only is she likable, but she is indubitably real; though she is portrayed casually and without effort, few other characters in American fiction equal her in absolute final reality. And Martin suffers only in comparison with Leora; although far more difficult than either Carol or Babbitt, he is more understandingly and more successfully portrayed. Yet even Leora interests Lewis less than his national portrait gallery of typical frauds and fakirs. He prefers to stay safely on the surface of social appearances. He shows little of Sherwood Anderson's hunger to delve into the lives of men and women.

The very mention of Anderson brings into sharp relief Lewis's limitations—his superficiality, his meretricious writing, his lack of passion and of thoughtfulness. If it were objected that the comparison has no point, Lewis being a satirist, I should reply that it is possible for a satirist to manifest penetration, strong feeling, and intellectual power, seeing that other satirists have obviously possessed these qualities. Yet I feel sure that Lewis has many unrealized capabilities. Underneath all the masks he puts on to rebuff or to placate the world, there seems to lurk a boyish artist, immature and shy and eager, full of fancy and sentiment, who has never grown up and ripened—denied his proper development, probably, by the necessity of manufacturing those protective masks. He is uncomfortable in the presence of other people, and feels at ease only with nature, on which he lavishes exquisite praise. The world would have none of him; so he will have none of the world. His world was a poor one at best, but he has denied himself even what little it might have offered. That is why he is still a boy, with a boy's insecurity and self-doubt hidden behind a forced rudeness and boldness.

In *Arrowsmith,* his seventh novel,[1] Lewis showed signs of beginning to develop a point of view, an inner standard of measurement. But that it is too late now for him to abandon his assumed attitudes and adopt the position proper to the artist, with the self-reliance which can come only from a sense of there being a pivot or point of rest in himself, *Elmer Gantry* is sufficient evidence. To the present, at any rate, Lewis is significant mainly as a social rather than as a literary phenomenon. And though this fact heightens his immediate importance, it detracts ultimately even from his social importance. While many of his contemporaries, who have succeeded in maintaining their integrity unimpaired, impart to their readers an intenser realization of the world they live in, the net result of Lewis's work is not a truer apprehension or a deeper insight, but an increase in mutual dissatisfaction: he has made Americans more outspoken and more hostile critics of one another. But perhaps after all it is better so: Lewis's romanticism and philistinism and vulgarity of style make him powerful because they make him popular. The attack on American practicality needs its shock troops—could we afford to give

[1] Eighth. [M.S.]

up so effective a critic for a better writer? Perhaps it is worth spoiling an artist to have him take so salutary a revenge. Lewis is the most successful critic of American society because he is himself the best proof that his charges are just.

Sinclair Lewis

by Walter Lippmann

I

The career of Mr. Lewis is usually divided into two periods: an earlier in which he wrote popular fiction without much success, and a later, beginning with *Main Street,* in which he tried only to please himself and had a huge success. Roughly speaking, this second period began with the inauguration of Warren Harding. Mr. Lewis has continued to flourish under Calvin Coolidge.

This is not, I imagine, a mere coincidence. The election of 1920 marked the close of that period of democratic idealism and of optimism about the perfectibility of American society, which began in its modern phase with Bryan, was expressed for a while by Roosevelt, and culminated in the exaltation and the spiritual disaster under Wilson. By 1920 the American people were thoroughly weary of their old faith that happiness could be found by public work, and very dubious about the wisdom of the people. They had found out that the problem of living is deeper and more complex than they had been accustomed to think it was. They had, moreover, become rich. They were ready for an examination of themselves.

Mr. Lewis was in a position to supply the demand. For he too had outlived his political illusions, having passed beyond the socialist idealism of Helicon Hall. At the moment when he sat down to please himself by writing *Main Street,* in the heroic mood of one who abandons the quest of money and applause, a vast multitude was waiting for him with more money and applause than he had ever dreamed about.

In this first success there was apparently no element of calculation. It so happened that the personal mood of Sinclair Lewis suited exactly the mood of a very large part of the American people. Very quickly he became a national figure. *Main Street, Babbitt,* and, in a certain measure, *Arrowsmith,* became source books for the new prejudices and rubber stamps with which we of the Harding-Coolidge era examined ourselves.

II

Although we are all endowed with eyes, few of us see very well. We see what we are accustomed to see, and what we are told to see. To the rest of what is about us we are largely anesthetic, for we live in a kind of hazy dream bent on our purposes. For the apprehension of the external world, and of that larger environment which is invisible, we are almost helpless until we are supplied with patterns of seeing which enable us to fix objects clearly amidst the illegible confusion of experience. When we find a pattern which works well, in that it allows us to feel that we have made a large area of reality our own, we are grateful, and we use that pattern until it is threadbare. For to invent new patterns requires more genius than most of us have, and to deal with life freshly in all its variety is much too much trouble for preoccupied men. As a mere matter of economy in time and trouble, we demand simple and apparently universal stereotypes with which to see the world.

Mr. Lewis has an extraordinary talent for inventing stereotypes. This talent is uninhibited, for he is wholly without that radical skepticism which might make a man of equal, or even greater, genius hesitate at substituting new prejudices for old. "This is America," he says in an italicized foreword; "this Main Street is the continuation of Main Streets everywhere." Now a writer without this dogmatism of the practical man, and with a greater instinct for reality, could not have written these words. He would have remembered that the world is not so simple. But what he would have gained in truthfulness, he would have lost in influence. He would probably not have induced a large part of the nation to adopt his line of stereotypes as a practical convenience for daily use along with the telephone, the radio, the syndicated newspaper, and similar mechanical contrivances for communicating with other men.

Mr. Lewis has prospered by inventing and marketing useful devices for seeing the American scene quickly. His psychological inventions are being used by millions of Americans to perceive and express their new, disillusioned sense of America. They are wholly mechanical and they are completely standardized now that they have passed into common use. Because of Mr. Lewis's success in fixing the conception of Main Street, it is now very difficult to see any particular Main Street with an innocent eye. A Babbitt is no longer a man; he is a prejudice.

The art of creating these prejudices consists, in Mr. Lewis's case, of an ability to assemble in one picture a collection of extraordinarily neat imitations of lifelike details. Had his gift been in a different medium he could have manufactured wax flowers that would make a man with hay fever sneeze; he could have crowed so much like a rooster that the hens would palpitate. He has a photo- and phonographic memory with an irresistible gift of mimicry. But since his business is the creation of types rather than of living characters, he does not photograph and mimic individuals. Babbitt is not a man; he is assembled out of many actual Babbitts. The effect is at once lifelike and weird. As with an almost perfect scarecrow the thing is so much like life that it nearly lives. Yet it is altogether dead. It is like an anatomical model of an average man, a purely theoretical concept which has no actual existence. For in any living man the average qualities are always found in some unique combination.

But just because Mr. Lewis's creations are composed of skillful imitations of details, they are extraordinarily successful as stereotypes. The Babbitt pattern covers no actual Babbitt perfectly, but it covers so many details in so many Babbitts that it is highly serviceable for practical purposes. The veracity in detail is so striking that there is no disposition to question the verity of the whole.

III

It is not going too far to say that Mr. Lewis has imposed his conception of America on a very considerable part of the reading and writing public. To-day they see what he has selected out of the whole vast scene. Now Mr. Lewis is a reformer. He does not assemble his collection of details with the disinterested desire to hold a mirror up to nature. He wishes to destroy what he dislikes and to put something better in its place; he is rarely relieved of an overpowering compulsion to make or break something. Yet this particular zeal is no necessary part of his great talents for mimicry. For he might conceivably have loved life more than his own purposes, and have written a human comedy. Or he might have felt that sense of their destiny which makes all human creatures tragic. Or he might have been filled with a feeling for the mystery that enshrouds so temporary a thing as man, and then he would have confessed that after you have studied their behavior no matter how accurately from the outside, there is much in all human souls that remains to be known. But Mr. Lewis is not a great artist. He has a great skill. He himself is a practical man with the practical man's illusion that by bending truth to your purposes, you can make life better.

There was a moment, I think, when Mr. Lewis was tempted to use his talent with that serene disinterestedness by which alone wisdom comes. I refer to that passage in one of the early chapters of *Main Street* when for the first time Mr. Lewis describes Main Street. Until I reread the book recently I had forgotten that in this early stage Mr. Lewis presents the reader with two quite contrasting versions of the same scene. One is the version we all remember, a dull, fly-specked, timidly gaudy spectacle of human vacuity. The other version, which he soon allows the reader to forget, is romantic, exciting, and full of promise. There is no doubt that at this juncture Mr. Lewis meant to say: What you see in Main Street will depend on what you are; it all depends on who is looking at it. In order to emphasize this notion he gives you first the Main Street which Carol Kennicott sees on her first walk in Gopher Prairie, and then immediately following the identical aspects of Main Street as seen by Bea Sorenson who is just off a lonely farm.

Carol is a comparatively sophisticated person; at least she does not belong to the prairies but to a town which with "its garden-sheltered streets and aisles of elms is white and green New England reborn." Carol, moreover, came from a cultivated home with a "brown library" in which she "absorbed" Balzac and Rabelais and Thoreau and Max Mueller. It might reasonably be objected, I know, that Carol never absorbed anything, let alone such heady stuff as Rabelais. But what Mr. Lewis meant to say is plain enough. It is that Carol came from a background which predisposed her to dislike the raw ugliness of Main Street civilization. And having said that, he introduced Bea by way of contrast and justice to show how delightful Main Street would look to a peasant mind.

"It chanced that Carol Kennicott and Bea Sorenson were viewing Main Street at the same time." Carol looks through the fly-specked windows of the Minniemashie House and sees only the row of rickety chairs with the brass cuspidors; Bea is thrilled by the swell traveling man in there —probably been to Chicago lots of times. At Dyer's drug store Carol sees a greasy marble soda fountain with an electric lamp of red and green and curdled-yellow mosaic shade; to Bea the soda fountain is all lovely marble with the biggest shade you ever saw—all different kinds of colored glass stuck together.

There is a humility in this passage which might have become the seed of a much richer wisdom than his regular practice exhibits. Here for a moment Mr. Lewis used his gift without self-righteousness. Here in this interlude he was willing to show some courtesy to the souls of other people. He was willing even to admit that their feelings are authentic. In this mood, had he been able to retain it, he might have risen above the irritations of his time and his clique, have given even the devil his due, and become the creator of a great American comedy of manners instead of the mere inventor of new prejudices.

But to have done that he would have had to care more about human beings than about his own attitude toward them. Apparently that was impossible for him. He cannot for long detach himself from the notion that what Sinclair Lewis feels about Main Street, about Babbittry, about the Protestant churches is of primary importance. What he feels would have more importance if he had great insight as well as great sight, if he had fine taste instead of sharp distastes, if he had salient intuition as to what moves people as well as an astounding memory of how they look to him when they move. Then his figures might have come alive, and been something more than a synthetic mass of detail which serves as the butt for the uncritical, rebellious yearning of the author.

Had he a real interest in character, and not such a preoccupation with behavior, he would have expressed his view of the world through all his characters, and not merely through one mouthpiece. He would have given you Main Street through Dr. Kennicott and Bea and Vida and Percy Bresnahan, instead of giving you Kennicott, Bea, Vida, and Bresnahan through Carol. For that young woman staggers under the burden of the weighty message she is forced to carry.

> There—she meditated—is the newest empire of the world; the Northern Middle West . . . an empire which feeds a quarter of the world—yet its work is merely begun. They are pioneers, these sweaty wayfarers, for all their telephones and bank accounts and automatic pianos and coöperative leagues. And for all its fat richness, theirs is a pioneer land. What is its future? she wondered.

She meditated! She wondered! Did she really, or did Sinclair Lewis? I ask the question in no captious spirit. This uncertainty as to who is talking and who is seeing the detail he reports pervades all of Mr. Lewis's books, and prevents him from achieving that "more conscious life" for which Carol yearns in phrases that are borrowed from H. G. Wells. When Mr. Lewis described Bea's walk on Main Street, he remembered for a moment what he usually forgets, that a more conscious life is one in which a man is conscious not only of what he sees, but of the prejudices with which he sees it.

IV

Though he is absorbed in his own vision of things, Mr. Lewis is curiously unaware of himself. He is aware only of the object out there. Carol, Babbitt, Arrowsmith and Frank Shallard have sharp eyes but vague spirits. Mr. Lewis is sophisticated enough to realize how they flounder about, and he laughs at them. But this laughter is not comic, it is protective. It is a gesture of defense by a man who knows that some mature reader, say Mr. Mencken, is going to laugh, and it is better to laugh first. It is not the carefree laughter of a man who is detached from the rather adolescent rebellion which he is describing. On the contrary, he is absorbed by it. Underneath their sardonic and brutal tone, these novels are extraordinarily earnest and striving. *Main Street, Babbitt* and *Arrowsmith* are stories of an individual who is trying to reform the world, or to find salvation by escaping it.

Carol fusses with "fanlights and Galsworthy," brightly painted furniture, and a separate bedroom. She runs away to Washington but returns to Gopher Prairie, saying: "I may not have fought the good fight but I have kept the faith." Babbitt on his sleeping porch dreams of the fairy child, frets with "veiled rebellions," escapes to the Maine woods, thinks he has been "converted to serenity," isn't, returns to Zenith, and, like Carol, at the end makes a speech: "Tell 'em to go to the devil." Martin Arrowsmith also takes to the woods, escaping from his wife's blue and gold velvet limousine, and at the end says: "We'll plug along for two or three years, and maybe we'll get something permanent—and probably we'll fail."

Dr. Arrowsmith is the only one who may have found what he wanted. He has fled from the barbarians and their gauds, he has left "a soft bed for a shanty bunk in order to be pure. For he had perceived the horror of the shrieking, bawdy thing called Success."

"I am sorry," says Gottlieb when he has to tell Arrowsmith that his great discovery belongs to someone else. "I am sorry you are not to have the fun of being pretentious and successful—for a while. . . . Martin, it is nice that you will corroborate D'Herelle. This is science: to work and not to care—too much—if somebody else gets the credit."

Arrowsmith is saved by embracing the religion of science. But for Carol and for Babbitt and for Shallard there is no religion available which they can embrace, and therefore, there is no salvation. Mr. Lewis knew what to do with Arrowsmith. For there is an ideal in science to which a modern man can give himself and find peace. But there is no ideal for Carol or Babbitt. They would not be helped by "believing in" science, no matter how devoutly. Only Arrowsmith who can do scientific work can be saved by it. Only Arrowsmith finds a god to love whom no man can possess and no man can cajole.

This is the point of Mr. Lewis's greatest insight into the human predicament. There is an unconscious pathos about it, for obviously the religion which Arrowsmith embraces, ascetic, disinterested, purified, is for Mr. Lewis like some fine mystery seen at a distance. That there might be a path of salvation like it for his ordinary characters, though in other ways, is too difficult for him to believe. It would be hard for me to believe. But it would have been possible to put the rebellion of Carol and the yearning of Babbitt in the perspective of an understanding of how, as Spinoza says, all things excellent are as difficult as they are rare. They might have failed, but their failure would have been measured against a spiritual insight as fine as Arrowsmith's. Then at least the author would have understood the failure of his characters to understand themselves.

That degree of insight Mr. Lewis does not attain. He can report what he sees; having known about the religion of science, he was able to report it in Arrowsmith. But in Carol and in Babbitt he was projecting only his own spirit, and when he attempts to make it articulate, he becomes literary and fumbling: "It was mystery which Carol had most lacked in Gopher Prairie . . . where there were no secret gates opening upon moors over which one might walk by moss-deadened paths to strange, high adventures in an ancient garden." Babbitt escapes from Zenith only when he is asleep, when he is drunk, and vicariously when his son tells the family to go to the devil. For Carol and Babbitt are worldlings, and for the worldling there is no personal salvation. He must either conquer the world and remake it, though in that he will almost surely fail, or he must escape into his dreams.

V

The America of Mr. Lewis is dominated by the prosperous descendants of the Puritan pioneers. He has fixed them at a moment when they have lost the civilized traditions their ancestors brought from Europe, and are groping to find new ways of life. Carol is the daughter of a New Englander who went west taking with him an English culture. In Carol that culture is little more than a dim memory of a more fastidious society; it merely confuses her when she tries to live by it in Gopher Prairie. Babbitt is the descendant of a pioneer; he is completely stripped of all association with an ordered and civilized life. He has no manners, no coherent code of morals, no religion, no piety, no patriotism, no knowledge of truth and no love of beauty. He is almost completely decivilized, if by civilization you mean an understanding of what is good, better and best in the satisfaction of desire, and a knowledge of the customs, the arts, and the objects which can give these satisfactions.

Carol and Babbitt inherit the culture of the pioneers who were preoccupied with the business of establishing themselves in a new world. But for them there is no wilderness to subdue, there are no Indians to fight, they have houses and sanitation and incomes. They have the leisure to be troubled; for they really have very little to do. They have nothing to do which exhausts them sufficiently to distract them when they ask themselves: What is it all about? Is it worth while? Their ancestors came as emigrants, and they divested themselves for the voyage of that burden of ancient customs which, with all its oppressions, made life a rite, and gave it shape and significance. For Carol and Babbitt this European heritage has been liquidated until all that remains of it is a series of prohibitions called morality, and a habit of church attendance without a god they adore or an ideal of holiness with which they can commune. Their religion has become a creed which they do not understand; it has ceased to be, as it was in Catholic Europe, or even in theocratic New England, a way of life, a channel of their hopes, an order with meaning. They are creatures of the passing moment who are vaguely unhappy in a boring and senseless existence that is without dignity, without grace, without purpose. They are driven by they know not what compulsions, they are ungoverned and yet unfree, the sap of life does not reach them, their taproots having been cut. In that great transplantation of peoples which has made America, not many have as yet struck down deep into the nourishing earth. And those who have not are only dimly alive, like Carol, like Babbitt, who are weedy and struggling to bloom.

The "splendid indefinite freedoms" for which Carol yearns are an emancipation from the frayed remnants of the heritage her Yankee forefathers brought with them to America. That stern culture nerved the pioneers to hardship. It merely makes Carol nervous. She will, however, soon be free of this bondage. In the big city, where her creator has preceded her, she will be bothered no longer. She will be a free metropolitan spirit, like Mr. Lewis, free to do anything, free to disbelieve, free to scorn her past, free to be free.

VI

The prophet of this metropolitan spirit, toward which Carol reaches out, is Mr. Mencken. Now Mr. Mencken is a true metropolitan. Mr. Lewis is a half-baked metropolitan. He has just arrived in the big city. He has the new sophistication of one who is bursting to write to the folks back home and let them know what tremendous fellows we are who live in the great capitals. There is more than a touch of the ex-naif in Mr. Lewis, not a little of the snobbery of the newly arrived. For he has as yet none of the radical skepticism of the true metropolitan. His iconoclasm is merely a way of being cocksure that the household gods of Gopher Prairie are a joke. There is no evidence in his writing that he knows or cares much about the good things which the world city contains, as Mr. Mencken does with his German music, his fine sense of learning, and his taste for speculation about genus homo apart from his manifestations on Main Street. Mr. Lewis is proud to belong to the great city, he enjoys the freedom from the Main Street tabus. But he is as restless in the big city as he is in Gopher Prairie. Unlike Mr. Mencken who is quite comfortable, happy, and well settled, as he shells the outer barbarians from his fastness at Baltimore, Mr. Lewis is forever running about the world and giving out interviews about how Main Street is to be found everywhere. He is probably right for he takes it with him wherever he goes.

The terrible judgments which he pronounces upon the provincial civilization of America flow from the bitterness of a revolted provincial. Mr. Mencken is savage at times, but there is a disinfectant on his battle-ax, because he is in no way turned morbidly in upon himself. Mr. Mencken is not a revolted Puritan. He is a happy mixture of German Gemütlichkeit and Maryland cavalier. But Mr. Lewis is still so enmeshed with the thing he is fighting that he can never quite strike at it gallantly and with a light heart. He is too much a part of the revolt he describes ever for long to understand it. That, it seems to me, is why he cannot distinguish between a sample of human ignorance and the deep-seated evil which is part of this world. Everything is in the foreground and in the same focus, ugly furniture and hypocrisy, dull talk and greed, silly mannerisms and treachery. This makes his books so monotonously clever. He will take the trouble to be as minutely devastating about poor Babbitt's fondness for a trick cigarette lighter as about the villainies of Elmer Gantry. He puts everything in the same perspective, because he has no perspective. Like Carol, he is annoyed by almost everything he sees in the provinces, and all his annoyances are about equally unpleasant to him.

For he is still in that phase of rebellion where the struggle to get free is all-absorbing. Of the struggle that comes after, of the infinitely subtler and more bewildering problems of mature men, he has written nothing, and not, I think, thought much. It cannot be an accident that in his whole picture gallery there is not the portrait of one wholly mature personality, of one man or woman who has either found his way in the new world, or knows clearly why he has not. There are such personalities in America, and Mr. Lewis is not a writer who tells less than he knows, or would fail to draw such a character if he had ever actually realized his existence. But Mr. Lewis's characters are all adolescent, and they express an adolescent rebellion.

VII

Mr. Lewis's revolt against the Puritan civilization had of course to include an attack on the evangelical churches.

> That small pasty-white Baptist Church had been the center of all his emotions, aside from hell-raising, hunger, sleepiness, and love. . . . He had, in fact, got everything from the Church and Sunday School, except, perhaps any longing whatever for decency and kindness and reason.

This is Mr. Lewis's conclusion at the beginning of *Elmer Gantry,* and the rest of the book is a sockdologer to prove it.

Had Mr. Lewis followed the pattern of the earlier novels he would have taken as his theme the struggle of an increasingly liberal clergyman to square his real faith with his creed. He would have made a clerical Arrowsmith. There is, in fact, such a character in the book, Frank Shallard, who symbolizes the central confusion of the churches. But Mr. Lewis merely sketches him in, and then lynches him with the help of the Ku Klux Klan. He was not greatly interested in Shallard. His hatred of the Protestant churches was too hot for any patient and sympathetic interest in the men who are somewhat vaguely trying to make organized religion suit the needs and doubts of modern men. He is not conscious as yet that somewhere in the ferment of religious discussion, Carol and Babbitt will have to find an equivalent for the salvation which Arrowsmith achieves. All that, which is after all the main question, Mr. Lewis ignores completely. For his central character he has chosen an absolute villain. And so *Elmer Gantry,* instead of being the story of a fundamentalist like Babbitt beset by doubts, or of a liberal like Carol, who has more impulse than direction, the book is a synthesis of all the villainies, short of murder, which the most villainous villain could commit.

Elmer Gantry is not, however, the portrait of a villain as such. It is the study of a fundamentalist clergyman in the United States, portrayed as utterly evil in order to injure the fundamentalists. The calumny is elaborate and deliberate. Mr. Lewis hates fundamentalists, and in his hatred he describes them as villains. This was, I believe, a most intolerant thing to do. It is intellectually of a piece with the sort of propaganda which says that John Smith is an atheist, and that he beats his wife; that Jones is a radical, and that he cheats at cards; that Robinson is a free trader, and that he robs the till.

Mr. Lewis is a maker of stereotypes. He had successfully fixed his versions of Main Street and of Babbittry on the American mind. Then, quite unscrupulously, it seems to me, he set out to stereotype the fundamentalist as an Elmer Gantry. His method was his old device of assembling details, but in his choice of details he was interested only in those which were utterly damning. It is as if he had gone to the clipping files of an atheist society, pored over the considerable collection of reports about preachers "arrested for selling fake stock, for seducing fourteen-year-old girls in orphanages under their care, for arson, for murder" and out of this material had then concocted the portrait of a clergyman. This is a stock method of the propagandist, and one of the least admirable. There is no truth in it. There is no human dignity in it. It is utterly irrational. If it succeeds it merely creates new prejudices for old, and if it fails it leaves a nasty smell behind it.

I have seen *Elmer Gantry* described as the greatest blow ever struck in America at religious hypocrisy. It may be a great blow. It may, for all I know, be another *Uncle Tom's Cabin*. But it is none the less a foul blow, and I do not think the cause of "decency, kindness and reason," which Mr. Lewis espouses on page 28, is greatly helped by adapting toward fundamentalists the essential spirit of the Ku Klux Klan. The practice of describing your opponent as a criminal ought to be reserved for low disordered minds with white sheets over their heads. A novelist who pretends to be writing in behalf of a civilized life ought not himself to behave like a barbarian.

The animating spirit of *Elmer Gantry* is the bigotry of the anti-religious, a bigotry which is clever but as blind as any other. Were it not that the discussion of religion seems always to stir up exceptional passions, the quality of this book might well alarm Mr. Lewis's friends. For until he wrote it, he had his hatred under control. *Main Street* is a rather sentimental book at bottom. *Babbitt* is pervaded by an almost serene kindliness. *Arrowsmith* reaches moments of spiritual understanding. But *Elmer Gantry* is written with a compulsion to malice as if the author could hardly hold himself. The industriousness of his hatred is extraordinary. He gives himself to an abandoned fury which is fascinating as a mere spectacle of sustained ferocity. You say to yourself: What endurance! What voluptuous delight this fellow takes in beating and kicking this effigy, and then beating him and kicking him again! If only he keeps it up, the sawdust in Gantry will be spilled all over the ground!

For in *Elmer Gantry* the revolted Puritan has become fanatical. The book is a witch-burning to make an atheist holiday.

VIII

There has been some curiosity as to what Mr. Lewis would tackle next. Bets have been laid, I hear, on the politician, the editor, the lawyer, the professor, the business executive. It is a fairly important question because Mr. Lewis is a very important man. But what interests me is whether Mr. Lewis will reach maturity, or remain arrested in his adolescent rebellion. After *Arrowsmith* one would have said that he was beginning to be free of that shapeless irritation and yearning which Carol Kennicott typifies. But after *Elmer Gantry* one cannot be so sure. The hatreds are turned inward, as if the effort to escape had failed and become morbid. There is some sort of crisis in this astonishing career, which is not yet resolved.

Our Photography: Sinclair Lewis

by E. M. Forster

"I would like to see Gopher Prairie," says the heroine of Mr. Sinclair Lewis's *Main Street,* and her husband promptly replies: "Trust me. Here she is. Brought some snapshots down to show you." That, in substance, is what Mr. Lewis has done himself. He has brought down some snapshots to show us and posterity. The collection is as vivid and stimulating as any writer who adopts this particular method can offer. Let us examine it; let us consider the method in general. And let us at once dismiss the notion that any fool can use a camera. Photography is a great gift, whether or not we rank it as an art. If we have not been to Gopher Prairie we cry: "So that's it!" on seeing the snap. If we have been we either cry: "How like it!" or "How perfectly disgraceful, not the least like it!" and in all three cases our vehemence shows that we are in the presence of something alive.

I have never been to Gopher Prairie, Nautilus, Zenith, or any of their big brothers and sisters, and my exclamations throughout are those of a non-American, and worthless as a comment on the facts. Nevertheless, I persist in exclaiming, for what Mr. Lewis has done for myself and thousands of others is to lodge a piece of a continent in our imagination. America, for many of us, used to mean a very large apron, covered with a pattern of lozenges, edged by a frill, and chastely suspended by a boundary tape round the ample waist of Canada. The frill, like the tape, we visualized slightly; on the New York side it puckered up into sky-scrapers, on the farther side it was a blend of cinemas and cowboys, and more or less down the middle of the preposterous garment we discerned a pleat associated with the humour of Mark Twain. But the apron proper, the lozenges of pale pink and pale green—they meant nothing at all: they were only something through which railways went and dividends occasionally came from, and which had been arbitrarily spattered with familiar names, like a lunar landscape. As we murmured "Syracuse, Cairo, London even, Macon, Memphis, Rochester, Plymouth," the titles, so charged with meaning in their old settings, cancelled each other out in their new, and helped to make the apron more unreal. And then Sinclair Lewis strode along, developed his films, and stopped our havering. The lozenges lived. We saw that they were composed of mud, dust, grass, crops, shops, clubs, hotels, railway stations, churches, universities, etc., which were sufficiently like their familiar counterparts to be real, and sufficiently unlike them to be extremely exciting. We saw men and women who were not quite ourselves, but ourselves modified by new surroundings, and we heard them talk a language which we could usually, but not always, understand. We enjoyed at once the thrills of intimacy and discovery, and for that and much else we are grateful, and posterity will echo our gratitude. Whether he has "got" the Middle West, only the Middle West can say, but he has made thousands of people all over the globe alive to its existence, and anxious for further news. Ought a statue of him, camera in hand, to be erected in every little town? This, again, is a question for the Middle West.

Let us watch the camera at work:

> In the flesh, Mrs. Opal Emerson Mudge fell somewhat short of a prophetic aspect. She was pony-built and plump, with the face of a haughty Pekinese, a button of a nose, and arms so short that, despite her most indignant endeavours, she could not clasp her hands in front of her as she sat on the platform waiting.
>
> Angus Duer came by, disdainful as a greyhound, and pushing on white gloves (which are the whitest and the most superciliously white objects on earth) . . .
>
> At the counter of the Greek Confectionery Parlour, while they [i.e. the local youths] ate dreadful messes of decayed bananas, acid cherries, whipped cream, and gelatinous ice cream, they screamed to one another: "Hey, lemme 'lone," "Quit dog-gone you, looka what you went and done, you almost spilled my glass swater," "Like hell I did," "Hey, gol darn your hide, don't you go sticking your coffin-nail in my i-scream."
>
> She saw that his hands were not in keeping with a Hellenic face. They were thick, roughened with needle and hot iron and plough handle. Even in the shop he persisted in his finery. He wore a silk shirt, a topaz scarf, thin tan shoes.
>
> The drain pipe was dripping, a dulcet and lively song: drippety-drip-drip-dribble; drippety-drip-drip-drip.

The method throughout is the photographic. Click, and the picture's ours. A less spontaneous or more fastidious writer would have tinkered at all of the above extracts, and ruined everything. The freshness and vigour would have gone, and nothing been put in their places. For all his knowingness about life, and commercially-travelled airs, Mr. Lewis is a novelist of the instinctive sort, he goes to his point direct. There is detachment, but not of the panoramic type: we are never lifted above the lozenges, Thomas Hardy fashion, to see the townlets seething beneath, never even given as wide a view as Arnold Bennett accords us of his Five Towns. It is rather the detachment of the close observer, of the man who stands half a dozen yards off his subject, or at any rate within easy speaking distance of it, and the absence of superiority and swank (which so pleasantly characterizes the books) is connected with this. Always in the same house or street as his characters, eating their foodstuffs, breathing their air, Mr. Lewis claims no special advantages; though frequently annoyed with them, he is never contemptuous, and though he can be ironic and even denunciatory, he has nothing of the aseptic awfulness of the seer. Neither for good nor evil is he lifted above his theme; he is neither a poet nor a preacher, but a fellow with a camera a few yards away.

Even a fellow with a camera has his favourite subjects, as we can see by looking through the Kodak-albums of our friends. One amateur prefers the family group, another bathing-scenes, another his own house taken from every possible point of view, another cows upon an alp, or kittens held upside down in the arms of a black-faced child. This tendency to choose one subject rather than another indicates the photographer's temperament. Nevertheless, his passion is for photography rather than for selection, a kitten will serve when no cows are present, and, if I interpret Mr. Lewis correctly, we must not lay too much stress on his attitude to life. He has an attitude; he is against dullness, heartiness and intolerance, a trinity of evils most closely entwined; he mistrusts Y.M.C.A. helpfulness and rotarian idealism; while as for a positive creed (if we can accept *Martin Arrowsmith*[1] as an unaided confession of faith) he believes in scientific research. "So many men, Martin, have been kind and helpful, so few have added to knowledge," complains the old bacteriologist. One can safely class him with writers termed "advanced," with people who prefer truth to comfort, passion to stability, prevention to cure. But the classification lets what is most vital in him escape; his attitude, though it exists, does not dwell in the depth of his being. His likes and dislikes mean less to him than the quickness of his eye, and though he tends to snapshot muscular Christians when they are attacked with cramp, he would sooner snap them amid clouds of angels than not at all. His commentary on society is constant, coherent, sincere; yet the reader's eye follows the author's eye rather than his voice, and when Main Street is quitted it is not its narrowness, but its existence that remains as a permanent possession.

His method of book-building is unaffected and appropriate. In a sense (a very faint sense) his novels are tales of unrest. He takes a character who is not quite at ease in his or her surroundings, contrives episodes that urge this way or that, and a final issue of revolt or acquiescence. In his earlier work both character and episodes are clear-cut; in his later—but let us postpone for a moment the painful problem of a photographer's old

[1] In England, *Arrowsmith* was published under this title. [M.S.]

age. Carol Kennicott, the heroine of his first important book, is a perfect medium, and also a living being. Her walks down Main Street are overwhelming; we see the houses, we see her against them, and when the dinginess breaks and Erik Valborg arises with his gallant clothes and poet's face, we, too, are seduced, and feel that such a world might well be lost for love. Never again is Mr. Lewis to be so poignant or to arrange his simple impressions so nearly in the order of high tragedy; "I may not have fought the good fight, but I have kept the faith" are Carol's final words, and how completely are they justified by all she has suffered and done! Babbitt follows her—of grosser clay, and a native while she was an exile, but even Babbitt sees that there is something better in life than graft and goodfellowship, though he acquiesces in them at the close. Martin Arrowsmith succeeds where Carol and Babbitt failed, because he is built strongly and prepared to sacrifice a home, but, regarded as a medium, he is identical with them, he can register their doubts and difficulties. And the same is true of Elmer Gantry; his heavy feet are turned to acquiescence from the first, but he, too, has moments of uneasiness, and hypocrisy; religious eroticism and superstition can be focussed through him. And so with Samuel Dodsworth in *Dodsworth*. He reacts this way and that among the main streets of Europe, and many pictures of them can be taken before he decides that they will not do.

Now, in the earlier books this method was a complete success, but with *Elmer Gantry* doubts begin; the theme is interesting, but the snapshots less remarkable. And in *Dodsworth* doubt becomes dismay. Dodsworth is a decent citizen of Zenith who retires early and goes to Europe with his wife. She is cultivated and snobby—a *rechaufée* of the second Mrs. Arrowsmith, but served upon an enormous dish. She talks, talks, flirts, patronizes, talks, and he, humble and observant, gradually realizes her inadequacies, but all the time he talks, talks, talks. The talk is rhetoric, the slang tired, the pictures blurred. The English country church, palace at Venice, restaurant at Paris, journey in an aeroplane, Bernese Oberland, back in New York, the right sort of American tourist, the wrong sort, is there a right sort, is it wrong to think there is a right sort? . . . on the story trundles, unprofitably broadminded and with unlucky thematic parallels to Henry James. The method remains, but something has died. The following quotation will show us what:

> He found that in certain French bathrooms one can have hot water without waiting for a geyser. He found that he needn't have brought two dozen tubes of his favorite (and very smelly) toothpaste from America—one actually could buy toothpaste, corn-plaster, New York Sunday papers, Bromo-Seltzer, Lucky Strikes, safety razor blades, and ice cream almost as easily as in the United States; and a man he met in Luigi's bar insisted that if one quested earnestly enough he could find B.V.D.'s.

What has happened? What has changed the Greek Confectionery Parlour at Gopher Prairie, where every decaying banana mattered, to this spiritless general catalogue? The explanation is all too plain: photography is a pursuit for the young. So long as a writer has the freshness of youth on him, he can work the snapshot method, but when it passes he has nothing to fall back upon. It is here that he differs from the artist. The artist has the power of retaining and digesting experiences, which, years later, he may bring forth in a different form; to the end of life he is accompanied by a secret store.

The artist may not be good. He may be very bad. He generally is. And it is not to celebrate him and to decry the photographer that I draw this distinction between them. But it does explain, I think, why quick spontaneous writers (the kind that give me more pleasure than any) are apt, when they lose their spontaneity, to have nothing left, and to be condemned by critics as superficial. They are not superficial, they are merely not artistic; they are members of a different profession, the photographic, and the historian of our future will cease to worry over this, will pick up the earlier and brighter volumes in which their genius is enshrined, and will find there not only that genius, but a record of our age.

Mr. Lewis is not our sole photographer. There is always Mr. H. G. Wells. They have just the same gift of hitting off a person or place in a few quick words; moreover, they share the same indifference to poetry, and pass much the same judgments on conduct. Consequently, one might have expected that their literary careers would be similar, that the authors of *Love and Mr. Lewisham* and *Main Street* would develop in the same way and at the same rate. They have diverged, and for an instructive reason. Wells is still kicking because photography was only one of his resources. When his early freshness wore off, he could bring into play his restless curiosity about the universe, and thus galvanize his later novels into life. In Mr. Lewis, curiosity about the universe has never been very strong. Only occasionally has he thought of the past, the future, international relationships, science, labour, the salvation or damnation of the globe. The people in the room and the houses across the street are what really interest him, and when the power to reproduce them sharply fails, he has nothing to do except to reproduce them dimly. If this view of his development is correct, the later stages of it are bound to be disappointing. However, there the early books are, done, safe, mankind's for ever; also, the longer one lives, the less important does "development" appear.

Dodsworth

by Ford Madox Ford

I wonder if one could not start a literary journal that should be contributed to solely by the unspoiled readers of books, since, from the standpoint of the novelist, it seems wholly inappropriate that he should criticize the work of his brothers who are, also, inevitably his rivals! However, since the critics are usually too lordly to bother their heads about anything so humble as the inside problems of mere novel-writing, it is difficult to see who is to do that rather necessary job. The most, therefore, that one ought to permit oneself is a friendly hail across space, using the press as it were as a sort of broadcasting apparatus. Then, one may give forth an exposition!

I shall, thus, permit myself to say that I like *Dodsworth* much better than *Elmer Gantry* and that I like Mr. Dodsworth much better than Mr. Babbitt as being the more convincing, the more human and, I daresay, more "felt" by his creator. With an immense admiration for *Babbitt* as a book, I always had behind me the dim feeling that Mr. Babbitt himself was a little of a Robot, moved here and there by his creator in an unimaginably real projection of Main Streets—the landscape, as it were, being in the major chord. Humanly speaking (I am not here attempting literary criticism), this is a relatively wrong way to look at a landscape. The fact is, if you go to look at a landscape or to observe a country you won't much do so, your impressions being too self-conscious; whereas, if you live and are your normal self and, above all, suffer in any given environment, that environment will eat itself into your mind and come back to you in moments of emotion and you will be part of that environment and you will know it. It is because Mr. Dodsworth suffers and endures in odd places all over the European and semi-European world that both he, as a person, and the settings in which he suffers, as settings, seem to me to be very real. Perhaps that is only saying that *Dodsworth* is a poem which *Babbitt* isn't.

Indeed, the title might just as well have been "Europa, an Epic." For Mr. Lewis presents to you practically all of Europe that counts in our civilization, including New York which isn't America. He also poetizes these places so admirably through the emotions of the sympathetic Mr. Dodsworth that when you have finished the book you, too, will have suffered and had your own emotions in the rue de la Paix—genuine emotions and not limited to the fact that in a shoe-shop they tried to charge you one hundred and fifteen francs for paste shoe-buckles instead of one hundred francs which is the price on the label. Indeed, I lately heard a lady say that Egypt was a rotten country because you could not get shredded wheat biscuits in Shepherd's Hotel, which was not true at that. I learn from another that Corsica is a bum island because the New York papers could not be had in an obscure mountain village, whereas it is a known fact that the birthplace of Napoleon might as well be sunk beneath the sea, but for American money.

That is the sociological value of *Dodsworth* and the benefit it may do to civilization. Indeed, I think it is safe to say that the superiority of Mr. Lewis as a sociological writer far in advance of others lies in the fact that he has a remarkable gift for rendering and the restraint which keeps him from pointing morals. Of course, his characters do indulge themselves in a great number of expository disquisitions but Mr. Lewis makes it sufficiently clear that he backs neither set of views when they do discourse. Thus, things remain very much as they were at the beginning and the final impression is one of a sort of solidarity of mankind from Altoona to the Adriatic and back.

That is a great achievement and I hope that *Dodsworth* will diffuse itself by the million on both sides of the Atlantic. It will do more to spread a knowledge of the world and its friendlinesses and freshness and attractions than a wilderness of Baedekers. Besides, it is a good novel, a good story. I found myself towards the end of the book really hoping that the hero might get his young woman—hoping against hope and turning to the last page to make sure. This is the real test—more particularly for a book that is going to do good: for it must be read for itself and the moral must sink in unperceived as do the morals that we draw from life itself. To that end, we must identify ourselves with the characters and live in the scenes.

I found myself, as I have said, hoping that Mr. Dodsworth might have his luck because, subconsciously, I regarded it as an omen that I might have mine; and that is to read a book as one read in the old good days before fifty or so winters and half a century or so of books had besieged these brows. That is the real, unconscious tribute and the real, true, friendly hail!

The America of Sinclair Lewis

by Lewis Mumford

The award of the Nobel Prize to Mr. Sinclair Lewis has sent many of us back to his novels for a fresh view of them. How far was the Swedish Academy right in setting Mr. Lewis's work ahead of Eugene O'Neill's in the drama, Sherwood Anderson's and Theodore Dreiser's in the novel, Robert Frost's and E. A. Robinson's in poetry, Paul Elmer More's in criticism? Putting aside for the moment a certain political bias in both the award and the chorus of European approval that has gone up in favor of it, one finds that Mr. Lewis's novels survive a reappraisal rather better than one had expected. At the end of the decade that brought forth his major works—I exclude such trial flights as *Free Air* and *The Job*—he remains the most effective satirist our country has produced. His achievement is no small one; and it merits a closer examination.

The two decades before the appearance of *Main Street* had been noteworthy for a succession of purely propagandist novels, inspired by a righteous indignation over the evils of American political and economic life. Although able pens had lent themselves to this literature, including writers like Frank Norris, Robert Herrick and Upton Sinclair, the total effect upon our life had been very small. Propaganda, agitation, reform —these were mere ripples of the wind upon the complacent bosom of our national life. Even Mr. Finley Peter Dunne's penetrating comments upon our follies and vices never quite struck home.

In 1920 Mr. Sinclair Lewis published *Main Street*. For the first time all the nebulous criticism and dissatisfaction, which had been accumulating over a long period, had found a voice, and what is more important, had been embodied in creatures of flesh and blood. The combat of Carol Kennicott with the stodgy, self-satisfied society of Gopher Prairie was symbolic of an underlying conflict that was going on all over the country. "Main Street," said Mr. Lewis in a brief introduction, "is the climax of civilization. That this Ford car might stand in front of the Bon Ton Store, Hannibal invaded Rome and Erasmus wrote in Oxford cloisters." The gossip of Main Street, the political beliefs of its bankers and grocers, the architecture of its railway station, the art of its movie palace—all this was for its inhabitants the essence of sound wisdom, the path of duty and progress.

What did Mr. Lewis show? He showed a dreary collection of hovels lined haphazardly along a shabby thoroughfare; a hard, pushing, aggressive economic life, in which the only admirable and spiritually independent figure was the town outcast, Miles Bjornstam; and upon the muddy surface of this society, like a few planks thrown desperately across the slippery ooze, a handful of wistful ignorant souls who aspired to gentleness and culture, but who were all too easily swallowed up in a vast and overpowering banality. The effectiveness of Mr. Lewis's portrait of Main Street was due to the fact that he was not an alien in this environment; his essential foreignness consisted in his ability to see Main Street for what it was, not for what it thought it was. Was it satire or was it portraiture? Plainly it was both; and the strength of the satire was in proportion to the universal reality of the portrait.

In *Main Street* an American had at last written of our life with something of the intellectual rigor and critical detachment that had seemed so cruel and unjustified when it had appeared in Dickens's *Notes* or in Arnold's *Civilization in the United States*. Young people had grown up in this environment, suffocated, stultified, helpless, but unable to find any reason for their spiritual discomfort. Mr. Lewis released them. He challenged the comfortable traditions and sure faiths of Main Street; he set its youths to speculating "whether there may not be other faiths." By piling up the details of this flat, commonplace, spiritually unleavened life, Mr. Lewis showed that it was humanly as monstrous as a nightmare. Main Street awoke from its sleep with the self-conscious grin of a man who realizes that he has been snoring in public.

What *Main Street* did for the small town, *Babbitt* did for the growing metropolis and for its typical hero, the middle-of-the-road business man, devoted to push and progress, to good fellowship and the latest devices in sanitation and hygiene, to playing safe in religion and preserving a religious respect for the latest inventions in industry.

Becoming more confident of his purposes, Mr. Lewis broadened the caricature of Babbitt and became even more savage in his attacks upon the dominant American idols. Babbitt, the realtor, was a recognizable type; he was a man caught in a civilization he believes in too heartily, who had never done a single thing that corresponded to his inner go: a willing victim to the blather and buncombe of American business life, but nevertheless a victim. Zenith, Babbitt's town, was Main Street, energized and aggressive, but at bottom equally futile; Babbitt was Dr. Kennicott, lacking the saving touch of heroism and poetry that goes into the doctor's operation upon an injured man on a lonely farm.

A weak figure, a ridiculous figure, caught in a civilization whose very virtues, hygiene and mechanical efficiency were, by their divorce from any complete conception of a humane life, as inimical to development as the dirt and inefficiency of other cultures—that was Babbitt, that was his country! Mr. Lewis had held the mirror up to middle-class America: so telling was the reflection that the name of his hero will probably go down in literature with Don Quixote and Tartuffe and Pecksniff. One such image is sometimes more important than volumes of more diffuse accomplishment. But Mr. Lewis's mirror was curiously built. At the centre it reflected accurately the person, the clumsy gestures, the vague speech of the principal character; around this were convex and concave surfaces which showed everything else in American life in vivid but distorted relationships. The surrounding caricatures—Chumley Frink, the "poet," and Dr. Littlefield, the intellectual apologist for the business classes—were as good as the realism of the central character. Littlefield and Frink could only snarl in helpless rage at their portraits; but Babbitt was genuinely touched and, being touched, he was on the defensive. A note of apology and self-derision crept into his attitude toward himself. Mr. Lewis had struck home.

In his next novel, *Arrowsmith,* Mr. Lewis produced his most mature and well-rounded picture of American society. It has more variety of pace and interest than *Main Street,* and its satire is quite as aggressive as in *Babbitt;* but it has that additional quality which belongs only to the higher levels of literature, the sense of facing the issues of life and death, and creating, in the very face of defeat, an inner assurance. Main Street, which threatens at the end to subdue Carol Kennicott, might leave one depressed over the dreadful odds; Babbitt might leave one cynical and contemptuous; while Arrowsmith, more tragically conceived, actually leaves one a little exalted.

In *Arrowsmith* Mr. Lewis depicted the odds against which the disinterested man of science labors in a society whose standards are those of pecuniary exploit and emulation. His hero, a physician with a bent toward research, encounters as many obstacles as did Pilgrim in his famous march; but, unlike lonely yearners such as Carol or, for that matter, Babbitt himself, Arrowsmith has company in his effort: Gottlieb, the pure scientist, an excellent portrait of Jacques Loeb, and Sondelius, the herculean fighter of plagues, and Terry Wickett, the hard-boiled research worker. Reaching out sympathetically toward these subordinate characters, Mr. Lewis created the most fully realized figure in his whole gallery—Leora, Arrowsmith's wife. Moreover, the satirist was after bigger game than the pusillanimities of the Thanatopsis Society; he showed the insidious betrayal of values in a great university and a great research foundation where, if anywhere, one might hope for disinterested motives and a free play of the intelligence. Was it altogether an accident, one wonders a little maliciously, that the Swedish Academy did not specifically mention the excellence of *Arrowsmith* when they bestowed their award?

The three novels that followed Arrowsmith may be dismissed briefly. *Mantrap, The Man Who Knew Coolidge* and *Elmer Gantry* do not belong to the same class as the first three that won Mr. Lewis distinction. Gantry, in fact, is almost a caricature of Mr. Lewis's method of caricature; and it shows by its utter lack of convincingness how the effect of Mr. Lewis's best work is based not upon external documentation alone but upon an inner sympathy and experience with his characters and his situations. When he writes well he writes out of the heart, and his satire is effective because his heart has been hurt.

In his most recent novel, *Dodsworth,* Mr. Lewis achieved, I think, the top of his excellence as a novelist, although the theme is less impressive than *Arrowsmith.* He returned, in a sense, to *Main Street* and *Babbitt,* with a new kindliness toward his central figure, the business man. Fran, Dodsworth's wife, is an odious counterpart of Carol Kennicott, with not a thought in the world but her own narrow ego, her own conquests and satisfaction; and Dodsworth himself is a Babbitt who has submitted to the prevailing standards without being enthralled by them. Not since Henry James had anyone so well portrayed the dilemmas of the untutored American in Europe, exposed to that irresponsive but quickening scene. I read this novel first in Geneva; and I remember how well Dodsworth survived this intimate ordeal. That very week I met Dodsworth in person, and felt that the reality had not been as deftly handled as the imaginary figure.

Are Mr. Lewis's novels representative of American life? Yes—if one is careful to qualify the meanings of these words. Mr. Lewis knows his own people of the Middle West very well; he writes as though at one period or another he had believed all their platitudes and participated in their worshipful mechanical routine. He has their intense practical sense and their wistfulness; the names of exotic places can stir him, and the chief defect of his style is the result of an effort to achieve glamour. His admiration for Joseph Hergesheimer and James Branch Cabell shows, I believe, what he would like to achieve in literature were he not, against his dearest efforts and convictions, immeasurably superior to these men.

Mr. Sinclair Lewis's satires have the value of photography, and to say this is not to disparage his achievements but to reinforce the claims of photography. His best satirical effects are obtained simply by holding in sharp focus something that actually exists, and forgetting, for the moment, all that historically or spatially enters into the object to qualify it. The art of photography is that of creative selection; it brings nothing into existence, except what is developed by the momentary act of abstraction. All the phenomena that Mr. Lewis shows are real; but, by the nature of his method, he is unable to indicate a more comprehensive reality. The sum total of America, as presented in the pages of Mr. Lewis, is less than that which a true poet, like Mr. Robinson Jeffers or Mr. Robert Frost, will indicate in a single page.

Do not be deceived—Mr. Lewis's satiric photographs have immense value; he has pried everywhere and caught people in ridiculous postures and feeble attitudes which in their blindness they mistook for normal human grace; and all in all he has been a sanative and healthy influence during the past decade. The pursuit of his particular satiric gifts, however, has led him to neglect his larger opportunities as a novelist. By now his satire is pat; we are familiar with the technique of his merciless mimicry and we know beforehand who will be hit by it; indeed, the satire, once perceived, avoids complete dullness only because of Mr. Lewis's skill as a creator of character. In this department, he has the immense fecundity of Dickens, with the additional advantage that he succeeds as well with thoroughly human figures, like Leora and Dodsworth, as with grotesques and oddities like the unforgettable Dr. Pickerbaugh. Were he not driven by some inner exacerbation to "get back at" the community that produced him, Mr. Lewis could give back much to it; for he has real insight and might easily create characters on a large scale who would exist in their own right, not merely as creatures in a malicious demonstration.

As satirist Mr. Lewis has demolished a good part of the scaffold of pretensions which conceals the flimsy structure of our institutions. Unfortunately, neither his critical intelligence nor his positive understanding is equal to the task of rebuilding this structure; nor is he willing to accept it as a whole, with all its virtues and defects, as Tolstoi accepted Russia, in order better to clarify its essence, its soul. The truth is that he lacks such imaginative profundity as would alter the whole centre of a person's life, such an alteration as Melville, Dostoevski, Van Gogh are capable of making. To define Mr. Sinclair Lewis's specific virtues is to acknowledge his limitations. He has been immersed in his milieu; he knows its dreadful human limitations; he has rebelled against them; but he has not mustered sufficient personal force or culture to overcome them in himself; the satirist, like the jailer, is the victim of his own system of punishment.

What, now, shall we say to Mr. Sinclair Lewis's achievement of the Nobel Prize? Purely on his literary merits, he would undoubtedly be one of the six or seven names that would come to mind as candidates for this prize. But Mr. Lewis's success in Europe has a political as well as a literary aspect. As a satirist he has created a picture of America that corresponds in a remarkable degree with the naïve caricature of America that all but the most enlightened and perceptive Europeans carry in their heads. In crowning Mr. Lewis's work the Swedish Academy has, in the form of a compliment, conveyed a subtle disparagement of the country they honored.

The comment of a Swedish newspaper on the award, to the effect that American writers are no longer to be regarded as "bread-hunting, sensation thirsty, uncultured Yankees," lets the cat out of the bag; for obviously, Mr. Lewis's novels do portray America in these terms—and this, apart from their genuine merits, accounts for his ready welcome abroad.

The very fact that the committee went out of its way to cite *Elmer Gantry*, Mr. Lewis's worst novel and grossest caricature, only increases one's suspicions of the unconscious forces at work. The European notion that the country which has produced a Melville, a Hawthorne, a Whitman, an Emerson, a Thoreau, a Dickinson, a Henry Adams, a James, must find itself a little flattered to be singled out for recognition in the person of Sinclair Lewis is ignorant enough and complacent enough to be accepted as merely funny. Had the Nobel Prize gone to the writer who, in his own person and work, embodies what is most precious and significant in contemporary American literature, it would doubtless have gone to Robert Frost. One has a notion, however, that Frost's America is a country of which the Swedish Academy has never heard.

Utopia, or Uncle Tom's Cabin

by Richard P. Blackmur

This[1] is a weapon of the intellect rather than a novel; there is hardly a literary question that it does not fail to raise and there is hardly a rule for the good conduct of novels that it does not break. Its success depends on incident not character, and on editorial interpretation not representation; depends most on the urgency of the theme and the emotion of the author in presenting it. There is nowhere in it the ultimate persuasiveness of language as an art, but a great deal of that vehemently presented fact which at the ripe time does as well.

It is not, then, a novel, not a seizure and showing forth of life, but, using for freedom the overt form of a novel, a declaration of things to come sprung from a faith of which the substance is things hated not hoped for. Out of the same impulse that in times of less dismay produced visions of Utopia Mr. Lewis has projected an inferno. We see the rise, in 1936, of an American fascist dictatorship, its inevitable progress in perfecting terror, maturing oppression, and developing a maximum corruption. The dictatorship passes through three persons: first, Senator Berzelius Windrip modeled on Huey Long and elected President with the aid of a Methodist bishop's League of Forgotten Men; second, Lee Sarason, his brilliant but morally depraved Secretary of State, who overthrows and expels Windrip; and, third, the revolted but no less bloody puritan Colonel Haik, the Secretary of War, who gains power by murdering Sarason and preserves it by warring on Mexico. With the first success of the fascist revolution there is the immediate rise of a counter-revolution, which sets out to create the American Cooperative Commonwealth under the leadership of Walt Trowbridge, the defeated Republican candidate of 1936, and later with the military aid of General Emmanuel Coon, who brings part of the regular army to support the spontaneous revolt of the Western farmers. Which wins, the Cooperative Commonwealth or the Corporate State, is conspicuously left in doubt.

Victory is round the corner, in the aroused or resurrected character of Doremus Jessup, Vermont editor and old-time liberal intellectual bour-

[1] *It Can't Happen Here.* [M.S.]

geois; victory is in the re-created character of Jessup and of you, the reader. That, if anything, is the purpose of Mr. Lewis's book: so to arouse his great audience—and no serious writer short of Walter Lippmann has a greater—that the horror of fascist revolution may be prevented. That—and the fact that Mr. Lewis has always been a publicist in fiction—is the reason that his book appears in the guise of a novel. The impact of the revolution is shown as it is felt by the Jessup family; its friends and associates, as they attempt under it, some to take advantage of new avenues to power, but most to live their ordinary lives in the small city of Fort Beulah, Vermont. The horror of fascism is shown by translating the Hitler terror and the earlier Italian terror into characteristic American terms and individuals. There is a history of terror in the bowels of every nation only awaiting the moment's impetus to be articulated and made general. People have, as Mr. Lewis remarks, a natural and unprejudiced love of violence—if not of violence itself, of seeing it, inciting it, and writing about it; so it is with surprising ease that Mr. Lewis's translations are made from European to American fascist violence; and it is almost superfluous to hear one of the minor characters remind Doremus Jessup, in their cell at a concentration camp, of such classic seminal examples as the Scottsboro boys, Tom Mooney, and the West Coast longshoremen. The credibility of the individuals and events in the novel is for the moment of reading enough. We see and know, as the time passes, for Doremus Jessup the slow expense of a disinterested mind as he gradually loses caste, his newspaper, and his peace of mind. We see him, with others, driven to start the N. U., the New Underground based on the old Underground Railway, to deliver fugitives and exiles to the safety of Canada. We see him toy with communism and desert it. We see him printing leaflets and pamphlets and distributing them at the risk of his life. We see his books burned, his college made a mockery. We see him discovered, beaten, and imprisoned; we see him escape to Canada with a shorn beard and dyed hair; and finally we see him return secretly to incite revolt in the Middle West. We see his son-in-law murdered, and his daughter in revenge commit murder. We see his other daughter almost raped for the cause. We see most of his friends imprisoned and some of them killed. And so on. We see for irony his son Philip become a stuffed shirt and a military judge of the Corporate State. And with all this and more we see intermittent reports of the responsible career of dictatorship through various acts of blood and folly in Washington and elsewhere.

So much will the reader of the moment see and, because it is in a novel, easily believe; and, the moment over, repeat, not at all disheartened, Mr. Lewis's title: It can't happen here. After all, Huey Long is dead. That is because the reader has missed the one lesson in the book worth learning; missed it largely because he was not the person to learn it, but partly because Mr. Lewis was not quite the person to teach it—although he has learned it himself. This is the lesson of American liberalism for liberals.

The career of Doremus Jessup, here all so strewn with blight and violence, has this emphasis: that only when the actuality of what he hated and distrusted destroyed the life he loved, only then did he convert his disinterested opinion into desperately interested action; and then, for all we know, it was too late. In more general terms, can it not be put that in a comparatively stable society the liberal can afford to be disinterested and is most valuable so, but in an unstable society disinterestedness is the very last thing he can afford if he is to live or be valuable at all? Or is liberalism only good for a prosperous society? Is it, after all, Utopia out of which Mr. Lewis has produced Doremus Jessup, and only there that, as the book ends by saying, "a Doremus Jessup can never die"?

Sinclair Lewis

by Robert Cantwell

With some fifteen novels to his credit at the age of fifty, together with enough short stories to fill several more volumes, Sinclair Lewis stands out as the most prolific author of his generation, with the mournful exception of Upton Sinclair. It is almost the worst thing you can say about him. For although Lewis has written at least two first-rate novels, and created a dozen powerful characters, and produced half-a-hundred masterly satirical sketches scattered throughout these books—as well as adding new words to the language and popularizing, more than anybody else, a new and skeptical slant on American life—he has also turned out as much journalistic rubbish as any good novelist has signed his name to, and he has written novels so shallow and dull they would have wrecked any reputation except his own.

He has, in fact, been one of the most plunging and erratic writers in our literary history; unpredictability, waywardness, unevenness are his distinguishing characteristics, as a brooding inconclusiveness is the mark of Sherwood Anderson. He has written the best novel of American business in *Babbitt,* only to make up for it by writing the worst in *Work of Art* and adding half-a-dozen wretched *Saturday Evening Post* stories on the same subject to the bargain. He has written the sharpest parodies of the lush, rococo, euphemistic sales-talk of American business life that we have, but he has also weighed down his novels with a heavy burden of unreal and exaggerated jargon, palmed off as common speech, with unfunny topical jokes, passed on as native humor, and the weight of that dated mockery grows heavier every year.

But Lewis has not only been the most uneven of American novelists; he has also been one of the most ambitious. There is an architectural symmetry in the order of the books that followed *Main Street.* Unlike his contemporaries, who seem always to have been improvising in the sequence of their work, Lewis apparently recognized a conscious program for his writing simultaneously with his recognition of his power, and seems to have driven toward its realization with something of the high-pressure intensity he has satirized so often. Where Dreiser gives the impression of having brooded, with a sort of ponderous aimlessness, over whatever lay close at hand, forever turning aside, distracted by every incidental issue; where Anderson and Vachel Lindsay, more than any of the others, were blown about in the cross-currents of American life until they were saturated with its apparently patternless variety, Lewis visualized on the strength of *Main Street* a cycle of novels comparable at least in scope to those of Zola and Balzac.

It was a spacious and inclusive project, bolder than anything an American novelist had tried to do, signalizing a final break with that narrowness of outlook which, exemplified in a thousand old swimming-hole sentimentalities, pathetic regionalisms and phony family dilemmas, had become almost the sole driving force of American fiction. And even now, when the limitations and shortcomings of that imaginative exploration are more apparent than its freshness and originality, it is still a little breath-taking to consider the broad outlines of the work that Lewis laid out for himself, to see that he planned nothing less than a catalogue of the interwoven worlds of American society, the small towns and cities, the worlds of business, of science, of religion, of education, and eventually the worlds of labor and professional politics, working it out at a time when the shabby, optimistic, patriotic smugness of the American literary tradition—the tradition of Henry Van Dyke[1] that, significantly, he attacked in his Nobel Prize address—still imprisoned the imaginations of so many of his contemporaries.

Lewis had a line on American society, and tenacity, if not much flexibility and resourcefulness, in following it. But more than that he had a sense of the physical variety and the cultural monotony of the country, an easy familiarity with the small towns and square cities, the real-estate developments and restricted residential areas, the small business men, the country doctors, the religious fakers, the clubwomen, the county office-holders, the village atheists and single-taxers, the schoolteachers, librarians, the windbags of the lower income groups, the crazy professors and the maddened, hyperthyroid, high-pressure salesmen—the main types of middle-class and lower-middle-class provincial society, conspicuous now because he has identified them so thoroughly. He had a grasp of these people and their environments, together with a sense of the country as a whole, where so many of his generation had nothing but an oppressed conviction of its emptiness or a dread of its rawness.

Only Vachel Lindsay and Upton Sinclair had seen so much of the country, in the elementary geographical sense of the term. Lewis had never taken any of the wild and pathetic zigzag journeys of Lindsay, dropping in on miners and hill-billies and reading poems for his supper, nor had he spent a season in the hell of the stockyards, as did Upton Sinclair, his first guide, at the beginning of a career no less extraordinary.

[1] The clerical academician (1852-1933) who made the most voluble lamentations about the Nobel award to Lewis. [M.S.]

But he had knocked around at an impressive variety of jobs after he left Yale in 1904—he had been a janitor in Upton Sinclair's Helicon Hall, a soda jerker,[2] a reporter on the *San Francisco Bulletin*—which was probably, under Fremont Older in the days before his capitulation, the best paper in the country to be a reporter on—a ghost writer for Jack London and an editor, in Washington, of a magazine for the deaf; he had taken the grand cruise of his generation on a cattle boat to England[3] and had hitch-hiked through the Middle West.[4] He had traveled over the face of the country and, although within pretty narrow limits, up and down through its social strata. And although his first four books were hack jobs, the native experiences he had packed away were too powerful to be satisfied with evocations of the joys of a stenographer's work, or of the wisdom of picturesque and homely old folks, or of an aristocratic Eastern girl made wholesome by contact with the great West—the substance of *The Job, The Innocents* and *Free Air*. Even as hack work those books are bad. They seem to tremble with some internal explosive disgust; in a way they are like the bad jokes and stale opinions that Babbitt and his friends take refuge in at their parties, when they dare not express even a little of what is going on in their minds, lest they betray their hatred of their environments, their boredom, their thwarted desire for change.

Apparently Lewis thought at the beginning of his career that the muse could be embraced and laid aside at will, and that she would not take her revenge by addling the wits of her ravisher—at least his first books prove nothing except that he did not believe the writing of fiction demanded a writer's full energy and his deepest understanding. That implicit irresponsibility has been his greatest limitation as a novelist and the source of much of the unevenness of his work. Even the broad project mentioned above—the cycle of novels following *Main Street*—is a vision of an imaginative survey of American life such as a glorified and supercompetent hack writer might conceive: a writer, that is, who thought of his writing, not in terms of its momentary inspirations and the pressure of living that played through him and upon him, but in terms of the accomplishment of a foreknown task; who thought of a novel of business, of religion, of science, as if he believed he could turn his art to any subject, regardless of how much it meant to him and how close to his heart it lay; who felt that it was within his power to "collect material" without becoming emotionally entangled in it or acting in response to what it implied. T. K. Whipple, who has written the only searching study of Lewis that we have, has compared his attitude in studying American society with that of a Red Indian stalking through the land of his enemies —it is a good description, for it suggests his wariness and vigilance, the surface accuracy of his observation, what can be called the heartlessness of

[2] No. [M.S.]
[3] Twice. [M.S.]
[4] No. [M.S.]

his approach, and above all his enforced detachment from the scene he viewed and the solitary and personal basis of his satire.

Now that the scandals that attended the publications of Lewis's books have been forgotten, the outlines of the world he created are clearer. On re-examination that world seems in a more advanced state of decay and disintegration than Lewis's first critics were willing to admit—it is, as Whipple has said, a city of the dead, in which the dead are above all determined that no one shall live. After *Main Street* his characters were still the long-winded, provincial, narrow-visioned old folks, the dreamy and timid job-holders, the clerks and salesmen and doctors—with here and there a workman from the semi-independent crafts—who figured in his first books and were all dominated by those strange, self-satisfied, self-possessed, jovially witless bankers and business men who loom so large in Lewis's world. But where such characters had been harmless and happy in the early novels, they were now vindictive, spiteful, vaguely threatening in their inertia and immobility.

Before the War, Lewis had written of their provincialism as if it were a source of serenity, however its expression might rasp on the sensibilities of the cultivated; for the provincials and the innocents themselves, it was an insulation against the cares of the world and not without its own homely poetry and wisdom. But with *Main Street* that provincialism was identified as an evil force, destructive not only to the Carol Kennicotts and Eric Valborgs, to Martin Arrowsmith and Paul Riesling—it was also poisoning the lives of those who clung to it and triumphed and, when their guards were down for a moment, were seen to be bewildered, distressed, clinging desperately to their appearance of smugness because they had nothing else to cling to. The problem of *Main Street* might have been "how much of Gopher Prairie's eleven miles of cement walk" was "made out of the tombstones of John Keatses"—but the message of *Babbitt, Arrowsmith, Elmer Gantry,* however Lewis might deny that it was his intention to preach it, was simply that American society was death to any disinterested effort, to any human tolerance, almost to any human sympathy; that it was regimented within an inch of its intellectual life; that any deviation from its norm of self-seeking, money-grubbing, career-making, throat-cutting, treachery, slander, blackmailing, was instantly punished with exile and disgrace; that spontaneity or generous emotions or a freedom from calculation, among the calculating wolves of business, amounted to suicide of a long-drawn-out and painful kind. Lewis drew a revolutionary picture of American middle-class life without coming to revolutionary conclusions above it, unlike Upton Sinclair, who leaped to revolutionary conclusions and then filled in the picture; he recognized the mechanics of capitalist control, and satirized them, without challenging the ends to which they were applied or visualizing any alternative except an escape—for those sensitive souls enlightened enough to be aware of their horror—into reverie and day-dreaming.

The moral atmosphere, with exceptions that will be noted, grew thicker and more poisonous with each succeeding book. Carol Kennicott's sensibilities were outraged by Gopher Prairie, and she was revolted by the hypocrisy and narrowness she found there, but the enemies she faced were largely passive—inertia, sluggishness and sullenness, the dominance of petrified prejudice. In comparison with *Babbitt* and the books that followed it, this is an almost pastoral view of life. The difference is not only in the greater violence of the later books, the general strike that interrupts *Babbitt* midway, the flare of melodrama in Riesling's attempt to murder his wife, the corruption and blackmail that accompany Babbitt's business career. It is rather in the cagey watchfulness with which Babbitt's friends of the service clubs bear down on each other for every deviation from their class line, and it is nowhere better dramatized than in the sequence that follows Riesling's tragedy—when Babbitt, shaken by it, develops an intermittent sort of tolerance, the others, particularly the sinister Vergil Gunch, get their knives ready for him at once, and the high point of the book, perhaps the highest point of Lewis's writing, is the realization that they are ready to spring, like the stronger wolves on a crippled member of the pack, at the first sign of Babbitt's confusion and dismay.

Yet even Babbitt's sacrifices for the good opinion of such prosperous thugs are nothing compared with the desperation of Angus Duer, in *Arrowsmith,* who tries to cut the throat of a watchman who has inadvertently threatened his career, and the indifference that Carol Kennicott faced in Gopher Prairie is nothing compared with the sustained enmity and malice that Arrowsmith faces in Wheatsylvania. The enemy—the provincial, conforming, suspicious enemy—is no longer merely passive and mocking; it has become aggressive, strident, criminal; it turns to blackmail and violence; it is ready to frame and destroy anyone who even raises questions that it cannot answer. And by the time *It Can't Happen Here* was written, Lewis's picture of the world was such that the violence with which the book is filled had become obsessive and perverse, divorced from any purpose and uncontrolled by any aim, an eruption of cruelty and horror and little more.

Spaced unevenly between the works in which this panorama of social damnation is drawn are those books of Lewis's that even his acquiescent critics usually overlook: *Mantrap, The Trail of the Hawk, Work of Art, Ann Vickers, Dodsworth,* the grotesque short stories that he wrote for the *Saturday Evening Post* and that seem particularly bad because there is so much evidence that Lewis knew so much better when he wrote them. He has never been a fastidious writer—he has a gift for slogans, a talent for mimicry, a kind of tormented delight in some of the cruder commonplaces of American speech, but he has always manipulated his people awkwardly to make them demonstrate what he wanted them to reveal about society, and his works have always been weakened, even in their moments of gravity, by a tumultuous and slapstick humor that seems less an expression of emotion than of a desire to escape it. As his career has developed he has relied more and more on his ability to capture the perishable local color of American life, the blaring and raucous Babbittry that surrounds his people, the pep-talks, the idiot drooling of advertisers and go-getters, instead of the indefinite but still sustained and consequential conflicts of Carol and her husband, of Babbitt and his friends—but this material, which was used in *Main Street* to show what a character who could not stomach it was up against, began to be used in the novels that followed almost for its own sake, until with *The Man Who Knew Coolidge* there was scarcely anything else in the book.

But precisely because Lewis has attached so little fundamental importance to such outpourings as Dr. Pickerbaugh's health sermons, or Chum Frink's poems, his increasing insistence on material of this sort is all the more clearly a sign of imaginative indecision and doubt. And how, after having so clearly shown the mechanics of American business control in *Babbitt,* and the psychological ravages of it, could he have drawn so unrealistic a figure of a millionaire as Dodsworth, or so romantic a business man as the Myron Weagle of *Work of Art*? In his best books Lewis had told us that the pursuit of wealth—or even a career in a business-dominated society—was a fierce and scrambling affair that killed its victims and crippled its victors; now he presented an industrialist whose unaccountable naïveté persisted (although he collected secret reports on the dissipations of his employees), and a starry-eyed, well meaning hotel manager whose poetic dreams revolved around the creation of more elaborate comforts for the exhausted Babbitts who could afford them—presented without art, without irony, at best with a kind of curdled romanticism that gave an impression of spleen and exasperation on the part of their author. With these books Lewis's explorations into American society stopped. His characters had become idealizations of the Babbitts he had previously condemned; his satire had degenerated to a kind of stylized mockery, closer in spirit to George Ade's "Fables in Slang" or to some of Mencken's less purposeful buffoonery than to the realities of American life—or it had become so broad and farcical that it had lost its point, just as, in his anti-fascist novel, his fascists were presented as so weird and unearthly that no practising strikebreakers, vigilantes, lynchers, anti-Semites, jingoes or acquiescent journalists need feel an instant's identification with them.

But with all this acknowledged, the positive contribution of Lewis's novels remains—and, in one sense, if books like *Dodsworth, Work of Art* or *Ann Vickers* seem so shallow, it is in large part because Lewis himself has made us conscious in his best work of the native realities that are absent in them. In his best books he has caught, better than anybody else, the desultory, inhibited, half-sad and half-contented middle-class life of the Middle West, a life of spiritless conflicts and drives in the country, of social gatherings as nerve-racking and exhausting as final examinations, of interminable business plots and fears of ruin, of frightened infidelities, limitless ambitions, of forced enthusiasms and false simplicities—a life hedged in behind social barriers set by the least enlightened members of the community and existing under a dictatorship that is no less powerful for being masked and unadmitted by those who bow to it. And even in his worst books Lewis has always been able to summon up some neglected, recognizable corner of the country—the run-down, red-leather hotel lobbies of *Work of Art,* the formaldehyde, oiled-floor, civil-service stench of public buildings in *Ann Vickers*—with such graphic power that he has always seemed to be setting the stage for some more momentous drama than he has ever shown taking place.

That effect may be the result of his inability clearly to imagine any antagonist capable of sustained struggle with the rulers of his city of the dead. He is more aware of the monstrous extent of the stables that must be cleaned than he is of the possibility of any Hercules ever cleaning them; and when he pictures people who are pitted against their environments he usually shows them struggling without much hope of victory, without allies, and often with ingrown doubts as to whether or not they are on the right side. And most often, when their feeble feints establish the strength of the enemy, they merely subside into that outward acquiescence and inward rebellion that is the death of drama—so Carol Kennicott, defeated in Gopher Prairie, dreams of a grass hut over some tropical river bank; Babbitt hungers for some wild woodland spirit as he awakens into the steel world of Zenith; Myron Weagle plans gigantic and flawless super-hotels as he fires the help of a run-down Florida boarding house, and these vague aspirations to escape their own environments are presented by Lewis as conferring some secret distinction on the people who hold them.

In denying that he is a satirist Lewis has said that he is a romantic, in much the same sense that these characters of his are romantics, and that he has rebelled against American society because it has none of the picturesque feudal remains that he associated with a rich and stable culture. But his characters are not romantic rebels committed to struggle. They are self-dramatists whose imaginations flower from their evasions of conflict—they are always posing before themselves and others, not in order to fulfill a consistent Byronic role, and to take the responsibility for it, but in order to conceal their true reactions and to hide the concerns that oppress them. They are always in the camp of their enemies; they cannot forget themselves for a moment, lest they reveal the depths of their revulsion. They dramatize themselves in order to endure the demands of a society that they have no hope of bettering and whose reality they cannot face, and they imagine themselves in all kinds of roles—except the ones they actually occupy—because they cannot get through their days without the help of such fantasy.

So the final testimony of Lewis's novels always seems a little grimmer than he apparently intended it to be, and never so grim as when he envisions the rebels and aspiring spirits who front the resolute conformists. He never comes so close to giving a clinical description of psychic breakdown as when he shows his characters making their peace with the world. It was a mistake of his critics to see in these novels evidence of that intellectual awakening and skeptical self-criticism which has become known as America's coming-of-age. For Lewis is the historian of America's catastrophic going-to-pieces—or at least of the going-to-pieces of her middle class—with no remedy to offer for the decline that he records; and he has dramatized the process of disintegration, as well as his own dilemma, in the outlines of his novels, in the progress of his characters, and sometimes, and most painfully, in the lapses of taste and precision that periodically weaken the structure of his prose.

The New Realism: Sherwood Anderson and Sinclair Lewis

by Alfred Kazin

"Oh, the briary bush
That pricks my heart so sore!
If ever I get out of the briary bush
I'll never get in any more!"
—Verse in FLOYD DELL'S *Moon-Calf*

"Cain made things hard for all of us that time he killed Abel at the edge of the field. He did it with a club. What a mistake it was carrying clubs about."—SHERWOOD ANDERSON, *Tar*

If it was the first trombone blasts from Mencken's *Prejudices* in 1919 that sounded the worldliness and pride of the new emancipation, it was two stories of revolt against small-town life in the Middle West—Sherwood Anderson's *Winesburg, Ohio* in 1919 and Sinclair Lewis's *Main Street* in 1920—that now brought new life into the American novel by dramatizing that emancipation in terms of common experience. Signalizing "the revolt from the village," as Carl Van Doren described it at a moment when Edgar Lee Masters's *Spoon River Anthology* had already set the tone of the new spiritual migration in the twenties, these two books signalized even more the coming of a fresh new realism into fiction. For up to 1920, the year Howells died and seemed to take what was left of the old realism with him, the fiddles had been tuning, tuning everywhere, but not in the novel. Between the death of Frank Norris and the suppression of *Sister Carrie* at the beginning of the century and the sensational success of *Main Street* in 1920, the realistic novelists had either lived underground or written the perishable social tracts of the Progressive period. When Howells died in 1920 on the eve of the new resurgence in fiction, he had survived himself for so many years that he had long since become a symbol of everything genteel and bloodless that the new novelists detested. Lewis was later in his Nobel Prize speech to use Howells as the measure of that whole "American Victorianism" against which the twenties rebelled; Anderson, growing up in small Ohio villages where the classic New England writers of the past beamed down like amiably remote divinities from their school-wall portraits, wondered whether Howells, the favorite child of the New England school, had ever been a realist at all. So far as they could see, in fact, the new realist had to learn from scratch. They had the example of Dreiser's courage and of Mrs. Wharton's devotion to craft (*Babbitt* was to be dedicated to her); yet though they were realists as a matter of course, they owed their realism more to the current of ideas during the "Little Renaissance" than to the first pioneers of realism in the novel.

The new realism that was ushered in with Anderson and Lewis had, in fact, only a formal relation to that first struggle for realism that had gone on in the eighties and nineties. It was the sudden current of liberation after the war that had set it in motion, and it was a realism, suddenly come free in the indulgent world of 1920, that no longer had to fight for its life. The old challenging rebelliousness remained; but realism had lost its hard, fierce tension. Where Norris and Dreiser had been philosophical naturalists of a sort, men who had taken up a position in defiance of the old traditions, naturalists who had been interested in the struggle for power, men like Anderson and Lewis were essentially as remote from naturalism as they were from the old Pollyanna romances against which they rebelled. For if theirs was a realism of revolt, the revolt was entirely domestic, as it were; it was a realism essentially instinctive, rambling and garrulous, and homespun. It was a realism that had emerged out of the struggle for freedom of conduct, a realism concerned not with the conflict of great social forces that had dominated the first naturalist generation, but with the sights and sounds of common life, with transcriptions of the average experience, with reproducing, sometimes parodying, but always participating in, the whole cluster of experiences which made up the native culture.

Though no two novelists were to prove more different than Lewis and Anderson, it was with them, as with that whole group of modern realists who now came into the twenties—writers so diverse as Floyd Dell, Zona Gale, and Ring Lardner—that the way was opened for the kind of realism that was to dominate American fiction, a realism that neither apologized for itself nor submitted to the despairs of naturalism, a realism that took itself for granted and swept at will over every sector of American life. No longer did the American realist have to storm the heavens, or in the grimness of creation build his books with massive blocks of stone. Realism had become familiar and absorbed in the world of familiarity; it had become a series of homely fabliaux, like the stories grasped out of common life that men had told one another in the Middle Ages; it had become the normal circuit. And though Anderson, and he alone among these realists, was later to learn from Gertrude Stein's literary ateliers in Paris—the learning process did not last very long—the new realists were essentially indifferent to the old dream of a perfect "work of art." For these writers did not usually think of themselves as "artists" in the European sense. They were participants in a common experience, newly liberated from what the young Sinclair Lewis called the "village virus" and writing for others like them. They had no desire to erect artistic monuments as such. They had emerged from the farms, the village seminaries, newspaper desks, with a fierce desire to assert their freedom and to describe the life they knew, and they wrote with the brisk or careless competence—Anderson sometimes did not seem interested in *writing* at all—that was necessary to their exploration of the national scene.

What this meant also, however, was that the new realists, by their very example and instinctive interests, gave the American novel over to the widest possible democracy of subject and theme. It was the homely average type—Sinclair Lewis's Babbitts and Chum Frinks, his Rotarians and business-ridden little men and Wheatsylvania farmers; Ring Lardner's dumb baseball players and Broadway producers and Long Island socialites; Zona Gale's unhappy young village couples; Sherwood Anderson's gallery of village librarians, horse-trainers, yearning young poets; even Edgar Lee Masters's farmers—it was these who now brought the savor and pain of common life back into the novel. Where Crane and Norris had gone to the depths to prove their realism, where Dreiser's naturalism had led him to massive realistic characters who were the embodiment of his profound sense of tragedy, the new realists brought into the novel the walking show of American life. For whether they wrote with the photographic exactness of Lewis, the often inchoate exultation of Anderson, or the harsh, glazed coldness of Lardner, they had a compelling interest in people, American people, of all varieties, sizes, temperaments, standards; and the interest was always direct.

It was this feeling for common talk and appreciation of common ways, so marked even in Lardner—perhaps especially in Lardner, though he seemed to hate everything he touched—that gave the new realists their hold over the popular imagination and made them so significant a cultural influence. Indeed, far from having to fight their public, the new realists often seemed to be associated with their readers in a certain camaraderie of taste and humor. Sinclair Lewis, as Constance Rourke said in her *American Humor,* could even in one sense be considered the first American novelist, for in his unflagging absorption of detail and his grasp of the life about him Lewis caught the tone, the speech, of the pervasive American existence; and it was significant that in his sharp attention to American speech—did anyone before him ever catch the American "uh"?—he brought back the comic and affectionate mimicry of the old frontier humor. There had been nothing of that humor in Dreiser, Crane, and Norris; and for all their superior weight, their more profound grasp of human life, nothing of the discovery of American fellowship that made for so significant a bond between novelist and reader in the new novels of the twenties. . . . For whatever else men like Anderson and Lewis may have lacked, they gave back, out of their candid and often bitter penetration of American life, a confidence to those who saw in their books the mirror of a common American existence. It was not an impersonal "America" that had stepped finally out onto the world's stage; it was Americans, millions of them—all the Americans who snickered at Babbitt yet knew him for their own; all the Americans who knew how authentic and tender was the world Sherwood Anderson illuminated in *Winesburg;* all the Americans who knew that if Carol Kennicott was not as great a creation as Emma Bovary, she was certainly more real to them, and lived next door. The American was here; he belonged; he was a character in the gallery of the world's great characters even if he did nothing more than sell Ford cars and live in a clapboard house. Even Babbitt inspired a kind of pride by his vividness; even the mean despotic village enemy in Chum Frink; and particularly all those Lincolnesque ghosts out of so many different Spoon River anthologies in the novel, village grocers and spinster aunts and thwarted farmers' wives, who addressed themselves so roundly to history, and so well. . . .

It was perhaps only a trick of time and the current of the new freedom after the war that put *Winesburg* and *Main Street* together, since no two novelists could have seemed more different than Anderson and Lewis. Yet it was just by those very differences, at a time when both seemed to be contributing together to the revolt from the old conventions and shibboleths, that they gave the new freedom, in their heyday, a perfect image of itself. For looking at Anderson and Lewis together, the drowsing village mystic and the garrulous village atheist, it seemed as if they had come from the opposite ends of the world (or from the same Midwestern street) to meet in the dead center of the postwar emancipation and be stopped there, wondering what came next. It was as if everything in American life had suddenly conspired to give them a moment's triumph and then betray them with it; to make them light-bringers, spokesmen of a needed modern wisdom, "cultural influences," even, and then leave them hanging pathetically in mid-air. Despite all their differences, Anderson and Lewis did sound in unison just the spirit of that revolt, of that yearning for freedom, which had been awaited; and if they made their triumph out of it, they were to share in the same humiliation—the humiliation of being remembered as "cultural influences" rather than as serious and growing artists; the humiliation of knowing that they had ceased to be significant, or even interesting, after seeing their first works go so deeply into the national mind and bring new words into the national language.

For Anderson, at least, this sense of anticlimax after his first important books in the early twenties was almost a private matter between Anderson and his kind of vision—a private failure to sustain what he had to give. There was always a failure of will in Anderson's books, a slow decomposition that had its source in some fatal stagnance. But Lewis, who enjoyed from the first a sense of public domination such as few novelists have ever known, suffered a different kind of humiliation. For there was nothing obviously "lacking" in him, as in Anderson. All the energy, the hard, bright wisdom, the tireless curiosity, that were in him reached maximum expression; all the public favor and understanding a writer could want he had. Far more than Anderson, far more than any other contemporary novelist, in fact, he had welded himself inextricably into the American scene. But Lewis had done his work so well, fitted the times so perfectly, that he became almost invisible *in* that scene; he had worked over the surface world so thoroughly, and with so contagious a wit and skepticism, that he became part of that surface. A more profound writer would not have had so assured a success; a less skillful one would not have been so influential in his success. But Lewis hit a certain average in art perfectly, as he hit off the native average—or what Americans like to think is the native average—so well in his characters; and that was at once his advantage and his misfortune. As his characters became public symbols, he came to seem more a public influence than a novelist; as his jokes against the old American ways became new American ways themselves, the barrier between his books and life in America came down altogether. George F. Babbitt had entered as completely into the national imagination as Daniel Boone, but with his emergence, as with every new archetype of American life Lewis brought in, some part of Lewis's usefulness seemed to be over.

To say this would seem to pay only the necessary tribute to Lewis's extraordinary place in modern American life and manners; but to define that success is at the same time to define his position as a writer and the resources he brought to the novel. For there is a certain irony in Lewis's career that is now impossible to miss, and one that illuminates it as a whole. Here was the bright modern satirist who wrote each of his early books as an assault on American smugness, provincialism, ignorance, and bigotry; and ended up by finding himself not an enemy, not a danger, but the folksiest and most comradely of American novelists. Here was the young rebel who had begun *Main Street* as his spiritual autobiography, who even wrote dashingly in his foreword that it preached "alien" doctrine and who painted that whole world of endless Main Streets where "dullness is made God"—and found that people merely chortled with delight over how well he had hit off the village butcher, the somnolent afternoons on Main Street, the hysterical Sunday-night suppers, and the genteel moneylender's wife, with her "bleached cheeks, bleached hair, bleached voice, and a bleached manner." Here was the crusading satirist who spared none of the hypocrisies by which Babbitt and his group lived, least of all their big and little cruelties, and gave Babbitt back to his people as a friendly, browbeaten, noisy good fellow. Here was the indignant critic of commercialism in science who portrayed the tragedy of Max Gottlieb in *Arrowsmith* and the struggles of Martin Arrowsmith against those who threatened his disinterested worship of truth, yet succeeded even more significantly in making out of Arrowsmith a gangling romantic American hero. Here was the topical novelist, with his genius for public opinion, who tried to describe the nightmare coming of Fascism to America in *It Can't Happen Here,* but really described his own American optimism in the affectionate portrait of Doremus Jessup, that good American small-town liberal.

In the first flush of his triumph in the twenties, when Lewis did seem to be the bad boy breaking out of school, the iconoclast who was Mencken's companion in breaking all the traditional American commandments, it was easy enough to enjoy his satiric bitterness and regard him as a purely irreverent figure. But today, when his characters have entered so completely into the national life and his iconoclasm has become so tedious and safe, it is impossible to look back at Lewis himself without seeing how much native fellowship he brought into the novel and how deeply he has always depended on the common life he satirized. The caricature will always be there, and the ugly terror that Babbitt felt when he tried to break away for a moment from the conventional life of his society. There is indeed more significant terror of a kind in Lewis's novels than in a writer like Faulkner or the hard-boiled novelists, for it is the terror immanent in the commonplace, the terror that arises out of the repressions, the meannesses, the hard jokes of the world Lewis had soaked into his pores. But in a larger sense his whole significance as a writer rests on just his absorption of all those commonplaces, for Lewis has seemed not merely to live on the surface of public reality, but for it. It was this that so many critics have felt when they have accused him of living intellectually from hand to mouth, and what T. K. Whipple meant when he so cleverly compared Lewis to a Red Indian stalking the country of his enemies. For Lewis has always led so mimetic an existence that his works have even come to seem an uncanny reproduction of surface reality. Not so much revelations of life as brilliant equivalents of it, his books have really given back to Americans a perfect symbolic myth, the central image of what they have believed themselves to be; and it is this which has always been the source of his raucous charm and his boisterous good-fellowship with the very people and ideas he has caricatured.

For what is it about Lewis that strikes one today but how deeply he has always enjoyed people in America? What is it but the proud gusto and pleasure behind his caricatures that have always made them so funny—and so comfortable? Only a novelist fundamentally uncritical of American life could have brought so much zest to its mechanics; only a novelist anxious not to surmount the visible scene, but to give it back brilliantly, could have presented so vivid an image of what Americans are or believe themselves to be. It was the satire that always gave Lewis's books their design, but the life that streamed out of them impressed people most by giving them a final *happy* recognition. Lewis caught the vulgarity and the perpetual salesmanship, and caught it as effortlessly as he caught the sights and sounds, the exact sound of a Ford car being cranked on a summer morning in Zenith in 1922, the exact resemblance of Chum Frink to Eddie Guest and of Sharon Falconer to Aimée Semple McPherson. But he caught also, as almost no one did before him, the boyish helplessness of a Babbitt, the stammering romance of a Martin Arrowsmith on his first day at the McGurk Institute, the loneliness of a great Sam Dodsworth before all those Europeans in Paris. Even his novel on Fascism reminded Americans that when an exiled American Hitler like Buzz Windrip goes to Paris, he yearns only for Lucky Strikes and the smoking-car jokes of his pals. Even his assault on small-town ignorance and bigotry in *Main Street* suggested that if Carol Kennicott was heroically unhappy on Main Street, she was just a little silly with her passion for uplift.

Yes, and for all their sharp thrusts and irritable mutterings, his books also confirmed in Americans the legend of their democratic humility, the suspicion that every stuffed shirt conceals a quaking heart, and the need of an industrial magnate like Sam Dodsworth or a scientist like Martin Arrowsmith to translate the most momentous problems of his craft into the jargon of a manly American fellowship. Lewis's men are boys at heart, living in a world in which boys are perpetually stealing through their disguise as men, and glad to know that a certain boyishness in the native atmosphere will always sustain them. Businessmen, scientists, clergymen, newspapermen, they are forever surprised at their attainment of status and seek a happiness that will encourage them to believe that they are important. They are frontiersmen suddenly ushered into the modern inheritance, and can giggle at themselves, as John Jay Chapman did on his grand tour of Europe in the eighties, by remembering all the derisive ancestors who stand behind them—"Dear old Grandpa, with his old cotton socks; wouldn't he be proud if he could see me hee-hawing and chaw-chawing with Roman princes!" But if Lewis's natives are boys, the Europeans in his books—Max Gottlieb, Bruno Zechlin, Fran Dodsworth's cousins in Berlin—though they are usually crushed by the native barbarians, are older than the rocks on which they sit, older and wiser than life, the sage miracle men of some ancient world of light and beauty and culture. Old Gottlieb in *Arrowsmith,* for example, was not merely a European scientist; he was *the* European scientist, the very incarnation of that indescribable cultivation and fathomless European wisdom—a man on speaking terms with Leonardo, Brahms, and Nietzsche; a scientist whose classic work on immunology only seven men in all the world could understand; a cosmopolitan who advised—sneeringly—his students to read *Marius the Epicurean* for "laboratory calmness," and could prepare exotic little sandwiches for his grubby co-workers.

Martin Arrowsmith himself, be it remembered, had no such skills. In fact, it was not until he came to Chicago (that halfway station to Europe?), shedding the provincialisms of Wheatsylvania and even Zenith, that he heard Mischa Elman, saw a Russian play, and—"learned to flirt without childishness." The Europeans in Lewis's novels never flirted with childishness; they had all the learning of the world at their fingertips; and as Gottlieb, or Bruno Zechlin in *Elmer Gantry,* proved by their inevitable humiliation and fall, they were almost too good to live in the parched American wilderness. Here was only one American folklore legend that Lewis made his own, a legend based on a conviction of native inferiority and subservience to Europe; and nowhere did it show so clearly as in Sam Dodsworth's encounter with Europe, a Europe that was the negation of Gottlieb's, yet cut out of the same cloth—a Europe too charming, too learned, treacherous and sly. Henry James's favorite story of American innocence abroad came back here with a vengeance. Yet it is interesting to note that a character like Gottlieb succeeded so brilliantly because he was so sentimentally realized a type. Gottlieb suggested so abundantly for Lewis just what many Americans would have supposed a German-Jewish scientist in Winnemac to be that he lived, as it were, precisely because he was a stock figure; lived because in him banality had been raised to the rank of creation.

Lewis's characters have often been criticized as "types," and they are, partly because he memorialized some of them as such, gave people in George F. Babbitt what seemed the central portrait of a businessman. But what is really significant in his use of types is that his mind moved creatively in their channels. With his ability to approximate American opinion, his lightning adaptability to the prejudices, the fears, the very tonal mood, as it were, of the contemporary American moment, Lewis has always been able to invest his tintypes with a careless energy that other writers would not have been able to understand, much less share, since they did not work so close to the surface. Lewis restored life; he did not create it. Yet what that means is that for him the creative process lay in the brilliance of that restoration—the ability to restore one Pickerbaugh, with his "he-males" and "she-males," out of the fledgling Pickerbaughs all over the American scene; the ability to set his villains or bores —Elmer Gantry, Chum Frink, especially Lowell Schmaltz—so to talking that though they were incredible, they attained a fantastic representative quality. It is doubtful, in fact, whether Lewis even wished to make Lowell Schmaltz credible in that long monologue, *The Man Who Knew Coolidge*. He wished only to hit him off perfectly, to make Lowell a kind of monstrous incarnate average, just as he wished to make Elmer Gantry an accumulative symbol of all the phoniness he hated in American life. With his lonely suffering rebels, however—Frank Shallard, Erik Valborg, Paul Riesling, Gottlieb and Zechlin—he attained not an average type but an average myth. For they are the protestants, the victims of the national life in which his other characters survive as a matter of course; and though Lewis admired them and suffered with them, the characters he gives them are just those which the artist-rebels, the men who are "different," would seem to possess by average standards.

Just as Lewis has always worked from type to type, embodying in them now the cruelty, now the sentimentality, now the high jinks, now the high-pressure salesmanship of one aspect of the national life after another, so he has always moved in his books from one topic to another, covering one sector of American life after another—the small town, Rotary, business, medicine, the smoking car, travel, religion, social work. More than any other American novelist since Frank Norris, he felt from the first the need to go from subject to subject that would lead him to cover the entire national scene. He knew that scene in all its range and could characteristically work up any subject; he had concentrated his whole ambition in the national life, and could hit the perfect moment again and again. In fact, like a sailor hitting ducks in a shooting gallery, Lewis gave the impression that he had only to level his aim, seize a new idea, a new flash of life in the American sector, and go after it. Yet this could work only up to a certain point, as the steady decline of his novels after *Dodsworth,* reaching a really abysmal low in *The Prodigal Parents,* has proved. For the ducks in the American shooting gallery soon stopped moving in convenient rotation. In a sense Lewis depended on an America in equilibrium, a young postwar America anxious to know itself, careless and indulgent to his friendly jokes against it, ambitious even to improve its provincial manners in the light of his criticism; but when that America lost its easy comfortable self-consciousness, Lewis's nervous mimicry merely brushed off against it.

It followed also from Lewis's whole conception of the novel that his brisk mimetic energy would become a trick repeating itself long after he had lost his sense of design and purpose. In some of the early brilliant descriptions in *Ann Vickers,* he seemed to be blocking out perfect scene after perfect scene that led to nothing; there is a forlorn flashiness about them that reveals Lewis running over his old technique even when he had little to say. In Lewis's first works his verve had always been able to light up an inconsequential book like *Elmer Gantry* with dozens of hilarious scenes, or, as in *The Man Who Knew Coolidge,* even to make one long monologue out of it; but now, with nothing more substantial to write about than Barney Dolphin in *Ann Vickers,* Myron Weagle in *Work of Art,* or Fred Cornplow in *The Prodigal Parents,* he could keep on bringing in his "trick," his special gift and charm, while the books merely sagged. They were tired, evasively sentimental books, and full of a hard surface irritability and uncertainty. Even *It Can't Happen Here,* for all its attempt to cover the imaginary coming of Fascism to America, was not a really ambitious book and certainly not a careful and deeply imagined one. Responding to the public terror that filled the air out of Hitler Germany as he had responded to a certain public mood he had known so well in the twenties, Lewis could catch only the surface terror, the surface violence; and they erupted mechanically in his book. But he could not really imagine Fascism in America, he had not really tried to; he had tried to hit the bell in 1936 as he hit it in 1920 with *Main Street* and in 1922 with *Babbitt,* to sound off a surface alarm and strike the public consciousness.

What these later works also signified, however, was not only Lewis's growing carelessness and fatigue, but an irritable formal recognition of his relation to American life. Far from even attempting iconoclastic satire, he wrote these books as moralities for a new time; and his new heroes—Myron Weagle, the poetic hotelkeeper; Doremus Jessup, the amiable and cautious liberal; Fred Cornplow, the good solid husband and father betrayed by his erring children—were the final symbols of everything Lewis had always loved best. He had lampooned Babbittry easily enough; but when the Babbitts themselves were threatened, he rushed forward to defend them. From his own point of view, indeed, there were no Babbitts now, or at least nothing to lampoon in them—Fred Cornplow was the mainstay of the times and Doremus Jessup a representative American hero.

Those who had missed Lewis's dependence from the first on the world Fred Cornplow represented, however, could only wonder at Lewis's sentimental tribute to him and his ugly caricature of those who mocked him. The thing didn't jibe; Lewis wasn't supposed to like Cornplow-Babbitt; and how could Doremus Jessup ever seem enough for him? Yet what was it but Doremus, with his fishing tackle and his wise little small-town editorials, that Lewis had ever known and loved? What was it but the Cornplows he had run after for twenty years, trying to catch the warts, the buffoonery up at the lodge on Wednesday nights, the pleasure of the open road on Sunday? The village rebels had all failed, and that was tragic; Gottlieb and Paul Riesling, Frank Shallard and Guy Pollack, had all gone down before meanness and ignorance and terror. But if the Fred Cornplows remained, they were not so bad after all; and Carol Kennicott really had been just a little silly. The village atheist ended his tirade, and sighed, and went on playing a friendly game of poker with the local deacons.

The Land of Faery

by Maxwell Geismar

"Until the nineteenth century, actors were classed as Rogues and Vagrants," says the inscription of Lewis's next novel [*Bethel Merriday*]." They were outside of respectable society—like Kings—and I am not sure but that this was better for their art and their happiness. . . ." It is interesting that the *Bethel Merriday* of 1940 should deal with the theatrical world. And although Lewis's rogues and vagrants still appear pre-eminently respectable, there is no doubt they are outside of their society.

As a matter of fact, Lewis consolidates his position here: he moves from an involuntary land of make-believe to a voluntary one:

> Five months after the six-year-old Bethel gave her imitation of the old lady, the Black Shirts marched bravely into the maws of the movie cameras in Rome, and five months after that, Hitler bounded out of a Munich beer garden. But perhaps it was as important that at this time John Barrymore was playing *Hamlet* and Pauline Lord *Anna Christie* and the Theatre Guild producing *Back to Methuselah*.

Now all the world's a stage, where everything is viewed, not only as illusion, but as an entertaining illusion, while that melancholy picture of "human crimes and misfortunes"—history itself—may serve to while away an interval between the acts.

For *Bethel Merriday* actually marks a deliberate and sustained attempt to reduce everything outside of the theater to inferior play-acting. "They were all serious children," Lewis tells us about Bethel's troupe—"very childish, very serious, and apparently the only people still existent, in a world of Hitler and Buchmanism, who enjoyed life. At every mistake, at every dropped line, they laughed and laughed together." Was a planet just then in tears? At least Lewis's laughter is truly "unembittered," while America has become a nation of one hundred and thirty million Neros. And in this final realization of the Free Life—"all magic and madness"—even the "talk" which has been the bugaboo of

Lewis's depictions of the Intellectual Life has become bearable. "It dealt entirely with the theatre."

Notice also the singularly remote quality of Lewis's theatrical world itself. The great achievement of Bethel's company—an achievement around which the novel is centered—is the production of *Romeo and Juliet*. The private lives of Lewis's figures are rigorously set, not only outside of the world of Hitler and Buchmanism, but almost outside of the whole modern age. "In the house was electricity; Mr. Merriday was reading about the tear-gas bombing of strikers in the aeroplane industry. . . . But Bethel and Charley sat on a porch in New England and . . . no one could have told them from their grandparents." In personal terms also the secret of Bethel's success as an actress isn't her knowledge of the world or her emotional experiences ("all those amateurs—they spend too much time working up an artificial sex stimulation"), but merely her infinite capacity to daydream:

> Like all artists—all painters, all musicians, all poets, even some of those plodding recorders, the novelists—actors are glorious children, with a child's unwearied delight in the same story over again, and the child's ability to make dragons grow in a suburban garden.

What is interesting is that a novel devoted with such an absolute and frightening simplicity to the "stage" should in the end reveal so little about the stage.[1] Probably Bethel's deepest fear—that she will remain an eternal amateur, that she will only "play at playing"—is based on her only genuine insight. But *Bethel Merriday* is by far the poorest of Lewis's late novels. Almost as though he were rebounding with a new vigor from this extreme of his fantasy life, Lewis's next two books are marked by a fresh and remarkable vitality.

In any case the Peony Jackson of *Gideon Planish*, in 1943, with her infantile morals, her adolescent values, and her mature body, is one of Lewis's most engaging if not altogether commendable heroines. What Peony wants out of life may not be very interesting, but the way she gets it is. As her wiles first entice and then trap poor, pompous Professor Planish, you may realize, almost for the first time in Lewis's work, the charms as well as the ironical tortures of the flesh. And as Peony starts her "Gidjums" going, and Gideon leaves his academic position to become a rising social worker in Des Moines and Chicago, an executive of "social reform" in New York, and a director of "Dynamos of

[1] Compare Bethel, for example, with the Esther Jack of Thomas Wolfe's *The Web and the Rock,* or, in a closely related art, the Thea Kronborg of Willa Cather's *The Song of the Lark*. In view of Lewis's own lifelong interest in the stage, it is hard to understand how his Civil War play, *The Jayhawker,* written in collaboration with Lloyd Lewis in 1935, could be *quite* so poor—unless, that is, one also understands that even Lewis's feeling for the theater is in its own way a sort of fantasy of a fantasy world.

Democratic Action" in Washington, U.S.A.—you feel the full extent of Gideon Planish's passion for his Peony, and the destructive power of the flesh.

For the theme which emerges from all the fantastic nonsense of *Gideon Planish*'s larger scene, cast as the novel is in the lunatic fringe of political action during the nineteen-thirties, is another variation on Lewis's familiar American Success Story. But for Lewis it is a very different variation.

The sensuous appeal of Peony is matched by her insatiable desire to "get ahead," and her ambition to glide in that "metropolitan stream of elegance, excitement, and fame" is matched only by her extravagance and bad taste. (The descriptions of Peony's various and always more expensive apartments are among the best of Lewis's visual reports on the American scene.) When the Planishes make the grade and become the intimates of the lords of the economic creation, and as the Planishes' income steadily increases, and so do their expenses, and Peony sings more exuberantly and only her "Gidjums" is bewildered, *Gideon Planish* also presents some of Lewis's best satiric portraits: among others, those of William T. Knife, the Okey-Dokey King, or Winifred Homeward, the Talking Woman, or Colonel Charles B. Marduc's group of promising young publicity men:

> Each of them allowed himself daily exactly twenty-seven cigarettes—carried in a quiet silver case—with two highballs, two cocktails, three cups of coffee, one Bromo Seltzer, and fifteen minutes of sharp and detestable exercise. They averaged 1½ spirited minutes of love per week, one rather unsatisfactory adultery per year, and one wife—always from a Good Family, usually a dark pretty girl whom you could never quite remember.

And when Doctor Planish finally comes to recognize the meaning of "the world of fame and philanthrobbery," and his own status amongst these native demagogues and fortune-hunters; when Planish begins to understand "how dead men feel," and Peony, still exulting, still driving him on, begins to grow increasingly indifferent to what his feelings are —in all this, *Gideon Planish* doesn't omit the implication of the Planishes' moral, as well as sexual, corruption: that whole darker side of human nature which up to this point has never been adequately represented in Lewis's work.

However, the earlier cultural observations of *Gideon Planish*—the description of Maple Grove, which had leaped from crossroad hamlet to small city "without ever having had the leisure to stop and be merely a pleasant village," or of Ipswich, which was "exactly like Chicago, except that it was only one two-hundred-and-fiftieth as large": these, also, show a deeper concern with what has been happening to the State of Winnemac. This is our introduction to the novel which marks the final return of Lewis to that midwestern scene which has been the real battleground of his work, the source of his divided emotions and the object of so much hidden as well as obvious conflict. And both the central figure and the milieu of *Cass Timberlane,* in 1945, represent Lewis's most sustained and mature attempt to record the virtues of a purely western way of life.

Judge Cass Timberlane himself surely typifies Lewis's highest order of native man in his background and descent as well as in his profession. In the security of inherited wealth and social position and in his larger indifference to wealth and social position, he is a cut above Sam Dodsworth; he is almost the *passive* as against the active middle-class aristocrat; and almost for the first time Lewis is able to visualize an aristocracy that is established rather than an aristocracy on the make.[2] There is little doubt as to the quality of Cass Timberlane's interest in his native city of Grand Republic; his "ancestral and proprietary right" to it, and his paternal and loving hopes for it:

> "It's just that I have some kind of an unformulated ideal that I want to be identified with Grand Republic—help in setting up a few stones in what may be a new Athens. It's this northern country—you know, stark and clean—and the brilliant lakes and the tremendous prairies to the westward—it may be a new kind of land for a new kind of people, and it's scarcely even started yet."

And in the panoramic view of Grand Republic which forms the background of the novel, such portraits as that of Boone Havock, whose success as a steel baron is due "less to his knowledge of how to handle steel than to his knowledge of how to battle with steel-workers"; or of those "fine, big, bouncing hussars" who are known to the ribald as the Zebra Sisters; or of Lilian Drover to whom, by contrast, the whole business of sex "had become a horror related to dark bedrooms and loud breathing"; or of Don Pennloss who "quarreled or made love or said the bacon was good or denounced the unions in exactly the same basso"; or of Rose Pennloss who wants to know just what is a woman to do

> who is still good-looking at thirty-six but not beautiful enough to make a career of it, clever enough to know she wouldn't be clever on any job, aware, through reading, of all the glamor and luxuries of life but with no money for them and no rich relatives to murder, active and yet contemptuous of amateur charities and artistic trifling and exhibitionistic sports, untrained in anything worth fifteen dollars a week on the labor market and not even, after years of marriage, a competent cook or nurse, no longer in love with her husband and bored by everything he does—and he always does it!—and

[2] A genuine *haute bourgeoisie,* that is, as against Lewis's aggressive and pushing *petit bourgeoisie* who consider themselves *haute bourgeoisie.*

> yet unwilling to have the thrill of being vengeful toward him or of hurting him intentionally, liking other men but not lecherous nor fond of taking risks, possessing a successful daughter and too interested in her to desert her —just what is this typical upper-middle-middle-class American Wife to do?

—certainly, in such portraits as these, Lewis is at last expressing something of the variety and mystery of that ordinary middle-western life which has been so largely ignored in his work, and which, even in the *Main Street,* upon whose heroine Rose Pennloss is now in a sense delivering a final verdict, was viewed within such a narrow framework of values.

It is worth mentioning that Lewis has located the city of Grand Republic in Minnesota rather than in that appalling chain-state of Winnemac—that in *Cass Timberlane* he has completed the whole cycle of East and West which we have been tracing and has come back full-circle to his earliest origins. . . . And yet it is a curious cycle, as we have seen, and, for all of the novel's merits, a somewhat ambiguous return.

Although Cass does belong to that older western tradition which is "informal but not rackety," it is also a middle-western scene where, in Cass's set, which is largely above the seven-thousand-dollar line, it is "as obligatory to dress for party dinners as in London." Unlike London, however, Lewis's Midwest views the "universal multiple revolution, just then, in the early nineteen-forties, from sulfa drugs and surrealism and semantics to Hitler" with complete and sublime indifference—an indifference that is marked, perhaps, when the fact of this revolution becomes inescapable, by just the slightest tinge of irritation. "Oh, curse the luck," says Cass when the news of Pearl Harbor bursts upon his honeymoon. It is a Midwest which shares Lewis's now firmly established conviction that love—married love—conquers all, and that the fate of Europe, as Cass decides, must be subordinated to the fate of his own marriage:

> If the world of the twentieth century, he vowed, cannot succeed in this one thing, married love, then it has committed suicide, all but the last moan, and whether Germany and France can live as neighbors is insignificant compared with whether Johan and Maria or Jean and Marie can live as lovers.

And finally this is a Midwest which has relegated all signs of its own troubles, as well as those foreign "incidents," to Lewis's new conception of a happy marriage as "a blissfully shared community of ignorance." It is true that Grand Republic has "leaped from clumsy youth to senility without ever having had a dignified manhood," and exists on western land that is almost exhausted, as Lewis says, from the uncouth robbery of forests and mines. Still wondering whether to become a ghost town or a living city, it is also marked by labor trouble, racial prejudice, and industrial unrest. Yet these elements are almost completely subordinated to the story of Cass, his "half-tamed hawk of a girl," and the hawk's little flights. And here it is difficult to understand just why the central love-story of the novel, developed as it is at the expense of every other theme in the novel, is so meretricious until one realizes that Lewis's Jinny Marsh is a postscript to his whole line of emancipated heroines: a last and more unpleasant figurehead of modern youth and of "Young Revolution" who, through her disastrous extra-marital romance, is forced to receive her just deserts, and repents.

Thus, in the final accounting of *Cass Timberlane,* Lewis's world is probably not well lost for love. But it is undoubtedly well lost. "Yep," says the Governor Blizzard of *Gideon Planish,* "I'm reverting to Main Street with some of the fastest reversion you ever saw." And this is in fact a "reversion" rather than a return to Lewis's western origins: a reversion that has partially sublimated, but hasn't altogether resolved, the familiar elements of Lewis's conflict: that is also directed against all thought and talk outside of Main Street, and that, dismissing the eastern metropolis quite as blindly as it had once embraced it,[3] has exalted the vices as well as the virtues of small-town life into the order of a completely detached, a wholly self-absorbed, an absolute cosmogony.

You may now realize the value of that recurrent image in these later Lewis novels: the vision of the northern Middle West as "the fabulous Great Land of the year 2000 A.D." For in a sense this land, with its brilliant lakes and tremendous prairies, its long bleak winters and rich hot bursting summers; this "stark and clean" midwestern land which Lewis has just begun to appreciate *is,* in Lewis's mind, already in the year 2000 A.D. Or anyhow it is well beyond the reverberations of either the European conflict or of that disturbed American industrial order whose material products and moral values seem everywhere to have conditioned it. This is a land of prefabricated prairies that float in a synthetic infinitude: a "new kind of land" indeed.

And "a new kind of people." There is an element of truth, again, in Lewis's almost complete reversion to the domestic affairs of his characters. Just because ordinary people insist on living ordinary lives in the midst of social catastrophes, they have managed to survive such catastrophes in the most incredible way. But were ever private lives *quite* so private as they are in Lewis's final philosophy—a philosophy that excludes not only the "more" that is dreamed of on heaven and earth, but almost the notion of heaven and earth itself? If this is to be the price for the survival of the human race, it is at the cost of practically

[3] New York is clearly described as "a jungle spawning of people and buildings, fierce and purposeless," while, as Lewis says, "anything printed, a timetable or the rich prose of a tomato-catsup label, is more stimulating than any talk, even the screaming of six economists and an intellectual actress." And particularly, one supposes, the screaming of the economists.

every feature that has made the race human. Moreover, just as *Gideon Planish* is the most vigorous and acute of Lewis's late novels in artistic terms, it is also the most explicit about his repudiation of all larger human values.[4]

For Lewis's "World of Philanthrobbery," the world outside of Main Street, includes not only those odious radicals or revolutionaries, but the most discreet liberalism, not only the lunatic fringe of social reform, but all social change, and not only the racketeers of the humanitarian impulse, but the humanitarian impulse itself. Probably *Gideon Planish*'s brightest satiric passage—

> So Gideon Planish firmly set his plump foot upon the upward path that would lead through the miasma of lecturing and the bleak wind of editing to the glory of cloud-cuckoo-land, yet, even unto the world of committees and conferences and organizations and leagues of implementing ideals and crystallizing public opinion and molding public opinion and producing informed public opinion and finding the greatest common denominator in all shades of opinion——
>
> Of grass roots and liberal thinking and blueprints for democracy and the system of free enterprise and far-flung armies and far-flung empires and far-flung money-raising campaigns, together with far-flung night-letter-telegrams about the imminence of the crisis and far-flung petitions to Congress about the state of politics in Chile or Iran, and ideologies and ideological warfare and in general the use of the word 'ideology' as meaning everything except Far-Flung and Coca-Cola, and the longing to serve and the need of discussion and constitutional measures and challenges and rallying-points and crises, lots of crises, practically daily crises, and basic appeals and spiritual ideals and the protection of the home, and the sickness in our civilization . . .

—such a passage most clearly illustrates the final nature of Lewis's Great World and his final reversion to "the comic strips and to anarchy."

In the age of Hitler and Expressionism, the bourgeois counter-revolution has run amok; this is the nightmare of a nihilist. . . . One cannot but admire the glitter of such passages as these; for eloquence and sheer vitality Lewis has probably done nothing better over a full quarter-century of his literary career, and notice that the structure and rhythms of Lewis's prose have become much more flexible and fluent. Similarly,

[4] Lewis's most recent novel, *Kingsblood Royal,* which deals specifically with the Negro problem, seems to be an exception to this rule. In part, it is a return to his earlier vein of social satire. But notice that the most vivid passages in the novel deal with the almost nightmarish horror of an eminently respectable Northern white man who is confronted by the dreadful possibility of becoming a Negro. . . . Just as in the case of *It Can't Happen Here,* the real elements of social conflict in *Kingsblood Royal* are subordinated to a childlike fantasy of social conflict, while the profoundly disturbing factor of mob violence in the United States today becomes, at the close of the novel, another sort of parlor game played with imaginary shotguns.

in the larger range of Lewis's work as a whole, one may admire that stubborn persistence which results, for example, in this least "feminine" of artists having established such a long line of feminine figureheads, or in this least sensuous of writers perpetually dealing with, and finally limiting himself almost purely to, the senses. Although Lewis's realism does not in the end compare with either Dreiser's or Dos Passos's, although his values are quite inadequate when compared with Willa Cather's or Sherwood Anderson's, there is a curious sort of solidity in his work, a fundamental sense of human decency, and a fundamental human perversity which is at the base of any mature individualism. It isn't, moreover, that Lewis is not always serious about the craft of a novelist. It is simply that he doesn't always know how serious the craft of a novelist can be.

Bethel Merriday, so the author tells us, had been reared "to the solid American Protestant belief in the glory and efficacy of human will power"—

> If anyone wanted enough to do anything, he would unquestionably do it, and his resoluteness was somehow very beautiful, if his ambition was to devour the moon or become the Queen of Sheba.

And in a sense this description of Lewis's actress, which illustrates so beautifully the vulgarization of the frontier ethos within the subsequent framework of Horatio Alger and Hollywood, is the clearest description of both Lewis's own source of power and his tragic limitations.

So all this wit and eloquence and artistic vitality operates in a sort of intellectual vacuum in the end. You could say that the whole import of Lewis's work shows that he has learned nothing, answered nothing, solved nothing: that those Lewis characters who, in his first novels, left the West for an imaginary East are the same characters who leave the East for the imaginary West of his last novels; and that Lewis himself, like his most typical figures, is the Eternal Amateur of the national letters. Even the intellectual and emotional break-throughs of his last period: the final touching upon the perennial human impulses in the love-story of *Gideon Planish,* or the insight into cultural patterns which is contained in that brief note on the Beluca, Indiana ("pop. 277,000; site state aviation sch; Beluca, Univ., Littlefield Art Museum cont. a Fra Angelico, an El Greco; mfrs. plumbing supplies. . . ."), of *Bethel Merriday,* or merely the description of that Howard Pyle-ish courthouse in *Cass Timberlane*—

> It was of a rich red raspberry brick trimmed with limestone, and it displayed a round tower, an octagonal tower, a minaret, a massive entrance with a portcullis, two lofty flying balconies of iron, colored-glass windows with tablets or stone petals in the niches above them, a green and yellow

mosaic roof with scarlet edging, and the breathless ornamental stairway from the street up to the main entrance without which no American public building would be altogether legal.

—perhaps such bright passages as these, more than anything else, only serve to light up the gap between what Lewis's work could have been and what it actually is.

Furthermore, the point isn't that Lewis lives so completely in illusion. This is one of the prime sources of an artist's power and one of the reasons why Lewis's work, for all its limitations, has its own appalling validity. The point is that the illusion which nourished Lewis was so inadequate, and in the last analysis so transient. . . . For the Happy End to Lewis's unhappy historical vision—the vision of Middle-Class Bliss which marks the entire last period of Lewis's work—came at almost the precise historical moment that marked the crack-up of the Middle-Class Empire in America; at least in its first natural exuberant form. And if Lewis sees clearly enough the failure of the Horatio Alger tradition in American life, it is just as true that the brand of economic individualism for which he yearns was, almost from the very start of his career, more of a vestigial than a vital force in his society: even then, in the dawning age of the cartels, a myth and a memory of the past.

Here, too, we can appreciate Lewis's curious relationship with the Younger Generation. In the last of the broken antitheses which form the real dialectic of Lewis's work, we have noticed how the writer who has sought after "youth" most fervently hardly expresses it with the greatest conviction. How prematurely sober Lewis's typical young people are, and how perennially gauche and infantile his adults are: almost as though, never having had a true youth, they can never achieve a true maturity. You might almost say that the typical Lewis hero is an adolescent with a paunch. And in this respect, rather like those western settlements which have jumped from crude hamlets to ersatz cities, Lewis's people are reflecting the broken life-line of the Middle-Class Empire itself—that uneasy empire whose own youth in America was capped by a hurried and frantic maturity, and for whose brief flourishing Lewis has been forced, in *The Prodigal Parents,* to substitute a mythical and timeless splendor.

And doesn't George F. Babbitt himself, the Grand Mogul of the Middle-Class Empire, take on an added glory simply because he was allowed such a brief span on history's moving stage? The dupe of time as well as of the great American fortunes, Lewis's single big creation is a pathetic clown in truth. The clock goes faster in the United States, too fast for both Lewis's many-volumed diary of the economic man and for the diarist too. . . . And it is interesting that the cultural lag in Lewis's work should be so marked: that just as the real social forces of his time are placed for the most part quite outside of his literary scene, so the real social changes of his time are reflected so cursorily and so late. The ordinary mark of a first-rank author is that his writing is generally in some degree ahead of its time; the typical characteristic of Lewis's writing is that it is generally, to a marked degree, behind its time. Very likely this is the final key to Lewis's achievement—the key which opens the secret chamber in this otherwise absolutely uninspiring middle-class mansion.

For it would appear that Lewis's whole literary world, so extraordinarily prosaic for the most part, so lacking in subtleties and shadows; a world of perpetual daytime, on which night, with its enigmas and mysteries, never falls—that this whole uniquely commonplace literary universe of Lewis's *is* in the end haunted by the sense of its own destiny. This is also a middle class which is essentially without a home life, without children, without religion, and, finally, without an economic status to speak of: a middle class which is without all the historical props of a middle class, and which, hardly established in power, has every appearance of dissolving—including the escape into a dream world of the middle class. . . . At any rate, that is the impression that Sinclair Lewis's work leaves with us, as it turns from the barricades to the Land of Faery, while the true and final fascination of his own career, as we have noticed, is the degree to which he has become identified with the illusions of this class.

Salute to an Old Landmark: Sinclair Lewis

by Edmund Wilson

This review of Sinclair Lewis's new novel—*Cass Timberlane*—is, I am afraid, going to be one of those articles in which the reviewer talks about himself, so if this irritates you, you might skip to the middle, where I really get to work on the book. Coming back a month ago to New York after visiting several countries of Europe, I found myself more alienated from the United States than I ever remembered to have been after any similar trip. This may have been due partly to the fact that in Europe I had constantly been thinking how much better off we were at home and had built up an ideal picture, and partly to the fact that making the trip by plane in two days from Naples to New York does not, if you are accustomed to the old-fashioned kind of travel, give you time to prepare yourself for the change from one continent to another. The old reflexes, conditioned by sea voyages, do not tell you that you are home again, and you feel that you are not really there, that the new place in which you seem to have alighted is some sort of simulacrum or mirage. In any case, it was almost like arriving in another foreign country. I noticed characteristics of the Americans of which I had not been aware when I left: they were much larger than Europeans, enormous; their faces seemed lacking in focus and their personalities devoid of flavor; and most of the things that they were doing seemed to me done in a boring way. I had looked forward to picking up my old interests and was baffled and disconcerted when I discovered that these no longer seemed interesting.

Then I saw that I had to make an adjustment quite different from the kind of adjustment that is involved in going abroad and learning one's way about. I already knew my way about at home, yet I could not find the values I had known, the values on which I depended; and I realized that what made the difference was that abroad you were always in the position of a spectator for whom the inhabitants were putting on a show. This show consists of their being foreigners and behaving in a foreign way, and it provides you with entertainment without your needing to do anything yourself. But at home you are no longer in the audience, you have to be one of the actors, and there will not be the old show unless you get back into your rôle. You have to contribute, yourself, to creating the interest and the values, and I was still in the state of mind of the passive looker-on. I had not begun working yet.

At this moment I read Sinclair Lewis, and I appreciated him in certain ways as I had never done before and as I perhaps should not otherwise have done. We have had Lewis around for so long, so consistently being himself, that he has become a familiar object, like Henry Ford or the Statue of Liberty, about which, if one has been living in America, one does not think very much. Up to his novel before this last one, I had not read him for years, and had heard little about him except routine complaints that he was repeating himself or going to pot. I did read his book before last, *Gideon Planish,* because I had heard it was about foundations and I had had enough experience of foundation workers to want to see Sinclair Lewis turned loose on them. *Gideon Planish* was an extremely funny caricature, and I saw that Lewis's writing had improved: he moved more swiftly, made his points with less effort, and had mastered a not common art of introducing colloquial American, with style, into literary prose. But I found in his new book, *Cass Timberlane,* some qualities that were new to me and that I had not expected. Lewis has returned to Minnesota to live and he has written about a small Middle Western city in a way that is quite distinct from anything in *Main Street* or *Babbitt.* These northern Middle Western cities, with their big lakes and their raw business buildings, their gloomy old houses of the eighties that run to fancy windows and towers, and their people playing bridge and drinking cocktails, kept warm by a new oil furnace, in the midst of their terrific winters, have a peculiar impressiveness and pathos which are sometimes rather hard to account for in terms of their constituent elements but which, despite all the crassness and dullness, are inherent in the relation of the people to the country. This Lewis has got into his novel. Gopher Prairie, of *Main Street,* he hated; Zenith, of *Babbitt,* he ridiculed; but Grand Republic, Minnesota, the scene of *Cass Timberlane,* has really been lived in and loved. And the book made me feel, when I read it, that I was back in touch with home again and made me realize that Sinclair Lewis, in spite of his notorious faults, is one of the people in the literary field who do create interest and values, that he has still gone on working at this when many others have broken down or quit, and that he is, in fact, at his best—what I never quite believed before—one of the national poets.

And what about the story itself? It is a story about a husband and wife and is very much the same sort of thing as such novels as H. G. Wells's *Marriage* and Arnold Bennett's *These Twain,* of the literary era in which Lewis grew up and to which he still more or less belongs. A judge in his early forties, a serious and upright man, falls in love with and succeeds in marrying a girl in her early twenties, pretty, clever, and rather perverse. They do all the usual things—there are clashes of taste and interest, quarrels and reconciliations, she has flirtations with other men and he makes her jealous scenes, she gives birth to a baby, which dies, and has a period of ill health and depression. When she recovers, he takes her to New York, and there she is unfaithful to him with an old friend turned city slicker. Back in middle-class Grand Republic, she decides that she will divorce the Judge and marry the other man, but when she goes to New York, she finds out that her lover has never taken her seriously. She falls ill; the Judge comes on and rescues her and takes her back to Grand Republic. She has learned to appreciate her husband and is prepared to like their neighbors better, and we assume that all will now go well.

What is new in Sinclair Lewis's picture is an attempt on the author's part to deal with a typical bright young woman of the forties, so different from the emancipated woman of the earlier decades of the century, the "Woman Who Did," that heroine who dared to get herself a job or be a social or political worker or desert her conventional husband for the unconventional man she loved. The new type of liberated young woman wants to compete with the man without learning any trade, is rebellious against marriage but does not want a job, leaves her husband but does not stick to her lover. Sinclair Lewis is trying to get hold of this type, and his perception of social phenomena is always alert and sharp; but the truth is that he does not like Jinny, is too old-fashioned, perhaps, to sympathize with her. He works hard to make her attractive, but her relentless cuteness and cleverness always sound off key and self-conscious. Does he know how obnoxious he has made her? At one point he remarks that if the Judge had not been so much in love, he might not have cared for Jinny's whimsicality; and we have an uncomfortable feeling that if the author changed his tone only a little, we should get one of his frank female caricatures, like the wife of Gideon Planish. Here is Jinny being cute in Florida: "Jinny eyed the crêpe myrtle, the roses, the obese wonder of a grapefruit growing, and looked at the Cass who had worked this magic for her. 'My Merlin!' she said." And here she is being clever on the subject of their going to New York: The Judge says, " 'We'll pick up New York and shake it.' 'Oh, but that headwaiter at the Marmoset Club, with eyes like a wet old dishrag, who looks at you just once and guesses exactly what your income is, and do you know any Astors.' 'Maybe we'd get to know a few Class B Astors, if we wanted to, which I doubt.' 'I'd love to know *lots* of Astors—big fat juicy ones, and little diamond-studded ones in sables!' . . . 'Jinny, you shall have all the Astors you want. Have Astors with your corn flakes.' 'And cream.' 'And extra cream, from the Ritz. God knows even a very rich Astor or Vanderbilt or Morgan, one nine feet tall with a robe made of securities, couldn't be more chilly than our local John William Prutts. Let's look their lodge over. I mean, before we actually decide whether I ever shall resign, I think we ought to go to New York and study it, to see whether, if we had a real home of our own there, we wouldn't enjoy the place.' 'And Cleo?' 'Naturally,'" Cleo is a dreadful kitten, who is carried all through the book and is supposed to reflect the moods of their marriage.

The ending is absolutely Victorian. Lewis stacks the cards against Jinny by making her lover such a cold-hearted scoundrel—he has the currish name of Bradd Criley—as has hardly been seen in serious fiction for a century, and he has her develop diabetes so that she will become a chronic invalid. Scorned by her seducer and confined to her bed, she has no choice but to go home with the Judge, and Lewis evades the problem of finding out what such a girl would do if she were well and had pleasanter friends. He leaves her reading *Dombey & Son,* where, in the story of Edith Dombey and Carker, she must have found a singular parallel to the destiny which her creator has invented for her.

But in handling the Judge himself, Sinclair Lewis is a good deal better. He is dealing here with something that he intimately knows, and the Judge in relation to his city is really thoroughly and admirably done. The most satisfactory section of the book is the early part, in which we see Timberlane, divorced from his first worthless wife, living alone in his sombre house, hearing cases and dining with friends, working out chess problems at home, and discovering the birdlike young girl, living among the local Bohemia, whom he is passionate enough to pursue but not young enough or supple enough to meet on her own ground. The best and subtlest thing in the novel is the effect on the Judge's behavior with his wife and his treacherous friend of the conception of justice and individual rights which he has trained himself to respect in the law. Judge Timberlane, too, in his personal as well as in his official life, is creating interest and values for his less conscious and responsible neighbors.

These neighbors, the social organism of Grand Republic, are shown not only in relation to the Timberlanes but also by a series of brief histories, interspersed through the book, of the married lives of certain citizens. Some are funny, some are touching, some are implausible or superficial. But the general effect is successful. These sketches build up the community and serve to set the Timberlanes off. Nor can it nowadays be said of Lewis—as Sherwood Anderson used to do—that he does not see inside his characters and appreciate their human merits. He does not slight their commonness and ugliness any more than he did in *Main Street,* but Grand Republic, Minnesota, is a place in which one can imagine living, not, like Main Street, a circle of Hell.

The Last Flight from Main Street

by Malcolm Cowley

When Sinclair Lewis died in Rome on January 10, 1951, just before his sixty-sixth birthday, he had published twenty-one novels over a period of thirty-seven years. He left behind him the corrected proofs of a twenty-second novel, *World So Wide,* as a sort of epilogue to his career. It is unfortunate for his reputation that *World So Wide* is possibly the weakest of all his books. I say "weakest," not "worst," because there is little in *World So Wide* that is actively bad in the fashion of *The Prodigal Parents* or in the different fashion of *The Man Who Knew Coolidge.* It is a pleasant and trifling story of which the chief fault is that, as a novel, it was never really written and doesn't quite exist.

It is the story of a year in the life of Hayden Chart, a successful young architect from Newlife (read Denver, Col.). When Hayden's objectionable wife is killed in an automobile accident, he leaves his office in charge of a partner and goes wandering through the "world so wide" like a college boy on summer vacation. In Florence he meets Sam Dodsworth, from an earlier Lewis novel, and falls in love with Dr. Olivia Lomond, an assistant professor in history at the University of Winnemac.

Week after week Hayden stays in Florence instead of continuing his travels. Olivia proves to be not so cool and cloistered as she had seemed. Dr. Lorenzo Lundsgard appears, with plans to produce historical motion pictures and with a big expense account from Cornucopia Films. There are descriptions of Florentine churches and restaurants and accounts of cocktail parties in the American colony. There is also some mild suspense: Will Hayden marry Olivia, who is obviously the wrong woman for him? Will Lundsgard succeed in his aim of becoming a Fascist leader among American scholars? Will Hayden succumb to the easy ways of Florence and become a permanent expatriate? In the last chapter all the questions are answered a little too briskly and Hayden and his bride (who isn't Olivia) start back for Newlife by way of India and Ceylon.

The reappearance of Sam Dodsworth in the story is the key to its real nature. Hayden Chart is simply a younger Dodsworth and Dr.

Olivia Lomond, after starting out to be a new character, becomes a childishly scheming and unfaithful woman like Dodsworth's first wife. *World So Wide* is *Dodsworth* retold in half the number of words, with half the expenditure of imagination and curiosity. I couldn't find any feature in which it marked an advance over the earlier novel.

Reading it I remembered a sentence in an old essay by Van Wyck Brooks, "The Literary Life in America," published in 1921. "Our writers," Brooks said, "all but universally lack the power of growth, the endurance that enables one to continue to produce personal work after the freshness of youth has gone." *World So Wide* is an example that would seem to support Brooks' statement, but there are writers contemporary with Lewis who could be used as arguments on the other side. Brooks himself is one of them. T. S. Eliot, Willa Cather and Eugene O'Neill have all shown a power of growth from one work to another.

Even Dreiser, who never learned to write better than he did in his first book, *Sister Carrie,* and whose later novels, except *An American Tragedy,* were all of them massive disappointments—even the Old Unteachable showed a sort of growth at the end and wrote the last chapter of his last novel, *The Bulwark,* on what was for him a completely new emotional level. He made his peace with the fathers and rounded out his story. On the other hand, Sherwood Anderson—and after him Thomas Wolfe—stood frantically still. They burst on our vision and amazed us, but then they simply kept bursting like Roman candles, with no surprises after the first pink star.

Lewis was different from any of the others and showed the power of growth for exactly eleven years of his career as a novelist. His work had the trajectory of a rocket in the sky: up, up, up, from *Our Mr. Wrenn* (1914) through *The Job* (1917) to *Main Street* (1920); then leveling off a little but still rising through *Babbitt* (1922) to its highest point in *Arrowsmith* (1925); then sinking, not too rapidly at first, through *Elmer Gantry* (1927) and *Dodsworth* (1929); then down, down, down, in the books of his later years.

In reality the descending curve of the rocket wasn't quite so steep as its rise and there were little peaks in it, as if new stores of powder had been ignited. Lewis was an effective pamphleteer, though not a far-sighted prophet or a wise politician, in *It Can't Happen Here* (1935), and he was a bold campaigner against race prejudice in *Kingsblood Royal* (1947). In the former he was afraid, in the latter he was angry, and in both cases the emotion lent fire to the writing. *Cass Timberlane* (1945) was deeply felt on a more intimate level and was perhaps the best of his later books. *Kingsblood Royal* was the most popular, with a sale in all editions of 1,497,000 copies.

Even in these three novels, which stand far above the others he wrote after 1930, one observes a flagging power of invention; instead of creating new characters he was, for the most part, reintroducing the old ones under different names. A worse fault was that he had ceased to listen to anyone but himself. His early novels had been faithful transcripts of middleclass Midwestern speech. That speech has changed in the last thirty years, has learned new words and adopted new mannerisms, but Sinclair Lewis's characters in *World So Wide* talk almost exactly like those in *Main Street* and *Babbitt.* The result is that they sound like survivors from a vanished world, like people just emerging from orphanages and prisons where they had listened for thirty years to nothing but tape recordings of Lewis novels.

That is the case against his later work—or part of the case—and yet I started by thinking of this article as a defense of Sinclair Lewis. The truth is that I do not believe his permanent reputation will rest on anything he has written since 1930. All his later work will be swept aside, and perhaps the sooner the better for his fame. It would be a grave mistake, however, to undervalue what he wrote and what he did in his early days.

In 1920 he had a chance that American writers have seldom received. The success of *Main Street* not only gave him more money than he had dreamed of, but it also made him the acknowledged center of a whole galaxy of gifted writers, the leader, so to speak, of a new generation. Looking back on his career I think he deserves credit for accepting the responsibility as well as the privileges of his new situation. He didn't write easy books after *Main Street.* He laid out for himself an extensive plan of work: he would invent the state of Winnemac, more typical than any real state in the Union, and in one book after another he would describe the representative activities of its inhabitants, until he had completed a wide survey of American society.

He carried the project forward in a series of four big novels, each of which must have been harder for him to write than the one that came before it. Meanwhile he acted as a sort of spokesman for his generation of American writers and took what seems to us now the right side in most of the disputes he entered. He also made a point of helping writers younger than himself. To some of them he gave money—acting as a sort of private and informal Guggenheim Foundation—while to all of them he gave their full share of praise.

It was not at all an accident that Sinclair Lewis was the first American to receive the Nobel Prize for Literature. He had done more than any other American of his time to make our literature known in Europe; and when the Swedish Academy, which awards the prize, at last decided that our literature deserved official recognition, Lewis was the writer to whom it naturally turned. In his acceptance speech, on December 12, 1930, he spoke for a whole generation of American writers and ended by saluting the younger writers who would succeed him.

That was the high point of his career, but I think we have been placing too much emphasis on the slow decline that followed. The truth is that most writers decline at some time or another. Writing is normally a hazardous profession and those who retain the power of growth from year to year are the fortunate exceptions. The real task of critics is not to explain the decline in each case, but rather to explain the height and nature of the achievement from which it started. In the case of Sinclair Lewis they still have a great deal to explain.

Sinclair Lewis

by Joseph Wood Krutch

Sinclair Lewis loved notoriety almost as much as he loved fame, and he sought one almost as ardently as the other. What looked like both came to him rather early—he was thirty-five years old in 1920 when *Main Street* was published—and he had not outlived his reputation when he died at sixty-six. Two years after *Main Street* came the equally sensational *Babbitt*; after that a diminishing series of novels which, nevertheless, included such successful books as *Arrowsmith, Elmer Gantry, Dodsworth,* and *It Can't Happen Here.* For all the disorderly vehemence of his life he was a hard worker, and he did not give up, as many another writer has done, when it became evident that he could never again enjoy such a furor as he had once created. But he must have asked himself the question which is inevitably asked now: Had he won some enduring fame or was it all mere notoriety?

Like H. L. Mencken—whose permanence seems much less open to question—Lewis was that not unfamiliar paradox, the writer whose name is made a household word by the very people whom it was his special delight to attack. Just as every member of the boobocracy knew Mencken's name and, likely enough, could quote him, so *Main Street* lay on the tables of half the Main Street parlors, and Babbitts defending babbittry used the term with which he had supplied them. That, of course, proves nothing against him, may indeed be a point in his favor, since the enduring novelists, more consistently perhaps than the enduring writers in any other form, have tended to win easily a large general public. But such readers are sometimes lost as quickly as they are won, and Lewis has probably lost most of them already. His chance for immortality rests now in other hands.

Many of the factors which contributed very largely to the creation of his notoriety will hardly affect his fame at all. A man who added two apparently permanent words to the English vocabulary can hardly be forgotten. But he need not, for that reason, be read. And very much the same thing can be said in connection with the "social situation" and the "cultural climate" which so strongly favored him. Lewis did not invent his theme, for what Carl Van Doren called so precisely "the revolt against the village" was already under way. Ten years later, after the events of '29, native criticism of American society commonly concerned itself with the alleged defects of our economic system, but at the beginning of Lewis's heyday the equally inevitable targets were our puritanism and our provinciality, our lack of sophistication and "culture" in the narrowest sense of that term. *Main Street,* especially, followed this line of attack so precisely, so uncritically, and, one might almost say, so naively that even then its author was compelled to protest, somewhat unconvincingly, that he had not, as his critics assumed, intended to present the rather priggishly self-conscious Carol Kennicott as a model of elegant intellectuality and that—if I may put it this way—he did not really mean to suggest that the substitution of petits fours for the inevitable angel food at village card parties would constitute an important step forward.

Thus if Lewis did not invent his theme he gave it such a clear and not over-subtle exposition abroad as well as at home and was so closely identified with it that when, in 1930, he became the first American to receive the Nobel Prize for literature, not a few of his countrymen felt that the prize was less an expression of Europe's admiration for an American writer than an attempt to put the stamp of official approval upon what was regarded as a definitive exposé of American civilization. In certain respects *Main Street* so strongly suggested *Madame Bovary* that Lewis found it worth while to deny publicly that he had, at the time when his book was being written, ever read Flaubert's novel. Yet, so far as I know, *Madame Bovary* was never regarded as a definitive picture of the Frenchman or Frenchwoman, and the fact that it was not suggests to just what extent Lewis's study of a small town was, and Flaubert's was not, essentially a journalistic polemic rather than primarily a work of art.

If the fact that they were so perfectly apropos made for the immediate success of *Main Street* and *Babbitt,* the sudden shift of criticism from concern with "culture" to concern with politics and economics may have abbreviated their vogue and raised earlier the insistent question of what qualities other than journalistic ones they and the later novels may have, and whether or not any such qualities are sufficient to assure that the books will be read and not merely remembered. Can one imagine any of Lewis's novels becoming, within the next half-century, the beneficiaries of a revival like that which has affected the works of Melville and James, or to a lesser extent those of Hawthorne and Stephen Crane? Will Lewis ever be "rediscovered"? He is historically important of course. But have his books "wit enough to keep them sweet"?

Of *Arrowsmith* (1925) and *Dodsworth* (1929), as well as of lesser efforts, I have only an old memory, which, nevertheless, I trust. Lewis tried to find a hero as well as a butt, and his heroes were the emergent heroes of the popular advanced thinkers—an aviator in one of his earliest books, then a scientist, and then a business man dimly aware of a world he could not really enter. It was easy to call *Arrowsmith* and *Dodsworth* better novels than his two most sensational successes, and perhaps in some sense they were; but their virtues were not sufficient to compensate for the lesser journalistic impact, and it is largely because of *Main Street* and *Babbitt* that they are still remembered. To these last two I have returned, and I find them not very different from my recollection of them.

Main Street begins with a magisterial prologue. "This town is, in our tale, called 'Gopher Prairie, Minnesota.' But its Main Street is the continuation of Main Streets everywhere. Main Street is the climax of civilization. That this Ford car might stand in front of the Bon Ton Store, Hannibal invaded Rome and Erasmus wrote in Oxford cloisters." It ends, just short of fatuously, with its heroine defeated by this same Main Street and proclaiming, "But I have won in this: I've never excused my failures by sneering at my aspirations. . . . I do not admit that Main Street is as beautiful as it should be! I do not admit that Gopher Prairie is greater or more generous than Europe!" *Babbitt* has the advantage of a protagonist who embodies the central conception more satisfactorily than do any of the actual persons in its predecessor. It is also shorter, broader, more extravagant, less dependent upon earnestness, more dependent upon ridicule. And it is, for all these reasons, better. Neither Carol Kennicott nor her husband is a memorable figure. As persons they are not even very impressively what they are. George F. Babbitt, on the other hand, has a certain daemonic air. He may be no truer to life, but he comes closer to being mythical. If he is not a Don Quixote or a Gargantua he is at least, let us say, a Dick Tracy or a Katzenjammer Kid.

Both books are, each in its own way, tremendously well done in the sense that it is easy enough to understand why they produced the effect they were intended to produce. Yet, except perhaps in the case of George Babbitt himself, neither very often suggests the aims or the methods of that higher sort of fiction which either creates or reveals something that the mere description of observed fact cannot convey. Though Lewis had to a remarkable degree mastered his method, that method is a good deal like the one so successfully employed in the writing of many present-day best-sellers—the method, I mean, which produces books that are not so much naturalistic novels as "documentaries," pseudo-fiction in which everything is recognizable as true but with the fidelity of a waxwork and no suggestion of any sort of autonomous life.

If Lewis's books look better now than most of the current crop of documentaries will look a quarter of a century hence, that is principally because of one mental quality possessed by the man himself and one literary gift which he developed to an extraordinary degree. Much as he loved fame and even notoriety, it was not the desire for either which moved him to write *Main Street*. He was passionately sincere, and he was engaged in a crusade which seemed to him profoundly important. He may have understood the culture of Main Street a great deal better than he understood the idealized European culture which he attempted to oppose to it. Indeed, there is something ludicrous in the way in which he falls back upon vague references to Europe, as if he were imagining some fabulous London, or Paris, or Vienna populated exclusively by cultured sophisticates. But he genuinely hated something which he saw very clearly; he genuinely loved something which he but dimly understood; and because of those two facts both *Main Street* and *Babbitt* are more than merely slick jobs.

The literary gift that he developed to an extraordinary degree was, of course, the gift for mimicry, which is as definitely something more than mere naturalistic reproduction as it is definitely something less than imaginative recreation. As he used to demonstrate in social gatherings—sometimes rather over-insistently—he could improvise at any length the conversation or the speech-making of a Babbitt on almost any topic, and his improvisations had, like what he wrote in the same style, an air of authenticity, heightened by touches of burlesque, which made them as astonishing in their way as anything of the sort ever achieved. Yet at the same time he rarely if ever escaped the limitations of mimicry as an artistic device. The typical fact or the typical gesture is one step above the merely authentic. But it is also one step below the symbolic. Lewis habitually achieved the one, habitually made one exclaim "How characteristic!" But rarely if ever did he rise to that point where a detail is so charged with meaning that it becomes a symbol whose significance all but defies analysis.

It is for this reason that his brilliant, parodistic mimicry must go on and on; so that Babbitt's speech at the Chamber of Commerce dinner continues for nine pages. Good as most of it is, no sentence or paragraph is good enough to make further elaboration unnecessary, and in the end one is reminded of that ultimate satire on the naturalistic method embodied in a stage direction for one of Ring Lardner's plays: "The curtain will descend for seven days to indicate the passage of a week." Lewis falls victim, therefore, to the mimic's nemesis, which condemns him to remain always insufficiently more entertaining than the victim of his mimicry. There is too much burlesque, not enough wit.

To realism in art there is a limitation which *Babbitt* all too frequently illustrates. A bore in literature should be different from a bore in real life in at least one respect: he should not be boring. If *Babbitt* is not really a classic, that is probably because in the midst of our laughter and admiration we are likely to remember Mr. Bennett's remark to his piano-playing daughter: "You have entertained us enough for one evening." [1]

[1] What Mr. Bennet in *Pride and Prejudice* says to Mary is: "That will do extremely well, child. You have delighted us long enough. Let the other young ladies have time to exhibit." [M.S.]

Sinclair Lewis: A Lost Romantic

by Geoffrey Moore

There can have been few American authors so famous as Sinclair Lewis. He wrote twenty-two novels; he contributed two new terms to the mythology of the Western world; and he won the Nobel Prize. He was, in fact, an important man. Yet as a novelist—and I choose, perhaps a little unfairly, to understand by the term a writer who is concerned to explore through the medium of the novel the profoundest possibilities of the human spirit—as a novelist in this sense, he was second rate. In two novels, surely—that is, in *Main Street* and *Babbitt*—and in three others, possibly—that is, in *Arrowsmith, Elmer Gantry,* and *Dodsworth*—he raised himself, by an exercise of the imagination, above the level of sensibility of the *Saturday Evening Post,* for which he wrote in his early days;[1] but so far as the remaining seventeen are concerned it seems to me that one would wish to preserve only a few speeches and a few character studies. Lewis is therefore by way of being a phenomenon and the question that his career raises is how one can be such a limited writer and also have such an important place in the history of Western literature.

What, I think, happened is this. Lewis was of a journalistic cast of mind, but he had rather more potentiality than is indicated by his early work, the pre-twenties novels and serials. He was an ideas man with ideals. He saw what could be done; he saw that the ordinary domestic American, the transatlantic equivalent of the Wells or Bennett character, had yet to be written about, and he did write about him—brightly, energetically, and with amateurish conviction.

Europeans greeted Lewis with cries of joy when the novels of the 'twenties—*Main Street, Babbitt, Arrowsmith,* and *Elmer Gantry*—came out. Many Americans, on the other hand, were inclined to throw themselves on him with cries of rage. Did he not attack American institutions? "There was one good pastor in California," said Lewis, "who, upon reading my *Elmer Gantry,* desired to lead a mob and lynch me, while another

[1] Sinclair Lewis wrote for this periodical and others like it throughout his entire career. His last contribution to the *Saturday Evening Post* appeared in 1935. [M.S.]

holy man in the State of Maine wondered if there was no respectable and righteous way of putting me in jail." Other Americans seemed to regard him as an out-and-out humorist; the very idea that there could be any truth in his literary stunts was unthinkable. There is always a place in our minds to which we can consign the sort of disturbing thoughts that Lewis's novels arouse.

The approbation of Europe was the more remarkable because it came not only from ordinary readers but from European literary critics, and because it was capped by that Victoria Cross or Congressional Medal of Honour of literature, the Nobel Prize. This shows just how much we were in the dark, in the 'twenties, about what to expect from modern American literature. Hugh Walpole, in his Introduction to the English edition of *Babbitt,* said:

> *Main Street,* the book with which Mr. Lewis won fame in the United States, seemed to many English readers an ugly book, dealing with ugly people. . . . At first sight it might seem as though *Babbitt* is guilty of the same crime. Let us admit at once that the English reader will find the first fifty pages difficult, the dialogue strange, the American business atmosphere obscure and complicated.

We have moved a long way from the days when Walpole could say that, as has been shown by the award of the Nobel Prize to Hemingway and to Faulkner, novelists of quite different calibre. But it took twenty more years of increasing familiarity, and another world war, to make Europeans aware of American standards. In fact, in the 1920's Americans themselves were only just beginning to believe that they might have a literature worthy to rank with the other literatures of the world. The revaluation of Melville was just beginning; Mark Twain was still a rather vulgar little humorist turned cynic who tried to settle down and write books that would come up to the standards of Nook Farm; Hemingway was that good-looking boxer and tennis player who worked for William Randolph Hearst in Paris; Faulkner was a boiler-room attendant in the University of Mississippi; the Fitzgerald of *This Side of Paradise* could hardly be taken seriously; and the decade of Steinbeck, Dos Passos, Wolfe, Caldwell, and Farrell had yet to come. Today, when the honourable roll of American novelists is called, the "Present" of Lewis sounds a little shrill beside the response of Hawthorne, Melville, Twain, James, Howells, Stephen Crane, Edith Wharton, Faulkner, and Hemingway. It is not merely a matter of inferior literary stature, obvious though that may be; it is a matter of emphasis too, and to understand why Lewis's limited point of view was so popular in the 'twenties we might briefly consider the social and intellectual climate of the second and third decades of the twentieth century in America.

For a decade before the first World War it seemed that something was happening in American literature. The first cuckoos had been heard long before 1912, the year of the "poetic renaissance" in Chicago, when Harriet Monroe was publishing Sandburg, Lindsay and Masters, Eliot and Wallace Stevens. True, the sweet singers, Richard Hovey and Bliss Carman, were still singing their vagabond and fanciful songs, but these were also the years of Mabel Dodge's salon on Fifth Avenue, of Gertrude Stein's *Three Lives*, and of the discovery of Freud. Eugene O'Neill was writing those early plays that he carried in the famous suitcase to the Provincetown Playhouse. Edna Millay was writing her first lyrics: "Renaissance," that bone of contention, was published in *The Lyric Year* in 1912, and it is a good indication of the flame which possessed the rather soul-conscious literary aspirants of the time:

> The soul can split the sky in two
> And let the face of God shine through,
> But East and West will pinch the heart
> That cannot keep them pushed apart;
> And he whose soul is flat—the sky
> Will cave in on him by and by.

These, too, were years of experiment with social ideas. In addition to *The Masses* and *New Republic* in New York, there was *Reedy's Mirror* in St. Louis, the magazine that published the first of Masters's poems, and Margaret Anderson's *Little Review* which turned like a weathervane to expound whatever creed or style might be fashionable at the moment. Lewis did not like the *Little Review*. "He hated," Grace Hegger Lewis recalls, "those arty, sophomoric little magazines." Yet, after all, the *Little Review* did publish, in addition to the silly people, Joyce, Yeats, Pound, and Gertrude Stein. This was, as Van Wyck Brooks put it, the time of America's "coming of age."

Then, after the war, that Cook's tour for some, that tomb for others, things were very different. The promise seemed to have gone, but the need for revolt was still there, and it was there in a harsher form; the mood was nihilistic. It was a transatlantic version of Dadaism, or the English "Owenism" and the rather grotesque fancies of the Sitwells. The younger writers flaunted their disillusion like an honourable wound. Fitzgerald flirted with his in *This Side of Paradise*, Hemingway hinted at his in *In Our Time*, and Faulkner agonised over his in *Soldiers' Pay*. This sense of disillusion seemed to some Europeans a little exaggerated, even histrionic, because of the minor degree to which America had suffered in the first World War, but it was, I think, a measure of America's idealism. This "lost" generation was in a sense also the "found" generation. What they found was a common spirit of criticism. They left for Paris or Rome, or, if they did not leave their country, spent their time attacking American habits and institutions. Of these detractors perhaps the most important is Mencken, the scourger of the "booboisie." Who were the "boobs"? They were the dull and hypocritical members of American society, not just Middle Westerners, although it is true that Mencken had little liking for and less understanding of the workings of the American mind beyond the Alleghenies. In the *Mercury* he did what the *New Yorker* does in a much milder way today, that is, pillory examples of muddled thinking and general crassness. Here, for example, is an extract, quoted by Mencken, from an ordinance passed by the Christian Legislators of Long Beach, California:

> No person shall indulge in caresses, hugging, fondling, embracing, spooning, kissing, or wrestling with any person or persons of the opposite sex . . . and no person shall sit or lie with his or her head, or any other portion of his or her person, upon any portion of a person or persons upon or near any of the said public places in the city of Long Beach.

In lampooning such attitudes Mencken was attacking what the young intellectuals of the time liked to call "puritanism." Apart from sexual connotations, puritanism signified practically anything one wished, like not enjoying Gertrude Stein, or never having heard the horn of Roland.

What was Lewis's attitude to all this? He was attracted to some of Mencken's ideas, though he seemed a little uneasy in this company. His ambivalent attitude may have had something to do with the matter of "art." Mencken, like Edna Millay and the other daring young things of the literary-bohemian set, regarded life as one thing and art as very much another. This point of view nearly always results in pretty-prettiness and attitudinising, and the bluff Middle Westerner in Lewis disliked it intensely—as his outburst against the *Little Review* showed. Yet all the time he had this very strain in him, as his early poems and stories reveal very clearly. He made the world triumph over Istra in *Our Mr. Wrenn*, but he allowed Fran Dodsworth and Carol Kennicott, who are much more sickeningly precious than Istra, to have their say. True, the world is made to triumph over them, too, in the end; but one feels that this was Lewis's reluctant following of the facts, rather than the result of a clear perception of exactly why and how Fran and Carol were wrong. To complicate matters, Lewis had firm convictions (although no very clear idea) about his own artistic achievement. As the result of a review by Carl Van Doren in *The Nation* in 1921 he wrote furiously to Alfred Harcourt, protesting against Van Doren's "two assumptions":

> (1) that I am merely a disciple of Edgar Lee Masters in writing *M. St.*—somewhat humorous in that I have never sat down and read *Spoon River Anthology*, but merely heard parts of it read aloud, and this not until 1917, whereas I first began to plan *Main St.* 1905; and (2) that I have always been a writer of "bright amusing chatter to be read at a brisk pace". I asked him if he had read *The Job* or *Our Mr. Wrenn* or *Trail of the*

> *Hawk,* or certain short stories which I enumerated; and I hinted, if I did not say directly, that if he hadn't read these he had one devil of a nerve, and he was one devil of a bad critic, to dare to sum me up thus . . . You or Spingarn might follow this up by sending him a copy of *The Job* and making him read it. . . . I think he ought to do an entirely new article about me in *The Nation* . . . certainly he must change this if he's going to publish these articles in book form.

In another letter to Harcourt ten years later and just a month after the award of the Nobel Prize we find him comparing "Heywood Broun's supercilious words" in the *New York Times* with "Arnold Zweig's brilliant essay . . . spoken on the radio in Berlin and then published in the German *Literatur*; the comment of *l'Europe Nouvelle* in France; essays in *Das Tagebuch* in Germany; Dr. Karfeldt's analysis of my work before the huge and distinguished crowd at the formal prize-giving, with all the royalty there. . . ."

In order to understand the frame of mind which led Lewis to make these comments we must, I think, go back a little way and consider what kind of man he was. He was born in 1885 in a village rather like the Gopher Prairie of *Main Street,* a place called Sauk Centre in Minnesota. His father began as a schoolteacher but saved up enough money to take a two-year medical course in Chicago. He practised in Wisconsin, then moved to Minnesota. Three sons were born before his wife died of tuberculosis—Fred, Claude, and Harry Sinclair. Harry was five at the time his mother died and two years later his father married again.[2] The population of Sauk Centre was 2,500, the people mostly German and Scandinavian in origin. Harry could never play as well as his brothers, and Grace Hegger Lewis in *With Love from Gracie* seems to think that the effect on him of his brothers' derisive "Go chase yourself" was noticeable in later life. He retired into a world of his own. He read *Robin Hood* and *Ivanhoe.* In his freshman year at Yale, in 1904, he wrote a story of which the title, "A Miracle Forsooth", is sufficiently descriptive to need no further comment. At twenty-eight years of age he was still writing "Tennyson-and-water" poems like this one, which begins:

> Princess, princess, silver maiden,
> Throw your casement open; see—
> On the terrace I am singing,
> Come and take the road with me.

William Lyon Phelps says in his *Autobiography with Letters* that Lewis was not disliked in college but "was regarded with amiable tolerance, as a freak . . . He was a complete and consistent individualist, going his own way, and talking only about things which interested

[2] Harry was six. His father remarried after one year. [M.S.]

him. . . ." He took some time off from Yale to join (as janitor) Upton Sinclair's co-operative socialist colony, Helicon Hall. Then he went off with a classmate; took a cattle-boat to England, a journey which gave him the subject of *Our Mr. Wrenn*;[3] went back to Yale; graduated; got various jobs on newspapers and in publishing firms; and finally settled down in New York, where he married Grace Hegger. It was while working as a publisher's editor and commuting daily from Long Island that he wrote his first five novels,[4] during which time he gained sufficient confidence to become a freelance.

Yet he was still a "faery child," a fact which seems to be of some importance in considering the nature of his satire. He was a piner for mysterious places, for courts of love with royal jesters. He wrote a prayer to Grace Hegger at the time, which begins: "Our Father, Thou who hast made the faces of little children glad, and the field to shine with wonder upon Christmas Day—Thou who art so great that of Thee and thy ways the Jester can have but tiny glimmerings at the sunset time, or in beholding the goodness of the Lady Grace . . ." In his books Lewis tended to set his women on a pedestal, as Milt Daggett does with Claire in *Free Air* and as Dr. Kennicott does with Carol in *Main Street.* The other side of this romantic idealisation was a taste for lechery and his wife records that the first draft of *Elmer Gantry* was marred by his relish of this facet of Gantry's character. But, then, Mrs. Lewis may herself have aggravated this dichotomy in Lewis's personality. She seems, by her own account, to have contributed something, at least, to Lewis's persistent portraits of the blonde Lady Fair who says: "Don't you think it's a little icky, this sudden passion for embracing me when you're —well, exhilarated? "

After *Our Mr. Wrenn* Lewis turned to novels which can, by and large, be called "romances." Then he achieved fame, with *Main Street,* and he was never the same after that. Someone like Ludwig Lewisohn had only to say, "Mr. Lewis can contribute a great deal to American literature" and he would drop his current *Saturday Evening Post* serial and furiously start writing some book that would change the face of American literature. As he went on, he became more and more restless. He commuted, not from Long Island to New York, but back and forth across the Atlantic. Finally, after the European accolade, this country boy who had made good (Lewis's style, attitude of mind, and public pronouncements invite the description) had earls to pick him up in their Rolls-Royces, and Bernard Shaw to ride up all pink and bearded on his bicycle to take tea with him. The Lewis story was, superficially, a success story, but as time went on the novels got worse and worse.

There is one pen portrait of him in the 'thirties that is very vivid—although of course romantically exaggerated—and that is the one by

[3] He had taken two cattle boat trips before going to Helicon Hall, none after. [M.S.]

[4] He left publishing at the end of 1915, after two novels. [M.S.]

Thomas Wolfe in *You Can't Go Home Again,* where he writes of Sinclair Lewis as Lloyd McHarg, and says:

> He was fantastically ugly, and to this ugliness was added a devastation of which George [George Webber, who is Wolfe] had never seen the equal. [In fact Lewis had developed skin cancer early in his married life and it was radium treatment which pockmarked his face and made it seem, as his wife said, "spilt."] The first and most violent impression was his astonishing redness. Everything about him was red—hair, large protuberant ears, eyebrows, eyelids, even his bony, freckled, knuckly hands. . . . Moreover, it was a most alarming redness. His face was so red that it seemed to throw off heat, and if at that moment smoke had begun to issue from his nostrils and he had burst out in flames all over, George would hardly have been surprised. . . .
>
> He came towards George quickly, with his bony, knuckled hand extended in greeting, his lips twitching and bared nervously over his large teeth, his face turned wryly upwards and to one side in an expression that was at once truculent, nervously apprehensive, and yet movingly eloquent of something fiercely and permanently wounded, something dreadfully lacerated, something so tender and unarmed in the soul and spirit of the man that life had got in on him at a thousand points and slashed him to ribbons. He took George's hand and shook it vigorously, at the same time bristling up to him with his wry and puckered face like a small boy to another before the fight begins, as if to say: "Go on, now, go on. Knock that chip off my shoulder. I dare and double-dare you." This was precisely his manner now, except that he said:
>
> "Why you—why you monkeyfied—why you monkeyfied bastard, you! Just look at him!" he cried suddenly in a high-pitched voice, half-turning to his companions. "Why you—who the hell ever told you you could write, anyway?" Then cordially: "George, how are you? Come on in, come on over here!"

I mentioned three stages in Lewis's work. One of them seems to me to extend from *Our Mr. Wrenn* (1914) to *Free Air* (1919)—the stage of the young Harry; another from *Main Street* (1920) to *The Man who Knew Coolidge* (1928)—the middle-aged Harry; and the third, the old Harry, from *Dodsworth* (1929) to *World So Wide* (1951). This is a tentative categorisation based on the areas of social life to which he devoted himself. One could make another set of categories depending on whether Lewis treated his characters from a rounded point of view, or satirically. In the first period the two novels that seem to me most important are *Our Mr. Wrenn* and *Free Air*. There is one peculiarly Lewis-like touch that is worth quoting from *Our Mr. Wrenn,* that tale of the rabbit-like man who took a cattle-boat across the Atlantic and, in another land, learned a little about life. Wrenn meets a Mr. Mittiford, Ph.D., in England, an American academic, and he says about him: "He wrote poetry which he filed away under the letter 'P' in his poetry file." Wrenn fights with the tough men on the ship, he meets a socialist called Harry Morton, and he meets Istra Nash, one of those icy-cold and yet attractive blonde bohemian types that turn up so frequently in Lewis's novels. Istra and he go for a "daring" walk at night through the English countryside to an equally daring colony. The "message" of this book is really the same as the "message" of all those early novels, and that is that the dull people are really the nicest people. At least they are honest. If you stray into the world of Bohemia, of "artiness," then you will come to phoniness and to grief. Wrenn is misled by his Istra but he settles down with the nice people, the man who sells tobacco round the corner, the people who tell crude jokes but who are really good at heart.

The Job of 1917 has a woman as heroine. It is a "forerunner" of *Main Street*. Una Golden is an office worker with the soul of a bluestocking. She revolts from the village (in Pennsylvania), and the novel is really devoted to trying to give you some feeling about the mystic function of business. One can see Lewis "trying out" various themes, the theme of revolt, for example, and of whether business is a suitable subject for a writing man with pretensions to "art."

When we come to Milt Daggett's story in *Free Air*—or Claire Boltwood's story; it could be called either—we have a number of indications of the central split in Lewis, the degree to which he wished to express his appreciation of the prairie people, and the degree, also, to which he felt abashed before the sophisticated, educated Easterners. There is one passage in which he seems to be describing himself:

> Who is this extraordinary Milt Daggett? Him? Oh, nobody 'specially. He's just a fellow down here at Schoenstrom. But we all know him. Goes to all the dances, thirty miles round. The thing about him is: if he sees something wrong, he picks out some poor fellow like me and says what he thinks.

And in another passage:

> With Mr. Jones (that is, James Martin Jones, B.A.) he discussed—no, ye Claires of Brooklyn Heights, this garage-man and this threadbare young superintendent of a paint-bare school, talking in a tongue that was only a comma on the line, did not discuss corn-growing, nor did they reckon to guess that by heck the constabule was carryin' on with Widdy Perkins. They spoke of fish-culture, Elihu Root, the spiritualistic evidences of immortality, government ownership, self-starters for flivvers and the stories of Irvin Cobb.

Through Claire Boltwood we find out a great deal about Lewis's Middle West, but we find out more later through Carol Kennicott. I consider *Main Street* the best book Lewis ever wrote, partly for this reason and partly because in it he achieved a compromise between the two viewpoints I have mentioned, which were also the two sides of his nature. These two sides of Sinclair Lewis are represented by Carol, who is the person who wants to bring culture to Gopher Prairie and yet is rather snobbish, superior, and fanciful; and Dr. Kennicott, who is homely and good-natured, dedicated and dull. The book leaps like an electric spark between the poles of Carol's disgust and Main Street's healthy philistinism.

With *Babbitt,* satire begins. It was the attempt that Lewis made to prove himself as an artist. The characters are more obviously caricatures, and the prose has the bite of winter air in Minnesota. The raw material of the novel is forced into a light-hearted pattern by the satiric intention. Lewis is not here "opening himself" to life; he is deciding what should be said and forcing his characters into this mould. It is a fantasy, really, on the theme of business, an attack on the hypocrisy of small businessmen, but with a certain undertone of friendliness.

In *Arrowsmith* we have a rather fuller picture despite a similar satirical intention. The heart of the book is a rather unsmiling portrait of the scientist, Lewis's great hero, Max Gottlieb. Otherwise, it is an indictment of how business can use research unscrupulously for its own end, and it side-swipes the great foundations. It might be said to be the story of Mr. Truthseeker.

Elmer Gantry is, by contrast, a novel about Mr. Opportunist. It satirises the misuse of religion and contains the unforgettable portrait of Frank Shallard, who is beaten up by religious people for speaking on behalf of free-thinking. Gantry falls in with Sharon Faulkner, the evangelist. The book is a study of hypocrisy; and I find myself going back, while reading it, to what Lawrence said in *Studies in Classical American Literature* about Hawthorne—how everything is fine on the surface while that blue-eyed *Wunderkind* of a Nathaniel keeps up the pretence, but how underneath there are things going on, disagreeable things. This is of course not an unknown phenomenon outside the United States, but although the matter of puritanism is sometimes exaggerated, it does seem as if the Calvinistic strain in American culture might have made the discrepancy between public and private morality more acute than elsewhere. There are two rebels in *Elmer Gantry*—Shallard and Zecklin. Zecklin, who is a man of the Max Gottlieb type, is against conformity. There is no underlying praise of the Middle Western ethos as there had been in *Main Street.* The life seems to have gone from these Middle Western people; they have sold out and gone to California.

The Man Who Knew Coolidge (1928) is a satire in dialogue. Babbitt has become rotten. This boom-man is cliché-ridden and disgusting. Babbitt did have good qualities; he was lovable as well as despicable. Lowell Schmaltz, however, has no good qualities, no aspirations, no brain—nothing but grossness. He represents the depths of Lewis's disgust, and Lewis tried to redeem the picture to some extent in his next novel, which, socially speaking, goes into what I have tentatively called the final period. *Dodsworth* is about an upper-class Babbitt with his good points left in, rather than sieved out to serve the purpose of satire. Sam Dodsworth is a motor manufacturer who cares intensely for what he is doing. He is a craftsman, almost an artist, but temperamentally he is incompatible with his wife, Fran, who is the daughter of a brewer and has cultural pretensions. In her one sees the familiar divorce of life and ideals. Her ideals do not arise out of the pattern of her life; they come from another culture entirely. It is European pretentiousness that she longs for and that she gets, disastrously, in the end. She commits adultery, wants to run off with her Austrian Count, and is only brought to her senses when the Count brings his mother along to get him out of it. Mother effectively prevents him marrying her; then she goes back to Sam, and everything is fine for a time. But at the end her selfishness drives him off. Sam is to blame a bit, because he thinks too constantly of the world of business and not enough of his wife. It is a picture of the American boy-man, the "mythical" archetype, the man who is emotionally unawakened but is at heart an idealist. *Dodsworth* is a novel that has a great deal in it, and one of Lewis's more important ones.

In *Ann Vickers* Lewis deals with the life of an emancipated woman who has an illegitimate child, and learns from her experience. He seems to be letting himself go in this book. It is, in fact, as if he were beginning to find out something about life and emotions. There is a rather intense concentration on things of the flesh.

The last books are watered-down versions of what Lewis had done before. Even *It Can't Happen Here,* which is about the best of them, has an off-centre, fantastic quality about it that makes one not able to believe in, to feel for, the novel as a whole. There are moments of wonderfully effective satire, as in the characterisation of Bishop Prang, but the other attitudes and conversations ring false; they are exaggerated beyond necessity, and the opposition of Doremus Jessup, the good editor, and Buzz Windrip, the dictator, somehow goes wrong.

Then, towards the last, we have the picture of Frederick William Cornplow in *The Prodigal Parents,* a Babbitt type: "Like most Americans he was profoundly democratic except perhaps as regards social standing, wealth, political power and club membership." But at least this book deals with "real" American life again. In *Bethel Merriday* Lewis turns to the theatrical world; in *Gideon Planish,* in 1943, to satire of "do good" institutions. Then we have the story of a judge in Minnesota (not the mythical State of Winnemac; it is called Minnesota in *Cass Timberlane*); *Kingsblood Royal* about the Negro situation, *The God-Seeker,* and finally *World So Wide,* in which a man kills his wife rather conveniently by accident, and then goes off to get an education in Italy.

If one can say that Lewis has a "typical" technique it is the technique of his satirical novels, in which the approach is theoretical and intellectual. He has more in common with the popular English writers of the period than with the American. He looked to H. G. Wells, to Galsworthy, to Hugh Walpole, indicating the difference between the American writer of the 'twenties and the American writer of today. Lewis's method was to choose an institution or a class of people, decide on a point of view, and then flatten his characters into the mould he desired. It is a sort of "wide spectrum" writing; the awareness is a "public" awareness; there is no "innerness." If you take the example of the alarm clock in *Babbitt,* he describes it from the point of view of its manufacture. When he treats emotional relationships he does so in rather the same sort of way, as, I suppose, a journalist would (I do not use the word *journalist* in a pejorative sense exactly, but rather to indicate the level of the discussion). There is evidence in his books, supported by what Grace Hegger says in *With Love from Gracie,* that it was not until the 1930's that he began finding out what life was all about; and then it was too late. His style had been set, and he could not go back.

In a way Lewis was a rebel with too many causes. He was rebelling against the idea that Middle Westerners were inferior to sophisticated, cultured Easterners in the early books, and he was rebelling against hypocrisy of all kinds in the later ones. One aspect of his rebellion he wrote about himself. *"Main Street,"* he said, "published late in 1920 was my first novel to rouse the embattled peasantry and it had a success of scandal. One of the most treasured American myths was that all American villagers were particularly noble and happy and here an American attacked the myth. Scandalous! Some hundreds of thousands read the book with the same masochistic pleasure that one has in sucking an aching tooth."

When he began *Main Street* he called it *The Village Virus.* He wrote three drafts, beginning the first one as early as 1905 when still at Yale.[5] The title is indicative. He was against the smugness and complacency of the prairie villages—but with love, because he was part of that world; then he switched from that to a class, the small businessman; then, to the medical profession, to the religious "profession," to "do good" institutions, to the Negro question, and so on. There were unlimited topics for him to choose from and, restlessly, he went from one to the other. He woke people up by dramatising social evils.

Like Wells, after whom he named his son, he had in him as much of the reformer as the novelist. Yet like Wells, too, he had his felicities as a writer and I should not feel that I had done justice to his achievement if I left the impression that, in my opinion, he was entirely without literary merit.

In the first place one must admit that he created a world of his own and peopled it with characters who make sense within its confines.

[5] No. He said later that he had, but he had not, in fact. [M.S.]

It is a Dickensian type of talent. This is why I usually find myself objecting to the unqualified use of the term *realistic* with which American literary historians so often label Lewis.

In a sense, yes, he is realistic, but not in the way in which this term is usually used in literary criticism. He is realistic in that he writes about ordinary people and ordinary happenings. In other words, I think that Mrs. Lewis is right when she says that "he was in a sense more typical of people in the twenties in America than Fitzgerald was." Alfred Kazin, reviewing *Main Street* in the *New York Times*,[6] picked this out and was very hard on it, but he was looking at literature from the point of view of art, whereas Mrs. Lewis, no literary critic, was looking on the book from the point of view of the ordinary reader, in terms of life itself. In terms of life, *Main Street* and *Babbitt* were nearer to ordinary American existence than *This Side of Paradise* and *The Great Gatsby*. It is this sense of life that Lewis manages to project despite the grotesqueness, despite the cardboard nature, of his characterisation. One can say that he did succeed in conveying the reality of Middle Western people, even though one has the starker example of Dreiser before him. Moreover, he is not as bad as all that, as a prose writer. One has only to look at the first paragraph of *Babbitt* to see that at his best he could write a clean, stripped-down kind of prose that is fanciful but avoids excesses.

> The towers of Zenith aspired above the morning mist; austere towers of steel and cement and limestone, sturdy as cliffs and delicate as silver rods. They were neither citadels nor churches, but frankly and beautifully office-buildings. The mist took pity on the fretted structures of earlier generations: the Post Office with its shingle-tortured mansard, the red-brick minarets of hulking old houses, factories with stingy and sooted windows, wooden tenements coloured like mud.

It is not the prose of "sensuous immediacy" but it is an emotive prose that has power to it and the attraction of lucidity as well as emotional undertones.

Did Lewis, as the Nobel Prize judges maintained, create new types and "high-class American humour"? His characters *seem* to be new types because they have strange manners, and they come from a strange place—strange to Europeans at that time, that is—but it seems to me that they are really types that we know about in Europe too. And as for American humour, yes, in a way, and yet there is not the roughness and the gusto of Artemus Ward or Mark Twain. The humour is a little thin. It is neither the Ring Lardner or *New Yorker* deadpan type of humour, nor the exaggerated humour of that older time; it falls un-

[6] The sentence should read: "Alfred Kazin, commenting on *Main Street* in his *New York Times* review of *With Love From Gracie*. . . ." [M.S.]

successfully between the two. However, I must remember that I had set myself at this point—out of a sense of duty to the very real force of this remarkable man—to pick out his good qualities. He does, let us say, give us portraits of Americans that we can, despite the fantasy of the scenes, believe in and understand. They are old types who have been transformed by a new country.

If I may sum up, then: in his early days Lewis was a romantic, a Booth Tarkington with a star in his eye, and he did better than he knew, particularly in *Main Street*. This changed him, and he attempted "art." He achieved fame because the American public was in a mood to hear the things he said, and because the European public, rather in the dark and also a little anti-American, admired *Babbitt* for reasons which were not exactly literary. He gave Europeans the sort of America they wanted to read about.

When I re-read Lewis I am struck by two strong and conflicting impressions. The first impression is one of annoyance. I am annoyed by the shallowness of his writing, by his lists of places seen and things done, by his attempt to capsule whole areas of emotion and render them in a single paragraph of reportorial neighbourliness, by those caricature-characterisations that Alfred Kazin called his "brilliant equivalents" of American people. And yet, for all this initial feeling of annoyance, I come back always to a feeling of sympathy for these grotesque people he created. This second impression is one that leads me to the man himself—I think it is without any intention on Lewis's part or any conscious intention on mine—to this cantankerous soul who was driven by the everlasting gospel of work and whose good heart shines through his work. All these books of his reflect back on him, but since he did not consciously intend it, the result is somehow acceptable. I feel that I can agree with Thomas Wolfe when he goes on in that account of Lewis-McHarg in *You Can't Go Home Again*:

> In spite of the brevity of their acquaintance, George had already seen clearly and unmistakably what a good and noble human being McHarg really was. He knew how much integrity and courage and honesty was contained in that tormented tenement of fury and lacerated hurts. Regardless of all that was jangled, snarled, and twisted in his life, regardless of all that had become bitter, harsh, and acrid, McHarg was obviously one of the truly good, the truly high, the truly great people of the world.

Max Gottlieb in *Arrowsmith,* the scientist, the kind of selfless, dedicated human being that Lewis admired, says:

> God give me a quiet and relentless anger at pretence and all pretentious work and all work left slack and unfinished. God give me a restlessness whereby I may neither sleep nor accept praise till my observed results equal

my calculated results or in pious glee I discover and assault my error. God give me strength not to trust in God!

Lewis's relentless anger and his restlessness lasted all his life, though we might have our doubts about some of the targets that he used these qualities against. In the end he had nothing to write about except the same watered-down old topics.

I am half-inclined to say that America has outgrown Lewis. In the Gopher Prairies of the 'fifties the bankers have been to Williams or to Yale and even the storekeepers have a degree from the State university. But it is more than just a matter of education. If *Main Street, Babbitt, Arrowsmith, Elmer Gantry,* and *The Man Who Knew Coolidge* capture anything of the spirit of their time, then the Middle West has changed a great deal in the past thirty years. Yet Lewis's characters were, after all, caricatures even for that time. In his early books he praised "small-town" qualities, and then he jumped on the bandwagon of the 'twenties and dramatically illustrated Mencken's prejudices. He might—and he did say this to a European audience—he might have loved the Babbitt of his youth, but Babbitt changed, and Lewis did not change with him. America, in other words, had proved herself bigger than Sinclair Lewis. He tried to tackle too many of the social and moral problems of America in his time and his attempts grew progressively more shallow and less successful. He was ambitious, hard-working, and idealistic, but he was not exceptionally intelligent or gifted; nor was he equipped with a sensibility or a power of understanding above the average. He could not feel greatly, and that was his limitation and also his strength. His picture is often distorted, therefore; the colours clash; the point of focus is wrong. He did a lot of harm, but he also did a lot of good, and, at the very least, one cannot help admiring the sheer effort of his attempt—or perhaps, more accurately, standing aghast at the feverish activity of this driven, impossibly lonely man. Mark Schorer tells us that when he had his last heart attack in Florence, the doctor who came to see him found that the decanter by his bed contained not water but straight Bourbon. I should not be surprised to learn that in the drawer of the bedside table there was a Gideon Bible. Lewis was a travelling man, and he had a lot in common with the drummers that he talks about in *Free Air*:

. . . not only were they the missionaries of business, supplementing the taking of orders by telling merchants how to build up trade, how to trim windows and treat customers like human beings, but also . . . they, as much as the local ministers and doctors and teachers and newspapermen, were the agents in spreading knowledge and justice. It was they who showed the young men how to have their hair cut—and to wash behind the ears and shave daily; they who encouraged villagers to rise from scandal and gossip

> to a perception of the Great World of politics and sports, and some measure of art and science.

"These travelling men," Lewis says, "were pioneers in spats," and I think it is a sufficiently incongruous and a sufficiently true image to stand as Lewis's epitaph. He was himself, in a sense, a pioneer in spats.

If we say that America has changed, in the sense that it has outgrown Lewis, his books will pass into history along with the flivvers and the Kittyhawks and the unfenced prairie. Yet even as I say this I can see the ghost of Lewis with his head cocked on one side saying: "Will they? Will they pass into history?" And this is the sort of healthy attitude one ought to be left with when one reaches any thumping conclusion. Has America outgrown Lewis? The banker, I said, goes to Yale and the storekeeper to the State university. A thousand increments of commercially or altruistically motivated lessons in culture, in learning, in sophistication, have transformed the social scene in America; yet hypocrisy, provincialism, prejudice, all forms of materialism, have only changed their clothes to mingle, as they have always done, with the crowd. New writers—Mary McCarthy, for example—are better equipped to describe these clothes. But the face—is it not the same face that Lewis saw? Perhaps also we ought to remember, when we use Lewis's novels in order to point sarcastically at America, that the attitudes of mind in *Main Street, Babbitt, Arrowsmith,* and *Elmer Gantry* are not peculiar to America. To point at America is also to point at ourselves.[7]

[7] It seemed desirable to conclude this collection with an essay that was written after Sinclair Lewis's death and summarized the entire career. Mr. Moore's essay may offend people who know modern American literature intimately, but I could find none about Lewis that was more adequate. I have corrected Mr. Moore's mistakes about Lewis's biography, but I have not, of course, commented on his interpretations. [M.S.]

Chronology of Important Dates

February 7, 1885	Birth in Sauk Centre, Minnesota.
1902-1903	To Oberlin Academy, Oberlin, Ohio.
1903	To Yale College.
1904	Cattleboat trip to Liverpool.
1906	Second cattleboat trip. To Upton Sinclair's utopian experiment in communal living, Helicon Hall, at Englewood, New Jersey; then New York City and Panama.
1908	Graduated from Yale College.
1908-1910	Waterloo, Iowa; New York City; California; Washington; New York—when employed, as a journalist.
1910-1915	Employed by New York publishers.
1914	Publication of first novel, *Our Mr. Wrenn.* Marriage to Grace Livingstone Hegger.
1914-1915	Port Washington, Long Island.
1915	*The Trail of the Hawk.*
1917	*The Innocents.* *The Job.* 309 Fifth Avenue, New York City, and birth of first son, Wells.
1918	516 Summit Avenue, St. Paul.
1918-1919	1801 James Avenue South, Minneapolis.
1919	*Free Air.*
1919-1921	1814 16th Street, N.W., and 1639 19th Street, N.W., Washington, D.C.
1920	*Main Street.*
1921-1922	*Babbitt.* 25 Belknap Road, Hartford, Connecticut.
1923	Caribbean cruise with Paul de Kruif.
1923-1925	Largely in Europe.

1925	*Arrowsmith.* *Mantrap.* First American to decline the Pulitzer Prize. Pequot, Minnesota. 3028 Q Street, N.W., Washington, D.C.
1927	Separation from first wife. *Elmer Gantry.*
1927-1928	Largely in Europe.
1928	Divorce, and marriage to Dorothy Thompson, London. *The Man Who Knew Coolidge.* Twin Farms, Barnard, Vermont; summers through 1937.
1928-1930	Winters mainly at 37 West 10th Street, New York City.
1929	*Dodsworth.*
1930	Birth of second son, Michael. First American to win the Nobel Prize in Literature.
1931-1932	Winters at 21 East 90th Street, New York City.
1932-1933	Largely in Europe.
1933	*Ann Vickers.*
1933-1937	Winters at 17 Wood End Lane, Bronxville, New York.
1934	*Work of Art.*
1935	*It Can't Happen Here.*
1936	Europe.
1937	Bermuda. Separation from second wife.
1937-1942	In these years he spent his winters in various Manhattan hotels, his summers in the neighborhood of various summer theaters, and made sporadic trips to the Midwest, Hollywood, Florida, and other places at home and abroad, as he would continue to do until his death.
1938	*The Prodigal Parents.*
1938-1939	On tour with his play, *Angela Is Twenty-Two.*
1940	*Bethel Merriday.* 1712 Summit Avenue, Madison, Wisconsin.
1942	Second divorce, no remarriage.
1942-1943	1500 Mt. Curve Avenue, Minneapolis.
1943-1946	Winters at 300 Central Park West, New York City.

1943	*Gideon Planish.*
1944	Death of first son in battle.
1944-1946	2601 East 2nd Street, Duluth, Minnesota.
1945	*Cass Timberlane.*
1946-1949	Thorvale Farm, Oblong Road, South Williamstown, Massachusetts.
1947	*Kingsblood Royal.*
1948-1949	Italy.
1949	*The God-Seeker.*
1949-1951	Largely in Europe.
January 10, 1951	Death in Rome, Italy.
1951	Posthumous publication of last novel, *World So Wide.*

Notes on the Editor and Contributors

Mark Schorer, novelist and critic, professor of English at the University of California, Berkeley, is the author of *Sinclair Lewis: An American Life.*

Sherwood Anderson, influential novelist and short story writer, is the author of *Winesburg, Ohio.*

Richard P. Blackmur is a professor of English in Princeton University and the author of *The Expense of Greatness, The Double Agent,* and *The Lion and the Honeycomb.*

Robert Cantwell, critic and novelist, most recently published *Nathaniel Hawthorne: The American Years.*

Malcolm Cowley, for many years the literary editor of *New Republic,* is the author of *Exile's Return* and *The Literary Situation.*

Ford Madox Ford was a collaborator of Joseph Conrad's and a prolific novelist whose major works are *The Good Soldier* and the tetralogy, *Parade's End.*

E. M. Forster, most distinguished living British man of letters, is the author of five novels, many essays, a biography, and *Aspects of the Novel.*

Maxwell Geismar is the author of *Writers in Crisis* and *The Last of the Provincials,* companion volumes about the modern American novel.

Alfred Kazin is the author of *On Native Grounds* and of several collections of essays on literary subjects as well as of the autobiographical *Walker in the City.*

Joseph Wood Krutch, long a professor of English at Columbia University, is an authority on the drama and the novel and widely known as a master of the contemplative essay.

Walter Lippmann, author of many books, is commonly regarded as the "dean" of American political journalists.

Robert Morss Lovett, for many years a professor of English in the University of Chicago, entered politics as government secretary of the Virgin Islands.

H. L. Mencken was the famous editor of *Smart Set* and *American Mercury,* and the author of many works including *The American Language.*

Geoffrey Moore is lecturer in American literature at the University of Manchester and author of the British Council pamphlet, *Poetry To-Day.*

Lewis Mumford, American cultural historian, most recently published the enormous and impressive work called *The City in History.*

Vernon L. Parrington, for many years professor of English at the University of Washington, was the author of *Main Currents in American Thought.*

Constance Rourke was a brilliant American cultural historian who died in 1941.

Rebecca West, British critic, journalist, and novelist, collected many of her essays in the volume called *The Strange Necessity.*

T. K. Whipple was a professor of English in the University of California, Berkeley, and the author of *Spokesmen* and *Study Out the Land.*

Edmund Wilson is perhaps the most important living American critic; his many works include *Axel's Castle, The Shores of Light,* and *Classics and Commercials.*

Bibliography

The best critical writing about Sinclair Lewis is contained in this book. A few published books about him can be mentioned, but the reader should be warned that the first three titles were commissioned by Lewis's publishers and are really promotion materials:

Stuart Pratt Sherman. *The Significance of Sinclair Lewis,* Harcourt, Brace & World, Inc., 1922.

"Oliver Harrison" (Harrison Smith). *Sinclair Lewis.* Harcourt, Brace & World, Inc., 1925.

Carl Van Doren. *Sinclair Lewis: A Biographical Sketch.* With a Bibliography by Harvey Taylor. Doubleday & Company, Inc., 1933. The bibliography is highly unreliable.

Curious readers may be interested in two works by Lewis's first wife:

Grace Hegger Lewis. *Half A Loaf.* Liveright Publishing Corp., 1931. A bizarre *roman à clef,* almost literally translated into the next work, a biographical memoir.

Grace Hegger Lewis. *With Love From Gracie.* Harcourt, Brace & World, Inc., 1955.

An interesting account of Lewis's attempt to write his labor novel is available in two forms:

Ramon Guthrie. "Sinclair Lewis and the 'Labor Novel,' " *Proceedings* (Second Series, Number Two), American Academy of Arts and Letters. New York, 1952.

"The 'Labor Novel' that Sinclair Lewis Never Wrote," New York *Herald Tribune Books.* February 10, 1952. A shorter version of the foregoing.

A persuasively written impression of Lewis's last days in Florence is:

Perry Miller. "The Incorruptible Sinclair Lewis," *The Atlantic,* April, 1951.

Less persuasive is an account by Lewis's last secretary:

Alexander Manson (as told to Helen Camp), "The Last Days of Sinclair Lewis," *Saturday Evening Post,* March 31, 1951.

The only full critical biography of Lewis is my own:

Mark Schorer. *Sinclair Lewis: An American Life.* McGraw-Hill Book Company, Inc., 1961. This book contains a reliable checklist of Lewis's publications.

Books by Sinclair Lewis himself, apart from his fiction, are:

The Man From Main Street: Selected Essays and Other Writings, 1904-1950. Edited by Harry E. Maule and Melville H. Cane. Random House, 1953.

From Main Street to Stockholm: Letters of Sinclair Lewis, 1919-1930. Edited by Harrison Smith. Harcourt, Brace & World, Inc., 1952.

SPECTRUM 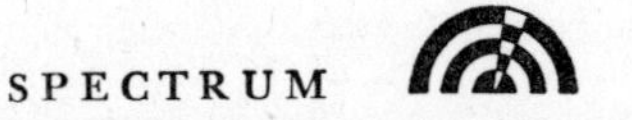 PAPERBACKS

Other SPECTRUM Books . . . quality paperbacks that meet the highest standards of scholarship and integrity.

S-18 Literature, Popular Culture, and Society, Leo Lowenthal, $1.95
S-19 Paradox and Promise: Essays on American Life and Education, Harry S. Broudy, *paper* $1.95, *cloth* $3.95
S-20 Religion in America: Past and Present, Clifton E. Olmstead, $1.95
S-21 Religion and the Knowledge of God, Gustave Weigel, S.J., and Arthur G. Madden, *paper* $1.95, *cloth* $3.95
S-22 Intuition and Science, Mario Bunge, $1.95
S-23 Revolution, Evolution, and the Economic Order, Allen M. Sievers, *paper* $1.95, *cloth* $3.95
S-24 An Anatomy for Conformity, Edward L. Walker and Roger Heyns, *paper* $1.95, *cloth* $3.95
S-25 Science and the Nation, J. Stefan Dupré and Sanford A. Lakoff, *paper* $1.95, *cloth* $3.95
S-26 Politics in Africa: Prospects South of the Sahara, Herbert J. Spiro, *paper* $1.95, *cloth* $3.95
S-27 The First Russian Revolution: Its Impact on Asia, Ivar Spector, *paper* $1.95, *cloth* $3.95
S-28 Mastery of the Metropolis, Webb S. Fiser, *paper* $1.95, *cloth* $3.95
S-29 Johann Sebastian Bach: An Introduction to his Life and Work, Russell H. Miles, *paper* $1.95, *cloth* $3.95
S-30 In Defense of Youth, Earl C. Kelley, *paper* $1.95, *cloth* $3.95
S-31 Heroes, Villains, and Fools: The Changing American Character, Orrin E. Klapp, *paper* $1.95, *cloth* $3.95
S-32 Communist China's Strategy in the Nuclear Era, Alice Langley Hsieh, *paper* $2.25, *cloth* $4.50
S-33 Sociologism and Existentialism, Edward A. Tiryakian, *paper* $1.95, *cloth* $3.95
S-34 Philosophy of Science, Philipp Frank, $2.45

The American Assembly Series

S-AA-1 THE FEDERAL GOVERNMENT AND HIGHER EDUCATION, edited by Douglas M. Knight, *paper* $1.95, *cloth* $3.50
S-AA-2 THE SECRETARY OF STATE, edited by Don K. Price, *paper* $1.95, *cloth* $3.50
S-AA-3 GOALS FOR AMERICANS, THE REPORT OF THE PRESIDENT'S COMMISSION ON NATIONAL GOALS, *paper* $1.00, *cloth* $3.50
S-AA-4 ARMS CONTROL ISSUES FOR THE PUBLIC, edited by Louis Henkin, *paper* $1.95, *cloth* $3.50
S-AA-5 OUTER SPACE, edited by Lincoln P. Bloomfield, *paper* $1.95, *cloth* $3.95
S-AA-6 THE UNITED STATES AND THE FAR EAST (Second Edition), edited by Willard L. Thorp, *paper* $1.95, *cloth* $3.95

Science and Technology Series

S-ST-1 THE ATOM AND ITS NUCLEUS, George Gamow, *paper* $1.95, *cloth* $3.75
S-ST-2 ROCKET DEVELOPMENT, Robert H. Goddard, *paper* $2.45, *cloth* $3.95

Classics in History Series

S-CH-1 FRONTIER AND SECTION: SELECTED ESSAYS OF FREDERICK JACKSON TURNER, *Introduction and notes by Ray Allen Billington, paper* $1.95, *cloth* $3.95

S-CH-2 DRIFT AND MASTERY: AN ATTEMPT TO DIAGNOSE THE CURRENT UNREST, Walter Lippman, *Introduction and notes by William Leuchtenburg,* $1.95

S-CH-3 THE NEW NATIONALISM, THEODORE ROOSEVELT, *Introduction and notes by William Leuchtenburg,* $1.95

S-CH-4 THE NEW FREEDOM: A CALL FOR THE EMANCIPATION OF THE GENEROUS ENERGIES OF A PEOPLE, WOODROW WILSON, *Introduction and notes by William Leuchtenburg,* $1.95

S-CH-5 SELECTED CORRESPONDENCE OF JOHN ADAMS AND THOMAS JEFFERSON, *Introduction and notes by Zoltán Haraszti, paper* $2.25, *cloth* $3.95

S-CH-6 THE SUPREME COURT AND THE CONSTITUTION, Charles A. Beard, *Introduction by Alan Westin, paper* $1.95, *cloth* $3.95

Twentieth-Century Views Series

S-TC-1 CAMUS, edited by Germaine Brée, *paper* $1.95, *cloth* $3.95
S-TC-2 T. S. ELIOT, edited by Hugh Kenner, *paper* $1.95, *cloth* $3.95
S-TC-3 ROBERT FROST, edited by James M. Cox, *paper* $1.95, *cloth* $3.95
S-TC-4 PROUST, edited by René Girard, *paper* $1.95, *cloth* $3.95
S-TC-5 WHITMAN, edited by Roy Harvey Pearce, *paper* $1.95, *cloth* $3.95
S-TC-6 SINCLAIR LEWIS, edited by Mark Schorer, *paper* $1.95, *cloth* $3.95
S-TC-7 STENDHAL, edited by Victor Brombert, *paper* $1.95, *cloth* $3.95
S-TC-8 HEMINGWAY, edited by Robert P. Weeks, *paper* $1.95, *cloth* $3.95
S-TC-9 FIELDING, edited by Ronald Paulson, *paper* $1.95, *cloth* $3.95
S-TC-10 THOREAU, edited by Sherman Paul, *paper* $1.95, *cloth* $3.95